1.50

Hidden Histories

HIDDEN HISTORIES

Palestine and the Eastern Mediterranean

Basem L. Ra'ad

PlutoPress
www.plutobooks.com

First published 2010 by Pluto Press
345 Archway Road, London N6 5AA and
175 Fifth Avenue, New York, NY 10010

www.plutobooks.com

Distributed in the United States of America exclusively by
Palgrave Macmillan, a division of St. Martin's Press LLC,
175 Fifth Avenue, New York, NY 10010

British Library Cataloguing in Publication Data
A catalogue record for this book is available from the British Library

ISBN   978 0 7453 2831 7   Hardback
ISBN   978 0 7453 2830 0   Paperback

Library of Congress Cataloging in Publication Data applied for

This book is printed on paper suitable for recycling and made from fully managed
and sustained forest sources. Logging, pulping and manufacturing processes are
expected to conform to the environmental standards of the country of origin.

10   9   8   7   6   5   4   3   2

Designed and produced for Pluto Press by
Chase Publishing Services Ltd, 33 Livonia Road, Sidmouth, EX10 9JB, England
Typeset from disk by Stanford DTP Services, Northampton, England
Printed and bound in the European Union by
CPI Antony Rowe, Chippenham and Eastbourne

From A to Z

Contents

List of Ilustrations

Credits

Archaeological objects: Figures 1.1, 1.2, 2.2, 3.1 are kept at the Louvre, Paris, France. Figure 2.1 courtesy of the National Museum, Damascus, Syria; Figure 2.3 courtesy of the British Museum, London, U.K.

Photos from books and other sources: Figure 1.3 "Capture," from John MacGregor's *The Rob Roy on the Jordan* (1870); Figure 2.4, courtesy of photographer Zev Radovan; old photo in Figure 3.2, courtesy of the École Biblique, Jerusalem, and new photo by George Rishmawi; Figure 4.1 reproduces a postcard from Syria; Figure 7.3, from *The Holy Land: A Unique Perspective* (1993), courtesy of RØHR Productions Ltd.; Figure 9.1, photo by Tom Powers; Figure 11.1, photo by Saadeh Saadeh; Figure 11.2, frontispiece, from E. A. Finn's *Home in the Holy Land* (London: John Nisbet, 1877).

Photos by the author: Figure 7.1 (from a dress owned by Ghassan Abdeen), Figure 7.2, 8.1, 9.2, 9.3 and 11.3.

Illustrations: Figures 5.1, 10.1, and 10.2 illustrated by Rana Bishara; Figures 4.2 and 5.1 additionally computer-enhanced by Khalil Jamous.

Palestinian art works: Figure 6.1, I, Isma'īl (Suleiman Mansour, clay, 1998); Figure 8.2, Wall in the Head (Ahmad Canaan, stone carving, 2007); Figure 8.3, Untitled (Mustafa el Hallaj); Figure 9.3, Cat and Jet (Farid Abu Shaqra, 2005); Figure 11.4 The Palestinian village of Deir Samet, Hebron region (Suleiman Mansour, 1982).

Front cover: Olive Grove (Suleiman Mansour, oil, 1980).

Back cover: Al Quds (Suleiman Mansour, oil, 1978).

Every effort has been made to clear necessary permissions for reproduction of copyrighted illustrations.

Preface

A corrective history of Palestine, its region, its people and its cultures has not yet been written. I am not speaking about the narration of recent events in Palestine and surrounding areas, but of a total vision that would encompass both ancient and modern times.

Briefly, a comprehensive history of this kind has been prevented by a combination of factors: the confusion between historical facts and religious narratives, divergent public perceptions in the West and in the region itself over centuries, the self-interested perpetuation of past misconceptions, and now the dissonant agendas of scholarship. The land has never been really free from colonization—whether in terms of control by successive empires or in terms of its association with religious imaginaries or political designs based on them. Its present fate—as a region divided into "countries" and a Palestine colonized by Israel—is largely the result of a misconstrued ancient history built on invention, misconception, and later conspiracy. There is a profound silence and suppression of knowledge concerning a past that continues to be misinterpreted. As a result, the real past remains unfulfilled. It demands to be retrieved and revealed. It wants to dispel a darkness that pretends to be light.

Scholarship has not been as helpful here as it has been in other situations. Mind-changing discoveries over the past 150 years have thrown previously held certainties into doubt and shown them to be unhistorical. Such discoveries offer the prospect of a revised and more enlightened understanding of the region. But because religious and now also political investments have become so entangled with mythic assumptions, there is enormous resistance to accepting the full implications of an increasing number of archaeological and epigraphic findings that, because they challenge mainstream thinking, continue to be ignored. The scholarship (whether Western, Israeli, or regional), being part of the dominant systems that generate and sustain it, remains largely either complicit or limited. It generally hangs onto old notions or interprets new findings within preset moulds, at the same time as nascent alternative approaches are either attacked or buried. Whether on the scholarly or public level, there is much to "unlearn" in what people have been led to believe or think they know—as a first step toward reframing attitudes, deepening insights and nourishing growth in human consciousness.

This book employs a diversity of means for extracting and interpreting information, as I explain in the introduction. Since it is more arduous to gather evidence when one's approach runs against the grain, it becomes necessary to extrapolate and to find alternative methods in order to recover as much as possible of the silenced past. Part One of the book, "Ancient Myths, Religions, and Cultures," synthesizes significant findings that dispel common cultural misconceptions and dismantle the usual monopolies associated with the three regional monotheisms. The assumption of a nicely sequenced "Abrahamic tradition" is the most treacherous trap in public thinking and the root of many unfounded claims. Another major source of misunderstanding about the region is the affiliated construct called "Western civilization," whose ingredients are analyzed in Chapter 1. The following chapters demonstrate that there are undeniable continuities between the three monotheisms and preceding polytheisms, and that the cultural contributions of the region are better recognized when approached without biased assumptions implicit in the monotheistic tradition and in elements of "Western civilization." Part Two, "Modern Myths and (De)Colonized History," moves from the past to its present symptoms and raises the question of how a colonized people can hope to write a useful history. Its chapters deal with issues related to identity formation, cultural appropriation, self-colonization, the political enforcement of place names, and the remnants of the past in present customs.

I should clarify here that I use the term "East Mediterranean" as a partial replacement for the colonial term "Middle East"—a term that political rhetoric has now expanded farther east to include even places like Iran, Afghanistan, and Pakistan. This alternative geographic designation, the East Mediterranean, includes, generally, what was previously called "the Levant." Specifically, it refers to an area that forms a kind of cultural crescent, extending from Greece, through Asia Minor (present Turkey) and Greater Syria (today's Syria, Lebanon, Jordan, and Palestine), inland to the east to incorporate present-day Iraq, and running southwest through the Sinai Desert into Egypt. I conceive of the eastern Mediterranean as a unit consisting of many socio-cultural intersections. In this way, I partly intend to remove the appropriation of ancient Greece into the construct called "Western civilization." My more immediate concern is with the region encompassing Greater Syria, Egypt, and what is called Mesopotamia—a region that originated much of "civilization" as we know it today.

In this region, Palestine stands as a real land bridge. It has been, also, the imaginary, the type, for holy constructions and unholy practices. It is ironic that a region usually described as "the cradle of civilization," and associated with crucial innovations in ancient times, should now be so enmeshed in troubles and in uncertainties about what is true and what is false, what is real and what is invented. It is clearly a region of contradictions that must concern everyone in the world today. More so than ever, its fate affects human principles and sanity, and demands a re-conceptualization of received ideas: how to approach historical knowledge and construct beliefs, how to expose fallacies, and how to interrogate or accept information. A renewed and more comprehensive understanding of Palestine and its region is urgently relevant to epistemic issues of all kinds.

Producing this book has involved a long journey, not so much in the actual time it took to write it as in what made its direction possible and necessary. It is a search for what remains of a people's history that has been effaced, buried, and is still ignored today. My years of study, travel, and daily life in North America and eastern Mediterranean regions led me to an insistent realization that more attention had to be directed to disentangling the implications of what has been said or written about historical Palestine in the context of the knowledge tools available now, rather than relying on religious convictions and acquired beliefs as substitutes for research and inquiry. It is essential to develop a language of questioning and to peel back the old accretions that have clouded perceptions.

The book's content is the result of a conflation of many circumstances and findings, among them happy coincidences and serendipities. I have been helped by a great number of people over the years—through discussions, reflections, and the sharing of ideas. I thank all those who helped for their support and suggestions. My close friends and family have been my greatest motivators and contributors to my work, and it is to them that I dedicate this book. Above all, I am grateful to the people of Palestine and the surrounding region, in villages and towns, who will not be aware quite how much they are the source of all that I have written.

Basem L. Ra'ad
Jerusalem

Introduction: Understanding the History of the Eastern Mediterranean

"Give me a book to read," demanded a student in a seminar I was teaching on travel writing relating to Palestine and the surrounding region. He was eager to learn, and wanted less random, more focused readings. It was impossible. In a region overrun by monolithic histories, shadowed by religious associations, and distorted by absolutist unhistorical claims, even the hundreds of presently available books on the subject would seem inadequate to hold it all together, let alone a single book. Those works that could be recommended are few and necessarily incomplete, while the library shelves remain weighted by innumerable tomes that are the product of past misconceptions and mainstream prejudices. The kind of book the student was looking for has not been written, and quite probably never could be. We are still waiting for the unsaid to be said, for the subaltern to be brought to the surface, and for excluded or censored knowledge to be consolidated into a whole. As such, the time is ripe for unlearning many inherited notions, charting alternative processes, and for developing a new cognitive framework.

That seminar on travel was in part what led to the writing of this book. It explored perceptions of Palestine, of the region and its people, as the students hear and experience them indirectly—in the texts of both ancient and recent travel accounts. At the same time, we discussed the many archaeological and historical findings that might influence our present understanding of the region's cultures and help to rewrite its history. It became apparent that the imagined "Palestine" (variously called "Canaan," the "Holy Land," or the "Land of Israel") is at irreconcilable odds with the actual history of the land and its people. Palestine represents a singular and intensified case of paradoxes in knowledge and history. Here, "knowledge," usually assumed to evolve, has instead regressed or stagnated, exploited by self-interested power to enshrine a monopoly on invention and to expand its systemic controls, while history has remained more laden than usual with spurious documents and mythologizing. In a land heavily invested with religious associations

1

by three monotheisms, and subject to both symbolic and actual colonization from ancient times to the present, it is not at all easy to differentiate fiction from fact. In very few other regions, if any, are observations by visitors so influenced by preconceptions, so much so that the physical is often perceived only through the screens of preformed imaginaries. Few places, if any, have been the subject of so many biased, inaccurate, or incomplete presentations in publications and the media.

This has only become more intensely the case since a previously imagined "Israel" was brought into unwieldy reality at the expense of an unwary Palestine. Strong religious and political investments both in the West and in Israel want to keep the old perceptions unchallenged—investments assisted by fundamentalism and the Judeo-Christian tradition. For Israel (which relied for its creation on biblical "history" and Western belief in it), the credibility of its justifications, the rationale for its existence, and the foundations of its identity are all at stake. As a result, recent discoveries promising to dislodge previously held notions and offer new insights are muffled, appropriated, or diverted. Furthermore, the region itself has been fragmented by colonially imposed divisions, its scholarship ill-equipped to formulate a response, and its people absorbed in self-colonizing identities that shorten their deep history and preclude any useful identification with it. On the regional side, there is a covering up of cultural depth with more recent identities, as well as an inflated exploitation by the Zionists of dominant accounts related to ancient times. This tension raises the question of how it might even be possible to retrieve a more accurate history.

That the case of Palestine demands a total revision in historical thinking is *not* only related to what happened in 1948 when the State of Israel was carved out, thereby creating a huge dislocation, a fragmenting and a dividing, which resulted in what Edward W. Said (in *The Question of Palestine*) calls "the cubistic form of Palestinian existence." Keith W. Whitelam describes what traditional biblical scholarship has done to its ancient history as a "silencing." Thomas L. Thompson deems that the "history" invented by biblicists should instead be read as literary fiction, as myth. A handful of Israeli scholars have also come to new realizations about both recent and ancient history. Going beyond the early nationalistic prerogatives of Israeli scholarship, historians and archaeologists such as Nachman Ben-Yehuda, Ze'ev Herzog, Ilan Pappe, Shlomo Sand, and Tom Segev have undermined many myth-based Zionist claims. Among them, they agree that there was no Exodus, no Israelite conquest, no dispersion and no Diaspora, no "Jewish people," no mythic Masada as portrayed in Zionist narratives, and that 1948 had more to do with the ethnic cleansing of Palestinians than with glorious independence. Others, like Meron Benvenisti and Tanya Reinhart, approach the conflict with a humanist orientation, in search of the truth about the past and in sympathy with what the Palestinians have endured. Gannit Ankori, an Israeli art critic, speaks (in *Palestinian Art*) of her eyes being opened such that she was "forced" to open her mind too, and change her perception. One wonders what keeps a wider public change of mind from occurring.

The problem is fundamentally related to how historical knowledge is formed, and how it is accepted, not only in relation to the past hundred, or indeed thousand, years but over the extent of recorded history. Added to this are the investments that systems and their followers have attached to the old perceptions, either as offering a comforting certainty or as conveniently serving their self-interest. The public continues to be bombarded with inaccuracies and falsehoods, and is unable to make the distinction between fiction and history. If most "scholarship" is complicit in the system, or unable to close major gaps in knowledge, what chance is there of saving the public mind from disorientation or distortion? The invasion of Palestine by the Zionists, the seizure of rights and properties on the basis of systemic inventions, the disruption of hundreds of thousands of lives, the deaths and suffering over decades, the West's support of Israel and the general silence of the rest of the world—all of this cannot easily be rationalized or accepted in either abstract or real terms. It makes one skeptical about human understanding and human values that such injustices might be made to appear less calamitous than they really are, or indeed might not appear at all.

If historical conceptions as they have evolved over centuries and millennia have produced this incubus, then the force of incredulity should drive us toward finding an explanation for the predicament of a people subjected to it. Faced with such a challenge, a mental paradigm shift toward an alternative perspective could help us escape the multifaceted accumulations that would otherwise continue to sustain an entrenched ignorance. Some have already begun to make this shift, working with little support against the backdrop of a well-organized and well-funded industry of invented history. Yet they have only begun to address, in their own special scholarship, what remains generally incomplete and ignored. In Chapter 1, under the heading "Old-New Scholarly Agendas," I classify scholars into five types: perpetuators, fabricators, mufflers, adapters, and challengers. Even with the last and highest category there are difficulties. While one scholar here and another there may supply valuable information or a commendable trend, the cumulative effect is insufficient, unfinished, not quite all that is needed. This can be said of the "Copenhagen School" which, for example, even as it takes the critical approach of looking at the Bible as a literary product of questionable historicity, often tends to overemphasize the biblical discussion. Furthermore, it adopts neither a specifically Palestinian nor a regional approach, with Palestinian or regional priorities. A scholar like Karen Armstrong has popularized a liberal discourse about religions and their pitfalls, and expanded views on the idea of God. Nonetheless, she often only repeats familiar myths and ends up relying too heavily on biblical quotations—to the point of offering an extended, almost romanticized rewriting of hyperbolized stories even as she suggests (somewhat infrequently) that they are unhistorical. Edward Said almost single-handedly opened up postcolonial discourse and was an eloquent defender of the Palestinian cause. Yet while he could discuss French and English travel writing at length and write about a Zionist novel by George Eliot, *Daniel Deronda*, he does not pay much attention to biblical orientalism, especially its U.S. variety. Indeed, in *Orientalism*, he dismisses in a couple of sentences the works of two authors, Herman Melville and Mark Twain, who were the greatest debunkers of "Holy Land" sacred geography and hence are worth investigating in detail (see Chapter 3). Even among the most enlightened people, there is a common failure to make the important distinction between "Israelites" and "Jews" (see Chapter 6). Arab scholars in the West sometimes shower fulsome praise on Israeli debunkers of biblical historicity but fail to see the danger in their proposed alternative theories (see Chapter 1, note 41). Finally, both popular culture and less familiar or buried sources, past and present, have as yet not been activated as legitimate means that might contribute to a less monolithic history of the region.

New methodologies are required. Given the erasures, distortions, and multiple scholarly and public agendas, finding a total picture that approximates the truth is difficult indeed. Hence an eclectic range of means has to be employed. First, it is necessary to situate oneself outside the investments of the system (or systems). From that position, one then has to read many books, articles, and references in several fields of study, whether these sources be informed or not so well informed, biased or unbiased, ancient or recent, mainstream or independent. Out of this mass of material, one needs to extract information that will challenge the invention of exclusivist claims and other habitual conflations of myth and history, and so replace these hegemonic accounts with an account that makes sense of the past of this land and its peoples. Finally, one must try to find evidence to fill the silences and help to reinstate real continuities. This can only be done by sifting through scattered details, reading between the lines, reconciling contradictions, and filling the cracks as far as possible with new ideas and original research. Two steps are essential to complement this process: first, exploring obscure or suppressed sources, bringing both recent findings and old forgotten facts into sharper focus while fully developing their implications; second, searching for any remnants of custom or language, or any other popular sources, that may be useful in reconstructing at least a part of the people's story that is missing from mainstream accounts. In other words, it will be necessary to extrapolate, and—in dealing with such varied, interdisciplinary strategies and cultural undertakings— to try to build up a more authentic picture of the whole.

Let me highlight here a few ways in which this book seeks to challenge commonly held cultural and religious notions, especially those that are exploited in support of Zionist claims. Most readers will know something of the ancient textual antecedents discovered in Mesopotamia and Egypt, since the middle of the nineteenth century—antecedents that demonstrated the existence of "parallels" to the biblical accounts until then thought to have been "unique." Even in the face of such evidence, biblical scholars and other monopolizers pursued strategies designed to maintain the Bible's "uniqueness" and assumptions about its divine source. Such misguided efforts, however, are nowadays less possible to sustain, given the additional evidence from Ugarit—a city from the second millennium BCE uncovered by a Syrian farmer—and the Dead Sea Scrolls, discovered in caves by a Bedouin shepherd boy. (With such accidental discoveries, history is giving itself back to the people, while Western scholarship rushes to readjust its previous knowledge system.)

How many people realize that, as I indicate in Chapter 2, there are at least two gods proclaimed in the Bible, Īl (El) and Yahweh, not one, and that the standard translations have camouflaged this fact? A key passage found in the Dead Sea Scrolls was altered in later scribal copying of the Bible to cover up the existence of a pantheon in which Yahweh is one of the sons of the chief god Īl (El). How many people know that the sacred monotheistic sites, exploited by today's politicians, are built on what were previously polytheistic sacred locations, or else are recent inventions (see Chapter 3)? Chapter 4, which looks at the evidence from the city of Ugarit, shows more clearly that so-called monotheism is derived from a prior polytheism, that the notion of "Zion" may have been transferred from northwest Syria, and that the god *yw* (Yahweh) was a member of the pantheon. Moreover, Ugaritic as a language is demonstrably closer not to Hebrew—as has been assumed and continues to be promulgated—but to Arabic. Popular language in Arabic today echoes Ugaritic and other ancient concepts and allusions.

These last two points have powerful implications that may refute much of what is taken for granted in classifications of "Semitic" languages and related theorizing. Ugaritic, originating in northwest Syria about 3500 years ago, has almost exactly the same sound system and vocabulary as present Arabic. This similarity disrupts many notions about the relationships between, and ages of, various ancient languages. It challenges the assumption that Ugaritic is to be used primarily to "understand" the Bible, and puts to shame Zionist pretensions that try to make Hebrew very ancient or to give it an ascendancy over other languages. As I show, at least in terms of script, there is no "Hebrew" before "square Hebrew," which is itself nothing but square Aramaic. Scholarly postulations about an "ancient Hebrew" are unfounded, except insofar as it was based on an appropriation of other ancient languages and scripts.

The evidence from Ugarit also suggests that Arabic did not just enter Palestine and the region as a kind of foreign language with the Muslim conquest in the seventh century CE, as Zionism wants to assume. Rather, Arabic is a live language that not only preserves the oldest "Semitic" features and vocabulary but is also the storehouse and fullest inventory of other ancient regional languages such as Canaʿanite/"Phoenician," Akkadian, and Aramaic. It should therefore be no great surprise to discover, both in an ancient source and modern commentary (see Chapter 2, note 24), the suggestion that the most exceptional and profound book in the Old Testament, the Book of Job (Ayyūb), has an Arabic source.

While such corrective facts can still come across here and there, their traces are fast disappearing under the weight of regressive, politically motivated scholarship in articles, books, and even encyclopedias. For example, while the currency called the "shekel" is commonly known to be Babylonian, it has recently been appropriated as being of "Hebrew" or "Jewish" origin in some apparently respectable dictionaries and encyclopedias (see Chapter

7). Similarly, the invention of the first alphabet has been subjected to appropriative readings and other biased agendas (see Chapter 5). Additionally, the assumption that ancient place names, thought to have been Arabized after the Muslims conquered Palestine (a convenient Zionist theory), need returning to their "original" biblical source is shown to be utterly misguided and misleading. Instead, some of the most ancient pre-biblical Cana'anite toponyms are almost exactly preserved in Arabic forms still used today, as they are elsewhere in the region (see Chapter 10). It is thus one of the aims of this book (and indeed is in humanity's interest) to both recognize and reward the region for its real contributions to civilization, culture, and thought, and thus to correct the historical balance sheet by reversing recent fabrications.

My emphasis on the Palestinian region is not without good reason. If Dimašq (Damascus) in Syria or Beirūt in Lebanon can retain their old names in the Arabic of today, why should Palestinian cities to the south—like 'Asqalān on the coast (mis-transcribed as "Ashkelon" in Western and Israeli usage), or 'Akka (distorted to "Acco" in Israeli usage, or "Acre" in Western usage)—not also retain their most ancient names? One of the most common myths is that Palestinians are "Arabs" ("Arab" being often equated with Muslim), and so are to be associated with the seventh-century Muslim conquest, which the Zionists tell us "distorted" the names in Palestine—though other similarly affected parts of the region did not show such purported distortion. Much of the Zionist claim system—including its terminologies, rationalizations, and scholarship—revolves around that contention. While the system has no difficulty accepting that the Lebanese could be descended from the "Phoenicians," or the Iraqis from the Babylonians, somehow Zionism wants a different theory for Palestine and the Palestinians. Zionists want to see Palestinians as migrant "Arabs" from the surrounding "countries," or from the Arabian Desert, to which they should return. Of course, when there were no borders, nothing prevented someone living in what is now Jordan from moving to live in Palestine, nor was it unusual for someone from Jerusalem to move to Dimašq or Ṣaida (Sidon).

The fact remains that people in villages and towns mostly stayed in place over the millennia, particularly in the small villages of Palestine and Greater Syria. Continuity is a lasting reality of the region, Palestine included. Now a foreign invader is claiming otherwise for its own purposes, pretending so avidly to be native whilst dispossessing the real native people, saying that it took over a barren depopulated land in order to make it green. For such claims to be believed by some, due to their own ignorance, greed, or religious obsession, only highlights the utter credulity of which the human mind is capable. "All who cultivate the soil in Palestine are Arabs," wrote a famous U.S. observer in 1857 (see Chapter 3). But even such testimony is unnecessary in order to refute the classic Zionist colonial justification, since the region has always had—as it continues to have—agricultural land coinciding with barren stretches, the sown and the desert combined, from which it derives much of its special status and lore.

The region had been a whole for millennia, just as Palestine was a continuous unit, disrupted only in the aftermath of World War I, with the division of the land into artificial states with neat border lines drawn up by the colonial powers, and by the creation in 1948 of a Zionist entity as an equally artificial body in its midst. In fact, the Palestinians, Lebanese, and Syrians are not only close to each other, but also in some of their cultural traits closer to people in, say, Cyprus or Greece, than they are to people in the Arabian Peninsula. The difference is that they now speak Arabic, and most of them belong to various Muslim or Christian sects. Though it is occasionally convenient for Christian fundamentalists and Zionists to identify the Palestinians as "Philistines" or "Canaanites" or "Ishmaelites" (all used in a derogatory sense, for demonizing purposes), more often the Palestinians are classified simply as "Arabs." At the same time, unlikely and dubious links are proposed between the unrelated idealized entities "Hebrew," "Israelite," and "Jew," even though the connection between the Jews of today and Judaism 2000 years ago has been negated in scholarship (see Chapter 6).

Then there is the bias that sees national "consciousness" (which amounts to blindness in most cases) as somehow a positive thing. That the Zionists imported a European nationalist ideology and adapted it to the colonization of Palestine, that they are obsessed with trying to establish any connection to the past, or with "collecting" heritage items, does not mean that their method of identity formation is somehow desirable or healthy or constructive. A latent, less self-conscious, more nuanced identity that is comfortable with itself requires no such perpetual self-justification; it is much more genuine than an invented, ideologically driven identity that entails aggression toward others and has to prove itself through the constant reinvention of structures of exclusiveness. The tragic irony here is that such an ideologically driven identity, based on an invented national myth, is sometimes able to subvert the more benign natural identity that is genuinely rooted in the land.

It is normal for Zionism to try constantly to justify itself through adaptive strategies that change over time. Zionists are particularly inventive and circumlocutory in their arguments, often unethically so at the expense of others. A more serious problem, however, is that other people in the region, including local scholars as well as those living in the West, sometimes fall into traps that Zionists are all too happy to see (especially self-colonizing traps arising out of the religious literature). Thus they adopt ideas and identities that effectively truncate their deep history, or fail to recognize the region's formative contributions to civilization (indeed, that it represents the *first* civilization as we know it today), or forget to value this deep history as part of their identity (thus allowing others to freely appropriate and exploit it). Such problems only highlight the urgent requirement to formulate a revised understanding of the region's ancient history and its impact on present understandings.

Hence both the structure and the purpose of the present book. After a lengthy introductory chapter explaining some of the models at work in both public and scholarly contexts, the four chapters that follow attempt to dispel myths related to religious and cultural history and to explore the implications of recent discoveries or old facts generally concealed or ignored. Chapter 2 examines some connections between polytheism and the three monotheistic faiths, Judaism, Christianity, and Islam. Chapters 3, 4, and 5 deal with the invention of sacred sites in the region, the important discoveries at Ugarit, and the development of the alphabet as a medium for writing. Opening the second part of the book, Chapter 6 introduces the transition from ancient history to modern identity construction. Chapters 7, 8 and 9 address the contemporary situation as it is revealed in the various complexes that plague people's understanding both of themselves and of others, such as appropriation and self-colonization. Chapter 10 provides alternative theories about how modern place names relate to ancient ones, and is intended to expose the Zionist policy of erasing the Palestinian map. The final chapter looks ahead to the prospects for finding evidence of continuities and for retrieving ancient remnants in today's popular language and customs. In this chapter as well as others I offer anecdotes and other illustrations from daily life that I hope will add an authentic cultural flavor to the scholarly documentation.

Rather than seeing this book as simply uncovering hidden and subaltern aspects of Palestinian history and culture, I would like it to be taken as part of a process of "unlearning" to be followed up with an endeavor to renew and re-conceptualize people's understanding of the region. Palestine's centrality to the region's future—and most of all to questions of historical truth and untruth—must be emphasized. It would not be a healthy development if all the past fictions about the "Holy Land," and now about Israel, ultimately succeed in being normalized and accepted as historical fact.

Palestine stands within modernity as the site where an old model of colonization has been applied using modern tools of power. Its Zionist occupiers cloak themselves in righteousness, while implementing a system that reviles another people and dispossesses them in a land hailed as holy. While it shares some characteristics with colonizing situations of the past (in the Americas, Africa, Australia, or India), the Palestinian situation carries its own burden of peculiarities. Both the land and the people have been subjected to continuous colonization from ancient times to the present, from rule by ancient Egypt and other later empires to the more recent Ottoman, then British, and now Zionist occupation. In addition, there are innumerable factors that continue to distort (in fact, almost disable) the voicing of a normal history. Primary among them are the shadows cast on Palestine as the site of varying religious understandings of "history"—its status as a "Holy Land" for three powerful monolatries, each with its own monopolies. The absence of a local "empire" that might have recorded its main history is another limiting factor—plus all the cultural and political biases in the conflict between Christian Europe and the Muslim East from the Crusades onwards. Mimicking the latter, Zionist ideology and its century-old implementations build on earlier fundamentalist notions, obsessions, and constructions, exhibited in a phenomenon called "Sacred Geography" (described in Chapters 1 and 3). Zionism attempts to distinguish itself by pretending its movement is based on a "return" to a native land, and so exploits on-the-ground Christian and Muslim sacred geography as a supplement to Jewish tradition. Zionists, in justifying and exercising their colonizing objectives, rely in effect on all these past inventions, preconceptions, and colonial strategies.

Unmasking such past inventions is crucial to locating Palestine's predicament within the colonial–postcolonial–neocolonial milieu. This is also central to the question of how a colonized people might write a coherent and useful history. Postcolonial theory is practiced worldwide, but with few exceptions there is little in the way of application to Palestine. For me, metaphorically speaking, more than half the world is still "Palestine," in the sense of being oppressed, hidden, and subaltern. Palestine is what has been forgotten and undervalued, what is distorted and now fractured, though it is still not completely covered over. The better we can detect the great deception, and the "history" made by that deception, the more we are able to recognize its doings and be prepared to head into the future at least aware of the possible traps. A fresh approach to Palestinian history could be a globally valuable enterprise in relation to enlarging human consciousness and perhaps achieving a modicum of human justice.

Part One
Ancient Myths, Religions, and Cultures

1
"Canaan Nails":
Idealized Perceptions and Their Uses

I use "Canaanite" as a metaphor applying to all those in a condition of being dispossessed and maligned, anywhere and everywhere. "Canaan," by contrast, denotes the "Promised Land" or the "Holy Land," as one of the names for Palestine and parts of the region. It is necessary to understand the workings of this dichotomy between an idealized land and a demonized people.

A few years ago, I was driving from my temporary apartment in Stony Brook, Long Island to deliver a lecture on the "Canaanites" at the State University of New York. I thought that as a visiting fellow it would be useful for me to speak to my U.S. audience, specialists in the humanities, about those ancient people and the new discoveries relating to them. I wanted also, as I do here, to suggest something about the tropes and imaginary perceptions that tend to hold sway over both the public mind and some scholarship—a mixed heritage handed down in the West over centuries, and which for a variety of reasons affects even otherwise thoughtful people. I began again to marvel at how this could be the case in societies saturated with heavy scholarly tomes and media technologies impassively received so far away from the sources of most of the myths they have accepted.

It was sheer serendipity that, as I stopped at an intersection, leaping out at me from a small shopping center was a sign that read: "Canaan Nails." What could it be? A hardware store that sold construction nails? An antique shop? What else? I parked and hurried into the place only to discover, to my mild embarrassment, and with some bemusement among those inside, that it was a manicuring salon. Is its name merely a reference to a town called "Canaan"? Or does it rather suggest that this is the place to go if one wants the perfect fingernails—ideal nails, a luxury of primal, self-indulgent appeal. Yet why "Canaan" Nails rather than Unique Nails, Paris Nails, or Power Nails?

IDEALIZED PERCEPTIONS: THEIR DEMONOLOGY

This trope captures many of the assumptions and terminologies that characterize the dominant history of the region where "civilization" began—the region I call the East Mediterranean, in preference to the famously colonial designation "Middle East." It has now become possible to deconstruct this dominant history more effectively than ever before, and to recognize that popular perceptions are based more on incessantly repeated inventions than on facts.

While researchers have struggled over the last hundred years or so to cope with mind-changing discoveries, the gap between old and new understandings and associations remains huge. Widened in the past by distance or ignorance or conflict, this gap is now even wider thanks to various self-interested parties investing in old myths and misconceptions in order to prop them up for political, economic, and social benefit. The actual history of the East Mediterranean is still shrouded in mystery, whether for people in the distant West or for people in the region laboring under imposed self-understandings.

Western perceptions of the East Mediterranean have been formed by a complex variety of factors, some imaginary, others real: 1700 years of idealized constructions and expectations concerning a "Holy Land" (mostly imaginary); European enmity toward and competition with Muslim empires (first Arab then Ottoman); the various kinds of crusades (starting from 1099); the assumptions inherent in that convenient paradigm called "Western civilization," which emerged only in the sixteenth century; the employment of biblical models of empowerment in various colonizing projects; the sacred geography of nineteenth-century Christian fundamentalists; writings by travelers, pilgrims, and orientalists; recent colonization by Western powers and the region's division into "countries"; and now the Zionist project in Palestine and its colonizing activities. Often, what has been implemented in the region originated in imagined religiously based notions, which were developed to evoke strong emotions and inspire blind "faith," and which in collusion with other colonial strategies achieved real gains on the ground.

At the heart of these perceptions lie operative models and notions about how to perceive the people and the land. It is convenient (and in many ways profitable) to have a demonizing model: "Canaan" is the ideal place, whereas the "Canaanites" themselves, whose fruitful land is craved, are unworthy demonic Pagans. For readers unfamiliar with the biblical stories, the "Canaanites" are (arbitrarily) supposed to descend from "Canaan," son of Ham, one of the sons of Noah. Canaan was cursed by Noah into slavery for no other reason than that Ham happened to see Noah's nakedness. This cursing is a preparatory step toward exclusion from the preferred genealogy—a procedure similar to what happens in the case of Isma'il/Ishmael, Moab, and others.[1] Biblical cursing extends to curses of destruction, acquiring a projection of divine approval, thereby functioning precisely as a strategy for the guilt-free murdering of people—including women and children—and acquiring coveted lands, homes, vineyards and olive groves, animals, gold, silver, and all the other loot or spoils from the "unworthy people" who had built, crafted, tended, husbanded, ploughed, planted, and harvested in a land that could then be deemed to be "flowing with milk and honey."

This notion of an idealized beneficent land—along with the concept of a people favored by a god and granted the right and privilege to take it from its unworthy occupants—has been variously exploited in colonizing projects in the Americas, South Africa, and Israel.[2] It also characterized the assumptions behind the Crusades, with "Canaanites" replaced by "Saracens" (Muslims, "Arabs," or "Moors"). In colonial America (as I will elaborate later), relying more heavily on the Old Testament than the New, the imagined unworthy "Canaanites" were now the native American peoples and the African slaves—the former being forced to give up the land, the latter to work it. A religious typology, which had earlier provided theological connections and inspiration, was translated in the woods and prairies to the living colonial experience of taming the wilderness.

In Europe, by contrast, especially pre-Reformation and Catholic Europe, there was purportedly greater emphasis on the Christian gospels, though that did not stop the Crusaders from making the same kind of land claims and launching their campaigns. European ideas about the perfect state, a paradise on earth, took different secular and religious forms, whether that of "utopia," "the republic," "the commonwealth," or "the City of God." Europeans, however, continued to view Palestine or "Canaan" as the "Holy" or "Promised Land" to which they had an entitlement through their association with the Christian story. Among British and other clerics, especially during the nineteenth century, it was not infrequent for Palestine to be claimed as "ours."[3]

NATIONAL MYTHS

Such uses of "Canaan" are neither accidental nor entirely innocent. They are built into the very construction of some national myths, most notably that of the U.S., and more generally of the concept of "Western civilization." It is essential to understand how scholarly agendas and dominant public perceptions operate, as well as how Zionism relied on these perceptions to create its own national notions and still deploys them in expedient images to suggest that "Western" and Israeli people enjoy shared values—even as such values are contradicted by practices that defy concepts of democracy, human rights, freedom, justice, or international law.

The U.S. identifies with certain events and covenants described in Genesis and Exodus, the details being copied into a national story about the ordeals of the "pilgrim fathers." Ever since 1492, and more particularly since 1620, the biblical model has mirrored America's colonizing project and its self-justifications. As others have pointed out, the early Puritan colonists identified themselves as the people newly "chosen" by God to be given a new "Promised Land," usurping for themselves (as others have done before and since) a purportedly God-sanctioned mythology that rationalized their acts and sustained them in their wilderness ordeal.[4] They were the true "Israel" destined to establish a commonwealth in a new "Canaan." What better tool is there than to link the words of a god to one's own special predicament? The Puritans' condition in Europe was likened to "enslavement" in Egypt, their ocean voyage across the Atlantic was an "exodus" through the desert; the landscape of their new world was rich and desirable (but also, paradoxically, a "desert" wilderness that God dictated must be tamed); its native people, or "Indians," were pagan Cana'anites, Philistines, Hittites, and other "enemies of God" who in the narratives are said to have fought the "chosen people."

In a story that has become part of Thanksgiving, the corn taken by the colonists from Indian stores was likened to the grapes carried back from other people's property by two spies in the biblical story (Numbers 13; compare spies in Joshua 2). (Today, this scene is schematized as the logo of the Israeli Ministry of Tourism.) The scouting "pilgrims" sent out to survey the riches of the envied territory—grapes or corn in each case, seen as evidence of the fatness of the land to be conquered—take the food and think it is God-sent rather than thank the natives who have saved them from starvation. Upon reaching Plymouth in 1620, William Bradford, one of the early pilgrim leaders, kept trying (like the fabled Moses) to find a Pisgah from which to view a promised land.[5]

When, in delivering a sermon on charity, John Winthrop spoke of those who should be excluded from the commonwealth of Massachusetts, he named them "Canaanites."[6] Colonial leaders and preachers fashioned themselves after Abraham in a New Jerusalem, or Moses on top of Pisgah. In Harriet Beecher Stowe's attack on slavery in *Uncle Tom's Cabin*, slave owners and the clergy employ the argument that black people are descendents of cursed "Canaan" and so, Old Testament-like, can be freely enslaved, to be used and abused. Stowe's use of "Canaan" is contradictory, however, for while a grave-looking clergyman dressed in black quotes Noah's "Cursed be Canaan; a servant of servants shall he be" to justify slavery, contradicting of course Christ's various injunctions, Eliza is made to run across the Ohio River ("like Jordan") to the "Canaan of her liberty."[7] *The Conquest of Canaan* is not about Joshua and his crossing of the Jordan River, but is a novel published in the U.S. in 1905. More recently, Ronald Reagan described "the city upon a hill," using words from Winthrop's sermon, which inconsistently quotes Christ's Sermon on the Mount, and Bill Clinton likened the peace process in the "Middle East" to "parting the Red Sea."

Geography, piety, and reality creation often converge. One of the earliest colonial towns in Massachusetts was named "Salem" (after Ur-Salem/Jerusalem, whose name derives from the pagan patron god of the city). Other biblical place names dot the U.S. landscape: Bethlehem, Jericho, Jordan, Joshua's Path, Mount Sinai, Damascus, Canaan, East Canaan, New Canaan, Babylon, and Palestine, among many others. In the late nineteenth century and early twentieth century the U.S. religious imagination transferred its "cultural myth" to "fantasized reality on the ground" in exhibits and parks reproducing Palestine and Bible lands for local "you-are-there" experiences, while actual travel, texts, Bible maps, and research eventually led this "geopiety" to establishing dedicated institutions in Palestine.[8]

Such mythic adaptations alert us to how myths travel, how they are gleaned for useful elements to execute new projects, to make "sense" of one group claiming to be chosen and privileging itself against others, and to create geographies. It is a pattern people should be aware could be usurped in the future, repeated by yet other "chosen" tribes to disadvantage more peaceful or less powerful groups. It is still quite rare today to find much of an inclination in the media to counteract this type of thinking that is a primary source of biases and prejudices. One should be pleased to see sympathy for native North Americans in films and media today, though it has only arrived when there is no longer a "threat," and is certainly too late to do much practical good. Similar patterns of demonizing and claiming, however, have transferred the oppression that went with the designation "Indians" to other people and places.[9]

Use of the "Promised Land" metaphor in national mythology was not, however, limited to the United States. For example, it has not been unusual to see Britain as the real land of "milk and honey," or General Allenby as a modern Abraham when he occupied Palestine in 1917, or Balfour's promise to Jews as a fulfillment of British national mythology and identification with the Bible as "an English classic," or indeed Canada as a larger and better "Canaan."[10]

WESTERN CIVILIZATION

"Western civilization" is a construct of European pedigree that evolved only during the sixteenth and seventeenth centuries, a period associated with the Renaissance and with the rise of colonialism, and that was later exported to the U.S. This notion of "Western civilization," as I describe it elsewhere, is "an appropriative complex in an amalgam constructed of select ancient Greek, Roman, and Judeo-Christian elements ... a triple paradigm [that] delivers history as a monolithic, sanitized chain of civilized descent to provide cultural depth, civil precedent, and serviceable truth."[11]

Ignoring ancient East Mediterranean antecedents and other traditions, the construct is designed to form a useful identity, and to serve the purposes of power and knowledge. Scholarship generally serves it, and any scholar who dares violate it by discussing instead the live connections between classical Greece or Rome and the East encounters "entrenched positions, uneasiness, apology[,] if not resentment," as Walter Burkert noted. The defenders of the canon reply with multiple strategies of "containment," with neglect, or with "a new line of defense" designed to minimize new discoveries.[12] Because it is selective, the established construct contains incompatibilities and contradictions, which are nevertheless rationalized. For example, it manages to reconcile Roman methods in politics with the principles of resistance to hegemonic power in biblical stories, or it combines an admiration for Greek and Roman mythology as "elevated" with a condemnation of other pagan myths of biblical enemies (from which, as I show in Chapter 2, the Greek pantheon and the three monotheisms primarily derive).[13]

To ensure greater consistency, the triple paradigm is purified of undesirable influences. Since its three elements are viewed as superior, it fabricates connections among them, appropriates from other cultures where necessary, while inheriting the peculiar enmities, stereotypes, and biases of each element in the construct.

Cana'anites are variously involved in these inescapable contradictions. The formation of civilization in Ancient Greece owed much to the Cana'anites (now euphemistically named "Phoenicians"): the introduction of the alphabet, mythological elements, and the first city state in Thebes, thus perhaps the beginnings of democracy. However, in Roman history the same Cana'anites are vilified because they are the competing Carthaginians, just as in the Bible they are demonized as idolaters whose slaughter is thus sanctioned.

Coincidentally useful is that all the combined prejudices of the three elements can be collapsed onto the now "Arab" region, including all the biases against Egyptians, Philistines, Carthaginians, Babylonians, and other ancient peoples of the region (most recently the Persians-Iranians) who are treated negatively for various acquisitive or other purposes whether in the biblical narratives, in Roman history, or in interpretations of Greek history.

APPROPRIATION

The Prologue to John Mandeville's *Travels* to Palestine and the Far East anticipates much that is to come. It is a fictitious account written in 1356 based on crusader and other medieval sources, relying on second- or third-hand information rather than an actual journey that Mandeville pretends to have made. Yet while it is now easy to disbelieve Mandeville's fanciful descriptions of the East, it is much more difficult to distinguish fact from fiction when it comes to his account of the "Holy Land."

Mandeville speaks of the "land of promise" as his "heritage" by virtue of being entitled to the site where a Christ sacrificed himself and spilled his blood to save humanity. It is thus his duty to "win it [this 'valuable property'] out of strange men's hands." It is more than a throwback to crusader feelings. It is an eerie foreshadowing of fundamentalist Christian attitudes in the nineteenth century and of Zionist assumptions that employed a religious Jewish tradition to construct an absolutist system of entitlement that in fact now follows, and often mimics or depends on, such earlier appropriations by Western travelers.[14]

A Palestinian, especially one of Christian background, more readily sees the teachings of Christ and Christianity differently. Anyone who truly follows Christ's attributed teachings would tend to view all demonizing and colonizing projects with "Canaanite eyes." Or one would at least recognize, as for example Herman Melville does in *Typee* and *Omoo*, that, despite lofty missions, colonizing projects remain rapacious processes motivated by self-interest and have destructive effects on native people and on the land—effects that contradict Christian values. Such a conclusion would apply equally to the conquest of the Americas, Polynesia, and Australia by Europeans, or the occupation of Palestine by the British, and its subsequent colonization by Zionists, all of which relied to varying degrees on legitimizing accounts from Old Testament books, as Michael Prior, a clergyman scholar, elaborates in *The Bible and Colonialism.*

The complexes infecting concepts like "Promised Land," "Holy Land" and "Canaan" sum up many nurtured misconceptions that plague the public mind, as well as systemic scholarship and its terminologies, as applied to the people and history of the East Mediterranean region. A callous attitude toward this region remains in place both among those who have visited and those who only imagine it from books. They see it as a geographical free-for-all, or feel they already own it, or see only a vacuum to be filled with their wishes and imaginaries, or brand it with their construction of knowledge. Paradoxically, because the East Mediterranean region was the "cradle of civilization," dismissive or demonizing attitudes toward its people are accompanied by a desire to appropriate without acknowledgement the formative cultural accomplishments that originated in the region. For how could great inventions like the writing system or the first epic poem or early scientific discoveries be left in the hands of the present descendents who are seen as such unworthy people? When these accomplishments are acknowledged, it is often done grudgingly or distractedly. As a result, some Western writers have baldly claimed, for example, that the Sumerian/Babylonian Epic of Gilgamesh is the first work of "Western literature," or that the current alphabet is really "Greco-Roman."[15]

Palestine or "Canaan" has been expropriated far more than any other part of the East Mediterranean, perhaps the world. As I describe in Chapter 7, everything in Palestine and about it has been confiscated—its foods and plants, its cultural heritage, its history, its very existence. Especially after the rise of Zionism, knowledge about the region has been manipulated and invented to accommodate and adapt to the Zionist project and its claim system, generating not a progress of knowledge but what can be described as a *regression*, recycling the old claims with further distortions and major fabrications, despite the discoveries that have shattered earlier assumptions. As I detail below and in later chapters, these discoveries have invariably been elided or distracted or camouflaged, their interpretations twisted to ensure that they fit the ownership system.

REAL "CANAAN"

I have placed "Canaan" and "Canaanite" in quotation marks because I do not want simply to reproduce how the words are written in the West (and the pronunciation is something else!). I prefer to include the guttural *'a* (ʕ). It makes a difference. Rather than the imaginary entity that derives its meaning from biblical stories, Cana'an was a real region in what is now Greater Syria where an ancient culture thrived for several millennia and radiated its influence across the whole of the Mediterranean basin and beyond.

Figure 1.1   Lid of a pyxis, Mistress of the Wild Animals, thirteenth century BCE, Ugarit

The name probably derives from the word *kana'a* (the first known occurrence in Akkadian cuneiform in the eighteenth century BCE reads close to *kinaahnu*), referring to the people in the region who were partly known for their trademark purple cloth, for which they used a dye extracted from seashells (thus probably also "Phoenician" [*phoiniké*] in Greek, used to refer to the coastal people who exported the purple cloth). As well as the biblical "Canaanite," they were also in later periods and locales given other names such as Carthaginian, "Phoenician" and "Arab" (terms for which I prefer to use scare quotes).[16]

Perhaps the people in the larger Cana'an region did not always identify themselves as a nation or a unified entity, since this was never an empire but only a grouping of city-states and communities in which, as Thomas L. Thompson says, power or imperial power "did not exist in any indigenous form."[17] After all, even today people living in villages and towns in the region tend to identify most strongly with their close environs. In terms of general identification, there is little difference in culture or language among these various "Cana'anites"—whether those called "Phoenicians" in some coastal cities (whether by the Greeks or by themselves, and during which period, remain in question), or the people living inland in the areas between Egypt and Mesopotamia, or those who migrated and established settlements across the whole Mediterranean. In the area of Carthage (now in Tunis), it is certain that the peasants identified themselves as Cana'anites as late as the fourth century CE, centuries after the destruction of the city by the Romans.[18]

As I explain in Chapter 5, it is in "Canaan" that the first alphabet was invented, a writing system that was to evolve into all the scripts used in the West and East. While usually under the sway of one empire or another, its city states often at odds with each other, Cana'an produced impressive material remains that we still see today.[19] In Chapter 2, I suggest how its mythology influenced the composition of the Greek pantheon and was the source from which derive the gods in the three monotheistic religions. Recent discoveries, such as Ugaritic and other texts (Chapter 4), have shattered many old notions and have turned biblical studies upside down, revealing more antecedents for biblical myths and stories.

From Cana'an much has been taken, much of which still needs to be recognized. To continue demonizing the Cana'anites (or the

Figure 1.2 Triangular pediment, sign of Tanit/ʿAnat, second century BCE, Constantina, North Africa

Philistines or Babylonians), while appropriating fundamental aspects of their creativity and their material culture without recognition, is an act of the utmost ingratitude.

As you read then these very words, you are in fact reading in Canaʿanite.

TRAVERSABLE TROPES

I am using "trope" specifically to suggest the creation of images that affect people's minds and embed patterns of thinking by association and repetition, often with the intent of forbidding questioning. Instead of being creative and original, the tropes I refer to here tend to be conditioned. Particularly, I apply "trope" to the rendering of cultural images and images of selected enemies, or those one desires to perceive as enemies, especially in historical narration. A traversable trope is a term I coin for a trope that travels, and so has multiple or contradictory edges in cultural usage. It is exploitable in more than one sense, as with "the desert," used negatively in some contexts ("wilderness"; "desolation"; "Arabs") and positively in others (desert purity; asceticism; "Israelites").

There is a multi-directional bias against the Cana'anites in these tropes, in each of the elements of Western civilization. In the Judeo-Christian tradition they are condemned for a variety of reasons—in Genesis and in later books (and also as it happens in the Qur'an). In one episode in the gospel of Matthew, in what seems inconsistent with his other teachings, Christ initially dismisses and belittles a "Canaanite woman" (Matthew 15: 21–28)—though the woman is "Greek" of local birth in Mark (7: 26).[20] Despite their formative influence on Greek civilization, Cana'anites become the subject of some animosity in a later period of ancient Greek nationalism. Since the Carthaginians were economic competitors and so enemies of the expanding Roman Empire, which finally conspired to destroy Carthage, they (as the "enemy") were accused of being dishonest traders and decadent child killers. "Punic" is still defined as "perfidious" in dictionaries.

Similarly, other ancient civilizations received stereotypical labels that are implicated in stories and assumed "historical" narratives: Babylonian (money-oriented keepers of temple prostitutes); Assyrian and Hittite (brutal empires); and "Phoenician" (cheap commercialists).[21] So while there is some acknowledgement of these important ancient civilizations, unavoidable as it is, it is accompanied or erased by perceptual prejudices.

Such systemic tropes are implemented in everyday language and in scholarly writing. The word "Philistine" is still used to imply crudity and lack of culture, in dictionaries, in general speech, and of course famously in Matthew Arnold's *Culture and Anarchy*. Present-day dictionary compilers have not yet deemed it necessary to designate such words as offensive or racist.

Current writing in the West is often dragged by habit or design to accentuate these language prejudices. A search for "Tower of Babel" on the internet throws up thousands of titles and allusions that associate Babel with a curse and with the "confusion" of tongues, on the basis of the story in the Book of Genesis. While there have recently been occasional positive allusions to "Babel" in connection with multiculturalism or translation, the dominant usage is one of vilification. In what seems like a closed cultural circle, an educated writer might venture to accuse rival pedantic critics of being "whores of Babylon." And Babylon is generally associated with corruption, money ("the Babylonian woe"), and profligacy, just as the ancient Egyptian and Assyrian empires are often shadowed by the biasing implications of biblical stories. Hollywood films exploit such notions to comment on contemporary U.S. culture, often pitting the stereotyped decadence and corruption of these ancient cultures against the presumed virtue in Old Testament values.[22]

The above examples are just a small sampling of the cruel liberties both popular and scholarly language takes with prejudices that are not noticed as such because they are emboldened by "tradition." Negative biblical and classical associations have become entrenched in the Western mind despite advances in historical and archaeological research that should have removed such cultural bias. Through ignorance of racist origins and connotations, or a desire to resuscitate older tropes, language continues to be used to surgically separate people into the valued and the unvalued.

It is rare to see alternative views exposing the way such tropes are employed to vilify, to express hate, to oppress, and to disinherit.[23]

TRAVERSABLE "ARAB"

The term "Arab" is very traversable and pliable in its connotations. That is partly due to its associations and its history. Like a natural feature subject to interpretation, the variable image of the "Arab" acts as a mirror of the perceiver's eye, mediated as it is by period and by cultural, religious or political factors. Its complexity and multi-faceted character, as demonstrated in travel writing and literature, ranges from provoking fear and demonization to identification and idealization. Ironically, "Arabs" themselves tend to fall into the traps of this ambiguous identity.

One dimension of its significance, of course, is the nomadic life, more specifically nomadic desert life. The desert in itself, like the sea or other open and fluid landscapes, generates a variety of impressions and interpretations. For the conservatively civilized or reserved religious mind, the desert is seen as dangerous and uncontrollable, a "desolation," and the nomad who lives in it is unpredictable, untamed, savage or evil, not much different from a beast. Paradoxically, the "desert" and its "desolation" may also be transferred to heavily forested regions, as in some Puritan writing which describes the treed landscape of North America as a "desert wilderness." For the Romantic spirit, however, the nomadic signifies a return to original primitive nature, as in Blake or Wordsworth or Shelley. For the ascetic spiritualist, the desert may be a place of purity, or of existential freedom. For many modernists, as in Melville's "Of Deserts" in *Clarel*, in the works of desert travelers, or in T. S. Eliot's *The Waste Land*, it is in response to the emptiness of the desert that people find peace or in reaction to it that they create religious certainty, or else the desert is either a reflection of or an escape from a differently barren civilization.

Throughout the history of its Western usage, "Arab" has been confused with various other designations such as "Saracen," "Muslim," "Turk," "Moor," and of course "Ishmaelite" and "Bedouin." Isma'īl/Ishmael, in Genesis 16 excluded from the main genealogy because of Sarah's jealousy (his "hand is against every man, and every man's hand against him"), is assumed to be the "father" of the Arabs (in this sense, desert Arabs or Bedouins). Arabic-speaking tribes from the Arabian Peninsula embraced Islam and moved out to conquer the region to the north in the seventh century, to Arabize what is now called the Arab World, and go further out to spread Islam among other nations who spoke different languages. The first region they conquered (what is now Jordan, Palestine, and Syria) was close in its spoken languages to Arabic, since they were Aramaic-speaking in general (Aramaic being related to Cana'anite/ "Phoenician"). The population was mostly Christian and mostly sedentary, not Bedouin, and it eventually also became "Arab." The Arabs in Andalus or Spain were later called Moors. The "Saracens" were Muslim but not all Arab, just as the Ottomans (or Turks) were Muslim but not "Arab." Some "Arabs" in the region remained Christian or Jewish in their religious affiliation.

The main problem is that the image of the "Arab" fluctuates between that of the romantic desert nomad and that of the dangerous savage, just as people using the word "Arab" often confuse Bedouins with other Arabized people in the region. It is easy to exploit this confusion, especially if the intention is to vilify the people of the region, who are then all portrayed as being "Arabs."

Yet, when the biblically obsessed read the narratives about the nomadic "Israelites" they identify with them and see their values in a positive light.

It was thus possible for an educated Englishman in the seventeenth century to transfer the Spanish term and refer to Palestinian villagers as "Moors," or for an eighteenth century traveler to fear the "Arabs" (Bedouins in this case) with no cause, and still assume the townspeople are all "Turks," or for a nineteenth-century Cambridge professor of Arabic (whose book tries to track a desert route taken by the nomadic "Israelites") to suggest that the "Bedawín" should be exterminated, or for a U.S. navy commander on an "expedition" to the Dead Sea to be instantly ready to shoot "Arabs" (whose image he meshes in his prejudiced mind with North American Indians and Blacks and ancient Moabites of "incestuous origin") on first suspicion of imagined "treachery."[24] Zionism relies on and employs all these associations.

LAND USE

The proximity of "land use" and "promised land" arguments for possession of a "Canaan" leaves little practical distinction between religious and colonizing ideas as they have been applied in various places and periods. The land use justification relies on an interpretation of the injunction to Adam in Genesis 1:28 to subdue and master the earth and all its resources. It is then supplemented by the assumption of chosen-ness in later stories and the permission given by Yahweh to slaughter or enslave the inhabitants of the desired land. Metaphysical poetry of the early seventeenth century denotes the religious typology in its intellectual and figurative senses. For example, crossing the Jordan River to the Promised Land meant reaching an aesthetic promised land or a blessed condition or "freedom" (there was no regard, in this aesthetic interpretation, given to the rights or wrongs of the invasions and multitudes of massacres reported in the biblical accounts).

An early prototype is Thomas Fuller's *A Pisgah-Sight of Palestine* (1650), an absentee description of Palestine ("Canaan") which uses the Bible as its only reference. There isn't a single real description of the land or its culture or contemporaneous situation in this large volume—only what may be gleaned from the pages of the Bible as to its purported boundaries, underground resources, and vegetation (its "wealth" as Fuller calls it). The gates or other details about Jerusalem are derived only from what he interprets as expressly mentioned in the Bible, without reference to the actual gates at the time. However, Fuller suggests that such details would be useful for a prospective conquest or crusade, though his express purpose is to extract "moral" lessons. One such lesson is a sanction to "destroy people" in accordance with what "God commands," framed by the biblical model for acquisition of lands and resources and the authority from God to destroy "the Inhabitants of this lesser Canaan."[25] The point of such thinking is not only to imagine oneself obeying the highest imaginable commands but also to absolve one's conscience of any criminal act or intent, having already accused "the Inhabitants" of evil and barbarism.

This intersection of religious and colonialist thinking is further illustrated in two seventeenth-century accounts, by George Sandys (1615) and William Bradford (1620). Sandys has been praised as a secularist, an expression of "English humanism in its fullest flowering," whose account of a visit to the Ottoman Empire and the "Holy Land" made in 1610 is considered a new measure of "accuracy" in travel writing.[26] (Sandys later became treasurer of the Jamestown Plantation in Virginia.) However, his prologue, "To the Prince," describes the land and inhabitants of the Ottoman Empire in language almost identical to that of the early "pilgrim" narrative of Bradford's *Of Plymouth Plantation*: the land is a wilderness (or a "wast[e]"), peopled by corrupt "wild beasts" (the Ottoman Turks, and natives everywhere), and therefore deserving to be possessed and redeemed. Sandys' map of the region is "accurate" in its topographic outline but elides contemporaneous geography in the eastern Mediterranean by using ancient and biblical toponyms, thus reflecting avoidance of existing realities. It is not unlike Bradford's imposition of a biblical map onto the eastern coast of what is now the United States. In Sandys, religious skepticism about sites in the "Holy Land" is a symptom of his anti-Catholicism and does not prevent his application of a Bradford-type paradigm to legitimate prospective colonization and to construct an ideologically preconceived perception of the land as neglected and condemned, under tyrannous control, and inhabited by unworthy occupants, and so ripe for conquest.

As he passes near Hebron, Sandys describes it as "for the most part uninhabited, but only for a few small and contemptible villages, possessed by barbarous *Moores*; who till no more than will serve to feed them: the grasse wast-high, unmowed, uneaten, and uselesly withering." Here, "Moores" are transferred to Palestine, and become the Palestinian villagers. Sandys is blind to the area's cultivated greenery because it contradicts his expectation of Arab or Muslim neglect; how else could he justify his claim that this "desert waste" must be taken over and turned into a useful garden? As he returns home, he concludes that England is the only country that is not "defective"; it (rather than America or "Canaan") is the "land that floweth with milke and honey."[27]

This denial of Palestinian labor, its invisibility, the assumption of "waste," similar to the failure of the Puritan settlers to see signs of native American farming, is a prejudice perpetuated by generations of travelers and later colonialists, up to and including the Zionists who argue that Palestine was barren and neglected until they arrived to plant and improve the land. (For more discussion, see Chapter 7 and Chapter 11.)

Such paradigmatic operations indicate how power systems work, how pure self-interest and greed are made to look good, how lofty principles cover up inglorious practices, and how the blinding imperatives of conquest drive people to various forms of exploitation. What easier way is there to deny the rights or achievements of the native inhabitants of a land one wants to possess than to assume that one is superior, is "civilized," while they are unworthy "savages," and to cite one's own god in support of their dispossession? Who then is better entitled to use the land than you, once you have assumed the natives are failing to exploit it to the extent that, on your interpretation, your own god requires? No one can else plant as well, and so own as well.

D. H. Lawrence explains how the Romans generated negative tropes about the Etruscans, whose arts and culture they had appropriated and whose cities they had conquered: "To the greedy man, everybody that is in the way of his greed is vice incarnate."[28]

SACRED GEOGRAPHY

It was not until around the middle of the nineteenth century that this religious-colonial phenomenon was transferred fully to sites in Palestine. In this new type of sacred geography, pious typology and colonial logic merged, leading also to a pseudo-archaeology that is still pervasive. Hundreds of British, European, and North American books published during the nineteenth century typify these religiously haunted attempts to trace the sites of biblical narratives—not to mention a variety of missionary, millennial, crusading, colonial, "archaeological," and other motives at work in this period. (I discuss the relevance of such motives to the invention of sites in Palestine in Chapter 3.)

The sharp rise in travel to the Levant was an extension of the Grand Tour, and was made easier by Ottoman concessions to Western powers in the 1840s in return for European help in ending the occupation of Greater Syria by Muhammad ʿAli's forces, led by his son Ibrahīm. Increasingly, the travel was accompanied by the expansion of missionary and millennial activities pursued as a counterweight to the skepticism generated by recent scientific discoveries. It initiated a strange hunt in the "Land of the Bible" for any evidence that would "verify Scriptural sites" and prove "the veracity of the sacred record."[29] European and U.S. travel and exploration books concerning Palestine and its vicinities proliferated during the century. Most notable are Edward Robinson's *Biblical Researches in Palestine* (1841), William Bartlett's *Walks about the City and Environs of Jerusalem* (1844) and *Forty Days in the Desert on the Tracks of the Israelites* (1845), Eliot Warburton's *The Crescent and the Cross* (1845), Arthur P. Stanley's *Sinai and Palestine* (1856), William M. Thomson's *The Land and the Book* (1859), and Edward Palmer's *The Desert of the Exodus* (1871). Thomson's popular book was an on-site recreation, 200 years after Fuller's absentee account *Pisgah-Sight of Palestine*, of the land both authors felt they could readily appropriate as their "heritage," just as had Mandeville 300 years before Fuller.

One curious work is John MacGregor's *The Rob Roy on the Jordan* (1870).[30] MacGregor is credited with "inventing" a sailing canoe, a product of his Canadian experience. In recounting his dubious canoeing trip down the Jordan River (there are indications that at least part of the trip was a hoax), he reproduces the prejudices he acquired during his North American sojourns. In one place, he describes a confrontation with "hostile natives" on the river famous for the baptismal ritual. An illustration accompanying the text (see Figure 1.3) shows half-naked "Arabs" attacking him, carrying bones as weapons and looking stereotypically like North American "Indians." On his return to Britain, MacGregor acted out his adventures for profit, wearing Eastern dress. Even today, an Israeli boat-renting company, Dor Kayak, commemorates MacGregor's presumed journey down the Jordan on the "Rob Roy" as a believable narrative (his book is described as "excellent"), or at least treats it as an association to be identified with as credible and saleable.

Figure 1.3 "Capture," 1870

Two other odd works are wide apart in setting but share a similar theme. E. A. Finn, the wife of a British consul in the second half of the nineteenth century, wrote *Palestinian Peasantry*, only published by her daughter in 1923, six years after Balfour's promise and the British occupation of Palestine. Mrs. Finn was involved in missionary activity for several decades, especially dedicated to converting Jews, and based in Christ's Church in the same compound as the consulate (still there for that purpose near Jaffa Gate in Jerusalem). Jerusalem was a hub of activity for assorted missionaries, Christian Hebrews, Millenarians, and Adventists, whose main purpose was the "restoration of the Jews," or, in the absence of that, the "conversion" of local Palestinian Christians to the "true faith" in anticipation of Christ's Second Coming.

In her introduction, the daughter, A. H. Finn, sets out a clear agenda: what is all this talk about an Arab majority that ought to be given "self-determination"? The Palestinians, whom her mother studied, are "most probably of Canaanite origin" and so are too ignorant and unworthy to be allowed any measure of self-government. Her mother provides examples of customs (often exaggerated or inaccurate) whereby Palestinian farmers violate Mosaic law, though she concedes some similarities to the Israelites (see Chapter 11). Her real purpose, however, is ultimately political: these people are easy to subjugate: "The agricultural Fellahheen of the present day would most easily and naturally fall into the same position [not full extermination but servitude] towards any nation of superior intelligence and cultivation who might enter into occupation of Palestine."[31]

The Reverend Lucas' *Canada and Canaan* (1904) provides a particular twist to parallels between "Canaan" and the New World, a constant theme earlier in the colonies of North America that became the United States. For Rev. Lucas, the "heritage" that God's providence has given to Canadians is "nearly five hundred times greater than was bestowed upon His chosen people"; the rivers are wider, the mountains are higher, and the wealth is greater than that of the original Promised Land: "Canada instead of Canaan! Moses would have danced with joy." Of course, the embarrassing question comes up (though not directly because the native people go unmentioned) of how this God could sanction the destruction of other human beings, including children, in order to allow the chosen ones to control the land. Repeating Fuller 250 years earlier, and confirming the beliefs of many missionaries, his explanation is intended to satisfy the religious conscience:

> Two things respecting the early taking off of these children [of the wicked Canaanites] reveal the mercy of God rather than His unrighteous wrath, as the skeptic thinks. Their removal [i.e. killing] before any actual transgression on their part left them eternally innocent. Their removal before they were able to perpetuate the sins of their fathers, sins the most beastly or the most devilish, was a blessing for us who came after.[32]

The Reverend was no doubt recalling accounts of similar dispatches of enemy children related in the Bible. In the background there is always the concept of a kind of balance sheet that such self-righteous people project as a godly will that they merely administer: land is an asset; people are a liability to be dispensed with or brought to servitude.

Such callous attitudes are still prevalent, constitute an underlying driving force in politics, and are played out in the actions and thinking surrounding the "Holy Land" and its people, as well as in relation to other colonized peoples in the region and elsewhere.

ZIONIST EMPLOYMENT

The Zionist project has both made use of and extended Western cultural and religious accumulations. It has exploited biblical accounts believed to be historical in the West, attempted to collapse the distinctions between "Arab" and Arabic-speaking regions, merged "Arab" into Muslim, employed the land-use argument and the myth about "turning the desert green," and perpetuated ancient biases essentially aimed at keeping the "Arab" World separate from the sites of the ancient civilizations with which it coincides. It has thus become useful for Israelis to insist on calling Palestinians "Arabs" in order to diminish their native legitimacy, imply they have a nomadic nature (i.e. are naturally landless), and to associate them with "Arab" countries elsewhere, where they can always go.

In inheriting and exploiting such thinking, Zionism has apparently succeeded in solidifying some of the ancient biblical biases that infect public and scholarly perceptions of Palestinians and in legitimating its claims to Palestine as the "Holy Land." That background in Western religiosity, as much as the later Zionist movement, enabled the eventual creation of the state of Israel. Not only was the Balfour Declaration of 1917 influenced by fundamentalist thinking, as Barbara Tuchman confirms in *Bible and Sword*, the first colonies in Palestine in the middle of the nineteenth century were established not by Zionists or Jews but by the wave of millennial and Adventist Protestant groups who were expecting the Second Coming and so needed to bring in Jews and convert them in preparation.

The Zionist movement merely, though skillfully, employed the misperceptions built up and perpetrated over centuries in the West, and it continues to do so. It amplifies all the stereotypes generated about ancient and modern peoples (from the Egyptians and Philistines to modern Arabs and Muslims), which are collapsed onto the now "Arab" region. Zionist lingo, especially when geared to North America, is replete with allusions to the usual biblical parallels (especially those derived from Exodus) and to "pioneers" and "settlement." Some of the most biased travel accounts have been reprinted by Zionist publishers, with the intention of promoting Zionist claims to a land awaiting its redemption and presenting negative images of the "Arabs" who inhabit the land but are unworthy of it.[33]

Simultaneously, Zionism is stuck in the logic of misconceptions inherited from Western and Jewish religious traditions as well as its own fabrications. In relation to "Palestine" and Palestinians, the biblical precedents on which Zionists base their claims are often applied in contradictory ways. Since the Palestinians lived on the land before the Zionists came to dispossess them, the paradigm is made to work in a multiplicity of ways. Zionists are often unsure whether to equate the Palestinians with Arabs, Philistines, or Cana'anites—all supposedly negatively conceived.

Are the Palestinians "Arabs" since they speak Arabic—"Arab" being traditionally associated with Isma'il/Ishmael, who is excluded in Old Testament genealogy? That the Zionists insist on calling the Palestinians "Arabs" is a convenient assumption on several counts. First, the association with Ishmael is uncomplimentary in the biblical Western or Jewish mind; second, "Arabs" as nomads (according to one definition) are not land-based and so the land-use argument can be applied to them (they don't use the land; we turn it green); and third, as "Arabs" the Palestinians can be dismissed as crude and unpredictable nomads who migrated from the Arabian Peninsula and other "Arab" countries to which they should be made to return.[34]

Or are they the Philistines of today (the name "filastīn" is close enough), who fought with the ancient Israelites according to the Old Testament, thus acquiring in biblical and Western imaginings (and dictionaries) a bad reputation of being crude, uncultured, and untrustworthy? It matters little that archaeological findings have revealed a different reality about the Philistines and their culture.

Or are Palestinians the cursed and pagan Cana'anites, who cannot be trusted to rule themselves, and whose lands and properties Yahweh decreed could be taken by the ancient Israelites (to whom present Jews presume to be somehow connected), who are also allowed to slaughter as many as they can and enslave the rest?[35]

"HOLY LAND" AND ITS DISPERSION

With the establishment of the State of Israel in 1948, along with the larger Zionist objective of "Eretz Yisrael" (Land of Israel), a process was begun that is designed to erase "Palestine" and replace it entirely with "Israel." Until 1948 and for at least 2500 years prior to that, at least since Herodotus, "Palestine" (in its earlier variants such as "Philistia," in Arabic "filastīn") was accepted by everyone as the name for the land. What had been one Palestine until 1948 is now divided into a mess of disconnected entities: Israel, the so-called "West Bank" (part of Jordan from 1950 to 1967), and the Gaza Strip (administered by Egypt from 1948 to 1967).

It was a gradual process. A couple of months before it occupied the region and set up a "Government of Palestine," Britain gave the Zionist movement Balfour's promise of a "national home," on condition that nothing would be done to prejudice the rights of the existing population. In 1936, a British commission mandated that one third of Palestine become a Jewish state, two thirds a Palestinian Arab state. In 1947, the formula changed to approximately half and half in the United Nations partition plan, coerced by the U.S., despite the fact that Palestinian Muslims and Christians still then formed the vast majority in relation to Jewish immigrants. In 1948, Israel occupied more than three quarters of historic Palestine, with 800,000 Palestinians turned into refugees, either being forced out or fleeing in fear of massacres, and more than 450 villages emptied or destroyed by the Zionists.[36] In 1967, Israel occupied the rest. Hundreds of ever-expanding Israeli colonies, special bypass roads, army outposts, and a concrete Wall have swallowed up more illegally confiscated land, making normal movement or contiguity impossible. And the project continues through organized Jewish immigration and strategies designed to force the remaining Palestinians to leave.

In archaeology and anthropology, even now, it is still fairly common to refer to "Palestine" when studying different aspects of this specific geographical area, from its ancient past to the present. However, within Israeli scholarship in general, the gradual trend (consistent with denial of the existence of Palestinians and "Palestine") has been to use "Eretz Yisrael." In fact, "Palestine" has been systematically avoided in Zionist circles (except recently by more "liberal" Zionists and some Palestinian Authority officials who limit "Palestine" to the West Bank and Gaza). In Israel, the step was taken to replace or imitate the "Palestine Exploration Fund" with the "Israel Exploration Fund."

The term "Holy Land" is often used as a kind of euphemism by Israeli or Zionist scholars publishing in the West in order to avoid using the term "Palestine" but also to associate "Holy Land" with "The Land of the Bible" and with "Eretz Yisrael." There are scores of apparently scholarly works that employ this euphemism. One of them, entitled *The Archaeology of Society in the Holy Land*, pretends to be a neutral presentation of studies within a Mediterranean context (it claims to follow the approach of the *Annales* school). In a careful review, Graham Philip finds this use of "Holy Land" to be "unfortunate," further commenting on the uneven distribution of chapters: "one chapter for the five hundred years of the Persian and Hellenistic periods, but five to the seven hundred years of the Iron Age." Of course, the Iron Age is given this much attention because it has been traditionally associated with the "Israelites," whom Philip calls one of those "idealized communities" from which future research should shift away its focus.[37] The difficulty is even more severe than Philip intimates. For the confused terminology is reflected in the essays themselves and in the terms used by contributors: "Canaan," "Palestine," "Israel" (a name strangely and of course inaccurately used even in essays on the Paleolithic and Neolithic periods), "Southern Levant," "Near East," and of course "Holy Land."[38]

ANTECEDENTS UNCOVERED

One main reason that "Holy Land" is particularly "unfortunate" is that it has become harder than ever before to think of it as a special term dedicated to a particular spot of land (why should this land rather than others be holy?). More particularly, discoveries over the past 150 years have shattered many old misconceptions and biblically based assumptions accumulated over two millennia, which used to privilege this land and think of the Bible as "unique." Initially, in the nineteenth century, it was geological and biological science and Higher Criticism that undermined the stories of creation and of the Flood, as well as biblical chronology in general. And things got gradually worse.

One by one the region unearthed its own truths—as if itself in revolt against all the untruths. Starting in the second half of the nineteenth century, many precursors to Bible notions and stories were discovered. As a result, previous preconceptions about the "uniqueness" of the Bible could not be maintained, except by those determined to insist on it despite proof to the contrary. First, there were the findings in Egypt and Mesopotamia, such as a duplicate of the Flood story 2000 years before the Bible was put together, then more recently Ugarit, the Dead Sea Scrolls and Kuntilet 'Ajrud. Such discoveries completely changed the picture of the region's history and its religious and cultural development. Second, archaeological research and other findings have wiped out and completely undermined the historical assumptions underlying Zionist claims to Palestine, such as the Exodus story or the conquest narrative or the existence of David.

As I discuss in the following chapters, these discoveries have certainly made it impossible for anyone to see the monotheistic religions in the same way as before, or to credit the usual claims made about the evolution of the concept of monotheism itself. Rather, it has become clear that "monotheism" arose out of a polytheistic context.

However, these discoveries and antecedents are also used as excuses for expanding the "Holy Land" by those for whom it is useful to maintain the old ideas (see Chapter 7, note 12). No longer content with just Palestine or its immediate environs, biblically obsessed study has extended the "Holy Land" to include the whole region and beyond, simultaneously attempting to ingrain biblical chronology and geography, incorporating Greater Syria as well as Egypt and Mesopotamia in terms like "Bible Lands," "Bible Times," "Land of the Bible," and "Biblical World."

OLD-NEW SCHOLARLY AGENDAS

It is not only common beliefs that are at odds with the new insights gained from recent discoveries; the scholarly responses have also been mixed—ranging from denial, circumlocution, and muffling to acceptance, interpretation, and insight. Discoveries relating to the evolution of monotheistic beliefs, ancient demography, historicity, archaeology, sacred places, and languages all provide the potential for rethinking earlier imaginary constructions that have since been turned into unwieldy facts. Because an old paradigm of civilization still prevails and a new state (Israel) was established on old assumptions, there are defensive, often regressive trends in mainstream scholarship that work hard to fit the new findings into old moulds or otherwise subvert them.

In the background of the new discoveries, modern scholarship concerning the region has attempted to negotiate its way. The tension shows itself in there being at least five types of scholars, classifiable as follows: perpetuators, fabricators, mufflers, adapters, and challengers. (I do not want to use the common distinctions, such as "maximalist" and "minimalist," because such terms are intended to measure how much credence is given to Bible historicity.)

Among the perpetuators of old thinking I include scholars who are dug deep into "biblical research" as a profession, and also institutions and university organs, religious or otherwise, that have dedicated their mission to that traditional pursuit and have a great investment in continuing to do so. It is a kind of self-generating industry that grew out of and now sustains the systemic workings of the dominant constructs.[39] The fabricators are more usually

Israelis searching for confirmation of Zionist claims or Western sympathizers with them (including all early traditional Israeli archaeologists and many of their current descendents). The concoction or stretching or suppression of evidence becomes particularly acute when it relates, say, to conclusions about David, a figure crucial to the Zionist national project and Israeli claims to Jerusalem as "the City of David."[40] Those I classify as mufflers are intent on not wanting to acknowledge the real implications the new information has for their self-interested understanding, and so engage in circumlocution or cover up. They could be called paradigm-benders because, rather than challenge any aspect of the old constructs, they incorporate new discoveries (in order to appear knowledgeable) but still insist on the old claims and models. A good example of muffling is how some scholars have dealt with the discovery of Ugaritic tablets in their reflections on biblical mythology, as they speak of "cognates" and "assimilation," thus skewing the value of the original on hard clay in favor of the less believable redacted derivative (see Chapter 2, the sections "Antecedents" and "Unique Muffling," and Chapter 4, "Muffling").

Adapters are somewhat different from mufflers in that they exploit the new findings and recognize the need to revise history but do so by way of generating new theories that only arrive at the same old claims more cleverly. Adaptation happens as a result of the admission that it is no longer possible to accept the historicity of the Bible, though the theories generated still hold on to the old claims. Faced with contradictory discoveries, scholars sometimes respond with modified justificatory strategies (however indirect), and so perpetuate the same old politics of entitlement and claims. For example, since the conquest theory (Joshua crossing the Jordan to conquer the "Promised Land" and exterminate or enslave the Cana'anites) is now defunct, there is an interpretation of the contrary evidence from archaeology that proposes a theory of "peaceful immigration" or of a peaceful transition, so that the "Israelites" become really the same as the earlier "Canaanites," and the change is seen as an ideological or religious one rather than a "conquest." In effect, such a theory tries to say something new by appropriating "Canaanite" material culture and so solving the problem of the lack of any "Israelite" cultural material. At the British Museum, for example, Egypt, Cana'an, and Mesopotamia have many items on exhibit, while "ancient Israel" is represented by a posted text (reportedly written by Jonathan Tubb) and no remains at all to show for it. Critics of biblical historicity therefore seem to compliment this theory, not realizing that it acts as a replacement which is worse than the conquest theory because it appropriates the culture and thus wants to gain a less immoral legitimacy.[41]

Finally, a relatively small minority are challengers of the old understandings and so attempt to deal with new information more even-handedly, or to start new trends, or construct a new history of the region. They are not all recent writers, since for a number of decades there have been some scholars working in various ways to recognize what has been covered up by dominant history—people like E. O. James, H. W. F. Saggs, Alan S. Kaye, Walter Burkert, and others. More recently, new approaches have developed, such as those studying even more intensely the influences of the East Mediterranean on Greece and Rome, or looking at the Bible primarily as a mythic or literary product with characters and stories copied from earlier sources, or simply questioning the Bible's historicity. Among the trendsetters one could cite (not wishing either to exclude others, or to express no reservations) Donald B. Redford, Mark S. Smith, Martin Bernal, Thomas L. Thompson, Philip R. Davies, Keith W. Whitelam, Ze'ev Herzog, and Shlomo Sand. As a result of their positive intentions and their challenge to the dominant constructs, some of them (especially Thompson and Whitelam) have regularly been attacked, improperly called "revisionists" ("searchers" would be a more appropriate term), and are regularly maligned in Zionist writing.

Somewhat surprisingly, regressive trends in information appear in the most standard references, in famous, presumably reliable encyclopedias, language dictionaries, and Bible commentaries (for examples, see especially Chapters 2, 5 and 7). What could be the reason, except that vested interests, political or religious, have infiltrated such sources in order to influence what people are supposed to "know" and to propagate notions that promote their interests?

Then there is scholarship in Arabic, which is in a critically impoverished state. In general, there is a vacuum. With the conditions on the ground and the turmoil, especially in Palestine, very few good scholars have developed in the Arab World, or are able to stand up to the pressure and "innovations" of Western and Israeli scholarly agendas.[42] Most of the material published in Arabic about ancient civilizations is copied, often with unaccredited reproduction of illustrations, from Western sources. Further, inadequate attention is given to ancient languages, which results in the unpalatable phenomenon of re-translating ancient works, such as Gilgamesh and the Ugaritic epics, originally written in languages related to Arabic, from Western translations in English, French, or German. Even more seriously, because of revitalized religious sensitivities, Arab scholars are wary of challenging religious doctrine, and in view of the proximity of biblical and qur'anic stories often end up falling into the traps of Zionist claims by giving credence to religious stories as historical. Here, the Israeli occupation enters even the geography of the mind, attempting to stifle any natural evolution in intellectual and spiritual space.

An important difference lies in the fact that the West and Israel are able to invest much more heavily in scholarship, in the propagation of old views and the systemic stifling of new ones, and so have a free reign to do what they want. In the Arab World, scholarship tends to be localized and is often limited to particular country-serving objectives (these countries having been divided along colonial lines) rather than regional or national priorities (so that Iraq is concerned with Babylon, Syria emphasizes Ugarit, Lebanon talks about "Phoenicians," while Egypt asserts its Pharaonic heritage). In general, Arab scholarship seems to have fallen victim to the colonial divide-and-conquer agenda, and is generally kept busy with its fragmented concerns and the recycling of self-colonizing information, beliefs, and attitudes.

POLITICS OF ANCIENT LANGUAGES

Whether in regard to present or past political entities, to language classification, or to periodization, the dominant strategy has been to keep the cultures of the region, ancient or modern, separate and discontinuous from each other, especially in relation to the continuity of the past with the present Arab region.

The greatest fallacy concerning ancient languages is the fallacy of script. Language is foremost sound, not script, the signs used to represent these sounds being merely conventions. Looking at the maps drawn up by colonial administrators, a region that was and still is culturally and linguistically connected appears discontinuous. For example, in terms of languages, Akkadian, Cana'anite, Ugaritic, "Phoenician," Aramaic, South Arabian, and Arabic are similar. Cana'anite, Ugaritic, South Arabian, and Arabic are identical in their sounds and the number of alphabetic signs (see Chapters 4 and 5). While theories about "Northwest Semitic" exclude Arabic, the Arabic of today is clearly closer than other languages to, say, Akkadian, Ugaritic, or "Phoenician." That the alphabet was abridged from 28 to 22 signs in Phoenician and Aramaic does not mean they are very different languages from Cana'anite, nor does the evolution of the Arabic script into its present form mean that the sounds are not the same as in older languages. If one puts the script aside and examines sounds, the languages become more closely connected.

One possible source of the bias has been the idea that somehow Arabic, the live storehouse of all ancient languages in the region, is merely a language of the Arabian Peninsula and the Muslim conquest. It was the traditional Western custom, and now Zionist interest, to diminish Arabic and exaggerate the importance of Hebrew by inflating its connection to other ancient languages. In fact, Hebrew (square Hebrew, the only real Hebrew) was merely a script variety of Aramaic; square Hebrew was/is nothing but an appropriation of a square Aramaic which developed in later periods. As a fossilized script for a long time, Hebrew (or rather the Aramaic script now called square Hebrew) has of course some shape similarities to the older scripts. But that does not mean that the takeover of ancient scripts can be extended back in time to assume that there is an "ancient Hebrew" when what is done is to take inscriptions that are Phoenician or Aramaic or Moabite and say they are "ancient Hebrew." As I detail in Chapters 5, 7, and 10, there are several habitual practices that, intentionally or not, exaggerate Hebrew at the expense of other languages, and in the process often appropriate other ancient languages.

Partly because of the reliance on Hebrew in old scholarly practices (in addition of course to Latin and Greek), and now Hebrew's revival in Israel, there are Zionist presumptions, almost imperialistic, that inflate the profile of Hebrew and its importance compared to other ancient languages and elide the extent of Arabic and its age. To summarize: "Hebrew can be understood as 'biblical Hebrew' and in that role it is an artificial, scholarly language that is derivative of fifth-century 'Judean'. It is definitely not a live language. Square Hebrew script is square Aramaic, nothing more! This is well known and shamefully silenced in biblical studies."[43]

Then there is the irritating habit of using square Hebrew to transcribe inscriptions from earlier ancient languages, such as "Phoenician." Such a practice is especially inappropriate (as examples show in Chapters 4, 5, 7, and 10) when a language like South Arabian or Ugaritic has the same expanded sound system as Arabic and Cana'anite and when the International Phonetic System would at least be more adequate. Another compulsive habit, more characteristic in writings by Zionists, is to use hyphenation to give ascendancy to Hebrew. Similar to the invariable order of "Jew and Arab," the hyphenated expression always places Hebrew first, as "Hebrew-Aramaic." Aramaic was the *lingua franca* of the whole region for many hundreds of years, before and during the limited currency of "square Hebrew" as a religious script. Placing Hebrew first, unalphabetically, is an attempt to gain importance by eliding actual historical evolution, as if this script variety is more major than the real regional language.[44]

A recent Zionist interpretation of a Philistine inscription even attempts to appropriate the enemy Philistine language (which used "Phoenician" for writing) by speaking of "Hebreo-Philistine."[45] In a blatant illustration, on a stone plaque added to the Pater Noster Church on the Mount of Olives, in occupied Jerusalem (illustrated in Chapter 7), Aramaic and Hebrew versions of the "Lord's Prayer" are placed next to each other and pointed out by Israeli tour guides as being the same—in order to show that it does not really matter if Jesus is said to have spoken Aramaic.

A side glance is necessary to observe how mis-transcription practices affect personal names. I have always found it somewhat humorous to hear names like "Joseph" and "John," whether used in English or by Arab Christians given these names. This is because the Germanic "J" was intended by early translators of the Bible to be the sound "Y," which is closer to the original ("Joseph" is really *Yūsef*). The names of regional kings and historical characters are also still given in their Greek or Roman or Hebrew forms, again quite distant from any original pronunciation. For example, the name of the famous Carthaginian general "Hannibal" would mean more if we realize it should most probably be *hani-ba'al* (meaning "one who pleases the god Ba'al" [more accurately transcribed as "bʕl"]). The name "Hani" is still common in Arabic, as is a similar compounding in personal names such as "Abdallah" (*'abd* for "servant," so "servant of God/Allah"). The name of a king like Sargon should more closely be *sarakhan*. Cadmus, who is famous as the one who introduced the Cana'anite ("Phoenician") alphabet to Greece and established its first city-state, Thebes (in reality, "Taybeh," still a common name for towns in the region, modeled in name on Taybeh in Egypt and in organization on his hometown of Ṣūr/Tyre), is given the Greek ending. However, the name "Cadmus" is likely to have been simply a combination of the three consonants *qdm*, to which the Greeks added *-us*. The name could have been assigned to symbolize his arrival in Greece (*qdm* could mean "one who arrives," as it still does in Arabic). His sister Europa, who in the myth is said to have been kidnapped by Zeus, gave a continent its name (probably originally *ghurba* or *ghuroub* or *erebu*, a Cana'anite or Akkadian word, which in Arabic still denotes "sunset" or "western").[46] It is ironic, then, that sometimes these mis-transcriptions and Westernized forms are imported back into their region of origin, so that in Syria both a bus company and a publishing house are called "Cadmus."

CONTINUITY

How might one bring some positive thinking into this situation of misunderstanding, callousness, presumptive attitudes, and public ignorance—in order to establish a clearer understanding of the past of the region that gave the world, including the West, what is called "civilization"? At present, dominant notions and fabricated connections are prevalent, having become familiar through repetition, at the same time as real continuities are denied and a truer picture of the region's history is hidden.

In concluding this introductory chapter, let me emphasize that one of my main purposes is to reinstate the continuity of our region with its ancient cultures. That continuity has been made difficult to see, and is unfortunately not widely recognized, in the separate "countries" that were created by colonial imposition. I attempt to retrieve and make sense of as much of the neglected past as possible, though not all the answers can be found and a lot of gaps will probably never be able to be filled. Certainly, the ancient people of this region did not disappear into nothingness: they are the same people who are now called by different names and given various designations. The irony (in the context of "imagined communities," to use Benedict Anderson's now famous phrase) is how some national identities are constructed by inventing or appropriating a historical depth, while others who indeed do have such deep ancient roots cannot employ them usefully as part of their identity formation.

In the process of creating constructed identities, mainstream Western civilization and the Zionist system have appropriated regional cultures for their own use and convenience, forcing them into a set paradigm in order to achieve their specific objectives of power and self-worth. Simultaneously, the people of the East Mediterranean region, both ancient and modern, have been demonized and devalued, subjected to tropes and strategies that should not remain unchallenged. To come out from under the shadow of centuries and many-layered past constructions will require a work of rediscovery and reinterpretation necessary to expand our knowledge of the East Mediterranean and to produce something closer to "real" history. Though the people genuinely try to surmount their condition now with sheer endurance, they eventually need to employ their whole history more usefully in forming the crucial elements of their identity and self-understanding.

2
Polytheistic Origins of Monotheism

In this chapter I explain how the eastern Mediterranean produced a peculiar kind of mythology that influenced all other mythologies across the region and eventually led to the three monotheistic religions that billions across the world now profess. Here I set out to synthesize recent findings and show what is possible to conclude from them. The so-called pagan religions of the ancient eastern Mediterranean, which developed over the three millennia BCE, are anchored in the specific regional landscapes, without which they could not have evolved the way they did. By their inclusive nature, they were able to provide a particularly essential and universal human appeal. As a result, all the monotheistic religions, as we know them today, are derived from and continuous with earlier polytheistic religions of the region.

This assertion has nothing to do with the existence of God, an idea present in all sorts of mythologies that developed across the earth. Whether that idea has an ultimate truth is impossible for us to know. The intention here, therefore, is neither atheistic nor agnostic. In fact, much recent atheistic talk seems misguided in its premises.[1] The point is rather to dispel the monopolies exercised by those who think they own the idea of "one god," within a framework that views Judaism as the first monotheism, and Christianity and Islam as derivatives or refinements of what is propagated as the first one-god religion (arguably, depending on whose perspective is taken). In this posture, there is an assumption of moral superiority, a monopoly of the truth, by one or the other religion, especially in the case of Judaism. However, as I shall demonstrate here, such monopolies are now impossible to hold in view of recent findings showing that the gods presented in monotheistic narratives have a specific polytheistic ancestry in a region that also produced the beginnings of "civilization" and "history." The enshrinement in one tradition of one god as the true God is, therefore, as misguided as notions of atheism.

NEW MYTHOLOGY

"A mythology reflects its region," wrote the great American poet, Wallace Stevens. He goes on to tell us that he lives in Connecticut at a time when mythology is no longer possible. He was both right and wrong. Even now mythologies are still created in different guises, as a result of internalizing the new landscapes of modernity— of highways, technology, and cyberspace. It is just that we seem less aware of this process as mythological, and so either become disillusioned agnostics or atheists, or find replacement religions (Western Buddhism, cabalism, scientology, etc.), or, as most do, hang on habitually or obsessively to fragments of the established belief systems by which they remain haunted.

People grope for a mythic sense in an arid environment, or find it in modern rituals, such as sports, since these are all that is left to replace the old sources of essential and genuine nature-based mythologies. In a poem by E. E. Cummings, "anyone lived in a pretty how town," the four seasons, the "sun moon stars rain"—all the referents of a more natural life, the original elements and the sources of mythologies—have lost their meaning in a society of technologies and conventional routines. In postmodernist fashion, humans become the product of a third artificial nature, beyond the first primitive nature and the second civilized nature.[2] This development was accelerated by what happened in the Americas, where the brutal colonial endeavor exploited religious models to justify itself, in the process squandering the last opportunity for humans to make a fresh start, and eventually prompting more drastic realizations about the old religions and their new mythological replacements.

Two types of mythology cohabit in the world today. First there are contemporary unfulfilling forms of myth that evolve out of the artificial and desultory environment of modernity. Second there are the remnants of organized religions that grew out of natural mythologies and were systematized by civilized societies. The older myths were not "untrue" in the common sense implied by "myth." Rather, they captured the human predicament and answered existential queries in varying ways across different cultures and societies. However, the more recent religions have now become separated from their natural sources, and so are text-bound and burdened with formalized rituals and obsessions.

Such obsessions arise because the old belief systems no longer have a basis in the landscape about us, and so cannot nourish us as they once did. The original creators of mythological stories did not generally intend for them to be taken as real, literal history, certainly not as we imagine history today. Rather, they told of events and conveyed ideas to express their understanding of the principles that govern humanity and the world. And because the idea of a transcendent god is nebulous, and by its nature irrefutable, it leads certain minds to cling in literal ways to religious stories that no longer have real foundations and to moralistic values that may no longer fit.

DESERT AND VEGETATION

The rain remains meaningful in "our" region—I mean the East Mediterranean. Just as in earlier mythologies, present customs are still informed by the seasons. People welcome the rain, calling it a blessing and saying, "With each year may good come to you." It is not so much that they personally all need the rain, though the farmers of course do, but this appreciation of it has been left in the genes. Habitual lifelines have by now become genetically inherited customs that connect, albeit less strongly than before, to seasonal cycles. In the summer the heat is *mōt* (death), so the people seek the shade; in the winter, they go to the sunny side. That summarizes our mythology. By September people start thinking "winter" although it is still warm. Our farmers look for the rain to come to launch a new planting season, and wait for more rain to nourish the plants. Our senses and our blood are still tuned to that rhythm set thousands of years ago, despite all the cars and all the plastic, which in many ways the people don't yet know how to manage.

It is this nature—the mountains, deserts, and seas, the weather and the seasons, the stars, moon, sun, rocks, and vegetation—that human beings faced in the primitive state and tried to understand whatever they could of the plants, animals, and environment they had to domesticate and tame. It was out of these that the original mythologies were created, as ways of helping human beings to live and feel safer and more protected in a strange, unpredictable, and sometimes hostile environment.

No wonder then that certain settled areas produced fabulous mythologies, particularly in Mesopotamia, the Nile Valley, the Indus Valley, and in the Americas. Out of contrasting elements people saw around them and outside them they created gods and stories to appease natural phenomena, to explain the beginning of the world, to control floods, to find comfort in a life after death, and to give purpose to existence. As a way to show gratitude or fear for what was not in their control, they created gods and goddesses for the natural cycles, a god of the sun, of the sea, a god (or goddess) of the moon, one for fertility, a god of rebirth, one for the rain and produce, and so on. As settlement advanced so did gods and kinship and centralization of religion in the nation, tribe, state, or empire.

So, out of the desert human beings emerged—"desert" in the largest sense: openness, nomadism, blankness, meaninglessness, uncertainty. Then humanity moved into the securities of controlled vegetation, protective shelter, and more concrete beliefs.

GREATER SYRIA

In between Mesopotamia and Egypt lies the area of "Greater Syria," which includes present-day Syria, Lebanon, Jordan, and Palestine (the last is now Israel and the other occupied territories, Gaza and the West Bank). While Egyptian and Mesopotamian civilizations grew in a strip of green surrounded by sandy or arid desert, Greater Syria has a mixed topography and a varied climate. Its landscape is diverse: coastal areas rising gradually to hills of medium elevation and a few mountains; the hills are reasonably well treed, and in places planted through the use of terrace agriculture, while the flatter elevated areas and plains are ploughed for grain and vegetable agriculture that is dependent on rain.

In Palestine in particular, partially barren hills descend eastward to a depression where the Jordan River runs into the Dead Sea. It is an iconographic landscape that has everything except green—or rather it is everything because it lacks green. In the hills and plains toward the coast, the land is more fertile and green, and in pockets around certain villages and towns the agriculture is prolific. To the south, there is a solid desert, a wasteland which blends eventually into the more fluid, sandier Sinai Desert.

The mythology that grew out of Greater Syria (mostly "Canaan" in ancient times) has elements the other two mythological systems in Egypt and Mesopotamia could not develop, though there are aspects of interdependence among them.[3] The sun is more powerful in Egypt, and is essential for the process of planting by irrigation. In Greater Syria, the sun is more of an enemy that in the summer burns the ground and so is represented as the death god Mōt, who is powerful and threatening and needs to be overcome by the fertility god Baʿal ("bʿl"). The regional pantheon eventually developed, more definitely by the second millennium BCE, into about

70 gods. Importantly, it had at its head a father god (Īl, written as El in scholarship) and a mother goddess ('Asherah); below them in the hierarchy were female and male gods who fulfilled necessary functions which varied in connection with particular areas or cities, and so individual gods had greater or lesser power, and sometimes different names, in one or another part of the region. Often, just as Īl (El) is used in personal names (Ismaʿīl/Ishma-el, which means "El hears"; Isra-el, a name for Jacob which probably means "El rules"; Dani-el; and so on), cities still have the names given to them after a god who was important in a particular area or was a patron god (as in Baalbek, Ur-Salem/Jerusalem, or Beit-Lahem/Bethlehem).

Figure 2.1   Supreme God Īl (El),
from Ugarit

Figure 2.2   Stele of king paying homage to Īl (El), Ugarit, thirteenth century BCE

Thus a distinctive mythology developed in this medial position, between Egypt and Mesopotamia, which was more diverse and eventually more continuous and lasting. Green and barren areas, the solid desert and the sown land, a few small rivers, hills and mountains, caves, springs, coastal plains, the coast of the Mediterranean, and other peculiarities and distinctions were more conducive to the development of city states, contiguous with tribal and nomadic groups, as opposed to the monolithic entities and imperial systems that controlled Egypt and Mesopotamia. The relative mildness of the weather, the availability of fertile areas dependent mostly on rain, open fields for grain, and a variety of fruit trees in orchards—all made for distinctions that could not be matched in the flood plains.

Not only did the features of the landscape produce the mythological elements, but the distinct areas, in their unique combination of separateness and connection, also resulted in the development of monolatry, or one god being worshipped more than others without denying the existence of possible other gods. While the chief god Īl (El) was important overall, one of his sons or daughters might become powerful in the daily life of people in a particular area or climate. Where seasonal rain was essential for agriculture in hilly regions, the people tended toward worship of Baʿal and his sister ʿAnat, whereas in a dryer or desert region to the south the choice was for Yaw/Yau or Yahweh; in other places, other gods or goddesses were preferred. The Bible is a late reflection of these accumulated mythologies in a region that featured earlier one-god religions.[4] It is possible that Jesus called on Īl (El) rather than Yahweh (see the section "Pagan Christs" below), and Islam seems to have returned to Abraham's god Īl (El). It is ironic that the Bible, the Old Testament and the New Testament, reached a Western populace who were unaware of such a background, and in whose environment such a mythology could not have emerged, and who thus developed and ingrained an essential attraction to it.

ANTECEDENTS

"Antecedent" in this context refers to a narrative or event that occurred before another that is narrated in more or less the same way. During the nineteenth century, the discovery of such literary and mythological precursors to biblical stories started to emerge from Mesopotamia and Egypt, with hundreds of archaeological and epigraphic findings. Among the first great finds by George Smith in Iraq in the second half of the nineteenth century were tablets in cuneiform that turned out to be part of the Epic of Gilgamesh. They contained an account of the Flood that is almost the same as the story of Noah. In 1876, Smith published *The Chaldean Account of Genesis*.[5]

More recently other parallels have come to light. Most significant, as I discuss in Chapter 4, are the religious texts from Ugarit in northwestern Syria, first uncovered in 1928, and what they reveal about the composition of the "West Semitic" or Canaʿanite pantheon as well as regional culture. Several scholars, among them Mark S. Smith, have probed some of these connections, which illustrate how the Ugaritic texts from the second millennium BCE show the extent to which present monotheistic religions—more specifically the "Israelite" religion—have their origin in the earlier polytheisms.[6]

It was not possible to come to such conclusions, at least definitively, before the latter half of the twentieth century. There were plenty of antecedents to be discovered and they were often devastating to the then received interpretations; their implications were also obvious to any reasonable mind. But there was/is always an argument that the overly religious will make against an antecedent, providing them with a way out; they cannot draw the obvious conclusions from the evidence because they want to hang on to their old ideas. One influential collation of antecedents was made by James Bennett

Pritchard in the 1950s.[7] As much so now as then, apologists for the Bible insist on seeing and not seeing the parallels. They look at them because they can't avoid them but then want to either deny them or point out that there are differences—that the Bible is still the product of divine inspiration by one god and that it has a superior moral message in comparison to the recovered earlier sources. So they say things like: the Bible was "unique" before we knew these things, my tradition tells me it is unique, my belief tells me it is unique, my job (especially if a clergyman or biblical scholar or otherwise personally invested) tells me to espouse its uniqueness.

As a result, discussion of antecedents was and continues to be biased by this notion of biblical "uniqueness" and by privileging assumptions about the Bible's historicity, or its "morality," or its God-given truth. With the Flood story, for example, the source found in the Epic of Gilgamesh came 2000 years before the Bible was put together, yet the details of the two stories are very similar (the pitch to seal the boat, the animals loaded onto the boat, the mountain where the boat lands, the birds sent out, and so on), though the names of the main characters are different and there are some differences such as in the number of days it rains and the order in which the birds are sent out. These minor differences are to be expected considering the time separating the two stories and the vagaries of copying, translation, and adaptation. However, biblical scholars and other commentators have been eager to argue that in Gilgamesh the gods are upset and want to destroy humans because they are disturbed by human "noise" (a detail nowhere to be found in the epic), whereas the story in the Bible, they say, has a moral purpose related to the punishment of human sinfulness. However, the morality in Gilgamesh is clear to a reader prepared to note that the god Ea defends his action to save Uta-naphishti and his family because, he insists, only those who transgress should be destroyed. In fact, in its narration of the hero's adventures, the Epic of Gilgamesh presents a natural balance of forces between civilization and wilderness that is more nuanced than the dogmatic morality of the Book of Genesis, which seems to give license to humans to control and exploit. In this sense, the original epic not only reflects that ancient setting but has much more relevance to our contemporary world and its environmental challenges.

The evidence on solid clay or stone of earlier originals ("parallels") has been interpreted by most "archaeologists" of the "Holy Land," by religious scholars, and by some literary critics as somehow of lesser value, as forming merely a "background" to the biblical narratives. Effectively, however, more and more concrete discoveries continue to shatter the old assumptions, so that the Bible is shown more clearly to be a mixture of modified precursors, and the god in it merely one in a regional pantheon. The Exodus account, of which there is no historical record or evidence of any kind, is most likely a recycled story about another people, and the story of Moses has a striking similarity to that of *Sarakhan* (Sargon).[8] And yet there is an increasingly defensive circumlocution among most biblical scholars, and malignity from Zionists, toward new historians who work to recover such lost knowledge. A discussion by one recent commentator is typical of recurrent clerical themes and of the circular logic of self-deceptive reassurance:

> Some parallels between Israel and ancient Near Eastern practices and beliefs suggest the possibility of a common origin ... through divine revelation the practices or beliefs were divested of their pagan distortions in order to use them as a proper vehicle to communicate the divine message. ... *Sometimes He [God] took a religious, cultic or legal regulation or practice and redefined or re-configured it in order to communicate, in a reliable way, His will to His people, or in order simply to adapt it to the theocracy. By acknowledging that God was directly involved in the process of rejecting, polemicizing, adapting, re-formulating, and incorporating some of the cultural, religious, cultic, and legal practices of the ancient Near East, we can honor the divine nature of Scripture and justify the need to submit to its authority.*[9]

Figure 2.3   Adam and Eve or "Temptation" seal, Mesopotamia, twenty-third century BCE

The denials often take even more extreme forms of circumlocution. George Smith came to reasonable conclusions almost 150 years ago after discovering the fragment of the Flood story from

Gilgamesh and a seal showing a female and male in front of a tree, which he identified with a story similar to Adam and Eve in the Garden of Eden. Curiously, a recent commentator, T. C. Mitchell, whose home is the British Museum (where the pieces are lodged) tries to deny the clear implications: "The date-palm between them and the snake may have had fertility significance and there is no reason to connect the scene with the Adam and Eve story." On the creation story, he surmises: "This account [*enuma eliš*] is typical of others and shows that, apart from individual details, the Mesopotamian creation stories have little in common with the early chapters of the Bible."[10] The non sequitur after "and" in the first case and the use of "typical" to downgrade earlier myths betray an illogical insistence on something special about biblical stories. Considering that periods of up to almost 2000 years separate the original sources from the biblical adaptations, it is only to be expected that plots or details would be altered with the passage of time and the process of copying. This muffling phenomenon betrays a simultaneous appropriating and demonizing of regional cultures, along with the privileging of the Bible. How could people invested in such devaluing assumptions ever recognize that "Israelite" religion (and thus subsequent monotheisms derived from that tradition) is not as distinct as they want to assume, or that the biblical god, the god that came down in the tradition that the West inherited and has believed in for so long, is merely one of the sons of the pantheon chief? E. C. B MacLaurin remarks on the "attempt in official religion to conceal the fact that El and YAHWEH were once worshipped as separate deities," not quite realizing at the time he wrote what has since become clearer, as I demonstrate below—that Yahweh is one of Īl's (El's) several sons.[11]

Other scholars may view the Bible as "literature," but still want to maintain its centrality. As Robert Alter and Frank Kermode say in *The Literary Guide to the Bible*, while its importance is a "historical accident," the Bible is something of the "strange" past that "we somehow must understand if we are to understand ourselves." This thinking is close to the effort at self-understanding that led to Northrop Frye's lifelong labor to explain the Bible's inscrutability in Western heritage, by "recreation" of inherited topography in literary theory, as in *The Great Code*.[12]

UNIQUE MUFFLING

It is not only this respect for "tradition" that has been responsible for muffling new findings or old facts. In the next few sections, I will discuss various issues related to how the implications of the biblical text itself have been covered up or muted, especially with regard to the Old Testament. I will also draw attention to matters related to accuracy in translating key passages, evidence of ancient and modern textual tampering (a matter far more drastic than the often discussed issue of "redaction"), earlier variants of biblical texts that reflect polytheistic origins, and the issue of a "pagan Christ."

The obvious and unavoidable reference to "the sons of God" (Genesis 6: 1–4) is present in old and new biblical translations, though it seems to have had no effect in alerting most readers. Crucial passages, discussed below, such as Exodus 6: 2–3 (where the god's name changes), psalms such as Psalm 82 (which, among others, contains evidence of a council of gods), and Deuteronomy 32: 8–9 (whose original text, indicating a pantheon, was altered later) are all too far-reaching in what they show for those who don't want to change their minds. As a result, the full implications are diluted by evasive interpretation in commentaries, biblical scholarship, and the various Bible translations.

Even before such clearer evidence emerged, a philosopher like David Hume could see the façade of monotheistic assumptions. His 1757 "Natural History of Religion" (for which he was threatened with excommunication) contrasts some of the characteristics of polytheism and monotheism. Hume considers polytheism to be "sociable" whereas all the monotheistic religions by their nature harbor "intolerance." He argues that "polytheism or idolatry was … the first and most ancient religion of mankind," not the "belief of invisible, intelligent power," and that "about 1700 years ago all mankind were idolaters." Alexander re-established polytheism in Babylon after his occupation of it, its former princes having made their religion monotheistic. If one thinks Judaism predates that, Hume explains: "Thus, notwithstanding the sublime ideas suggested by *Moses* and the inspired writers, many vulgar *Jews* seem still to have conceived the supreme Being as a mere topical deity or national protector."[13]

Hume arrived at these conclusions on the basis of philosophical thinking and the then available scholarship. He did not know of course that discoveries and scholarship more than 200 years later would confirm much more even than his conclusions—specifically that Judaism was merely a small offshoot of polytheistic religions in Greater Syria, that it worships one of the gods in a pantheon, that many characteristics of Christ pre-existed in pagan religion, and that all three monotheisms in various ways have polytheistic ancestry.

Figure 2.4 ʿAsherah, mother goddess and consort of Īl (El), clay figurine, circa eighth-century BCE

The pantheon was not very clear until relatively recently. The discoveries came out of the blue, so to speak. Two of the most important (Ugarit in 1928 and the Dead Sea Scrolls in 1947) were uncovered accidentally—by a local farmer in the first case and a shepherd boy in the second. It was some time before their implications were fully appreciated. Not only was translation difficult but the scholars themselves had to struggle with the implications. Further, inscriptions such as those from Kuntilet ʿAjrud and Khirbet el-Qōm (about the eighth century BCE) leave no doubt as to the existence of syncretistic cults which incorporated various beliefs in the south of Palestine, where Yahweh was worshipped along with Īl (El), Baʿal, and the goddess ʿAsherah. In fact, a discovery such as that at Kuntilet ʿAjrud unmoors the traditional narrative so much that some traditional Zionist-inclined scholars attempted to "remove the name of ʿAsherah from the inscriptions."[14] Ancient editors as well had "attempted to eliminate the evidence of her [ʿAsherah's] worship among the Israelites."[15]

MISLEADING TRANSLATION

Translation has been a major obstacle to recognizing the polytheistic underpinnings of the Bible, particularly textual allusions that indicate the existence of a divine assembly or council of gods, a pantheon in other words, and the prominence of two gods from that pantheon. The misleading use of "Lord" (for Yahweh) and "God" (where Il/El occurs) has created the impression that the two gods are the same.

Before elaborating on these translation issues, it is necessary to provide a brief description of the sources for available translations of the Bible (the Pentateuch and other books in the Old Testament, and the New Testament). Translation difficulties with the New Testament are typical of any translation work, in this case from Greek, although it is well known that church authorities removed certain books and passages to produce the texts we have today. On the other hand, the Old Testament has a more complicated and intractable history of transmission and redaction. "Redaction" is a long-standing subject of study, to determine what was written when and by whom, which in effect has shown the lack of actual historical sequencing in the various books in terms of date of writing. However, that is not my main concern here.

Until recently, the major manuscript authority from Hebrew was the Masoretic text and its surviving copy, the Leningrad Codex, which is about 1000 years old. The only older manuscript tradition was the Septuagint, a translation into Greek done in the second century BCE. Translators into common languages such as German and English used the Masoretic text since they assumed the Hebrew to be more reliable or "original" than the Septuagint. They did not of course know that the Dead Sea Scrolls would be discovered in the middle of the twentieth century.

At least two types of errors resulted. First, the translators either did not notice or purposely sought to avoid certain unconventional implications, such as the presence of more than one god in the biblical text itself. The second error occurred because in using the Masoretic text the translators inadvertently worked with passages where the original was altered or suppressed for theological reasons.

ĪL (EL), YAHWEH, AND THE PANTHEON

Translators and "editors" either did not recognize or wanted to avoid polytheistic suggestions, so they failed to distinguish or suppressed the distinction between the god Īl (El) and the god Yahweh. Instead, they used "God" where Īl (El) is mentioned in Hebrew and "Lord" for Yahweh or equivalent ("Lord" is a translation of "Adonai").[16] Contrary to the New Revised Standard Version (NRSV) and other presumably standard translations, such as the New American Bible (NAB) and the Revised English Bible (REB), the New Jerusalem Bible (NJB) is the only church-affiliated translation today that clarifies the common confusion between "God" (Īl / El) and "Lord" (Yahweh):

1   Exodus 6: 2–3 NRSV (~REB, NAB):

    God also spoke to Moses and said to him: "I am the LORD. I appeared to Abraham, Isaac, and Jacob as God Almighty, but by my name 'the Lord' I did not make myself known to them."

2   Exodus 6: 2–3 NJB:

    God spoke to Moses and said to him, "I am Yahweh. To Abraham, Isaac and Jacob I appeared as El Shaddai, but I did not make my name Yahweh known to them."

This passage can most likely be explained as an instance where the god of the Old Testament, Yahweh, a son of the chief deity Īl / El (cf. Allah), is made to subsume the father god and thus claim an exclusive role in one tradition, in a manner similar to what happened in other regional pantheons and in the Greek pantheon. Traditional translations (and modern popularizing ones) in rendering "Yahweh" as "Lord" and "Īl / El" as "God" end up hiding the difference between the two deities. This confusion of the two is kept not only in traditional and religious sources but also by contemporary analysts of religion who elide the differences by assuming that the gods in the three monotheisms ("God," "Yahweh," "Lord," and "Allah") are one and the same.[17]

PROOF DEFINITE

The common idea that monotheism goes back to the presumed time of Abraham and Jacob or of Moses (or even, so some revise, a later period associated with "reformers" like Josiah) cannot be sustained. It is not just that, as shown above, the sole worship of Yahweh was not developed in the seventh century BCE—a period much later than "Moses" or "David," as evidenced by Kuntilet 'Ajrud. The very polytheistic recognition that Yahweh was one of the sons of Īl (El) was present in the Old Testament itself as late as the second and first centuries BCE.

This has come to certain light more clearly since the discovery of the Dead Sea Scrolls in 1947, though the translation took several decades to filter through. Among other things, as shown below, Deuteronomy 32: 8–9 demonstrates that a scribe or scribal committee fabricated a change in the text in order to suppress any polytheistic suggestion. The altered text (what became the Masoretic) was the one used in later centuries in translation of the Bible into all the common languages that we read today.

Even without comparison with the Dead Sea Scrolls, other parts of the Old Testament imply a pantheon. Such buried suggestions of polytheism in the biblical texts have now become clearer. As an example, the best translation of the beginning of Psalm 82 is as follows: "Yahweh takes his stand in the Council of El to deliver judgment among the gods." Such a translation not only agrees with the text but also shows that the psalm's sense is muddled in any other translation, sometimes apparently on purpose.[18]

The crucial passage from Qumran (Dead Sea Scrolls, second–first century BCE) is Deuteronomy 32: 8–9. Let me quote it in four translations: the first is a traditional one based on the Masoretic text (the most common and widely used), the second is from a recent Jewish source, and the third and fourth take account of the Dead Sea Scrolls.

1 When the Most High divided to the nations their inheritance, when he separated the sons of Adam, he set the bounds of the people according to the number of the children of Israel. For the LORD'S portion [is] his people; Jacob [is] the lot of his inheritance.
(King James Version, 1611)

2 When the Supreme One gave the nations their inheritance.
when He separated the children of man,
He set the borders of the peoples
according to the number of the Children of Israel.

> For *HASHEM*'s [*HASHEM*, "the Name," to avoid pronouncing the god's name] portion is His people: Jacob is the measure of His inheritance.
> (*The Tanach*, Stone Edition, New York: Mesorah Publications, 1996)

3 When the Most High apportioned the nations, when he divided humankind, he fixed the boundaries of the peoples according to the number of the gods; the LORD'S own portion was his people, Jacob his allotted share.
(New Revised Standard, 1989, 1995)

4 When the Most High gave the nations each their heritage, when he partitioned out the human race, he assigned the boundaries of nations according to the number of the children of God, but Yahweh's portion was his people, Jacob was to be the measure of his inheritance.
(New Jerusalem Bible, 1985)

What the above demonstrates is that polytheistic implications in the original text were altered to reflect, or more accurately appropriate, an exclusive monotheistic notion. Further, some present sources that are invested in this monopoly want to maintain that impression today rather than to acknowledge the truth. (The Stone Edition seems to benefit from recent translations, except the most sensitive phrases, as it reinstates "Children of Israel" instead of the original "Children of God.") What is amazing is that the Dead Sea Scrolls (and now the NJB) agree with the Septuagint in the rendering of these lines. The change or priestly editing must have been made some time after the first century BCE, so that eventually the eleventh century CE Hebrew copy preserved that alteration and transferred it to later translators and readers. Who changed the text of Deuteronomy 32: 8–9 and when is still undetermined; probably not the Masoretes but some other scribes before the time of Jerome, since Jerome uses "sons of Israel" rather than the original "sons of God (El)" in his translation to the Latin vulgate in the late fourth century CE.

It is transparent in the original Qumran passage that Īl (El) is the father god who distributes the world and its peoples among his sons—one of whom is Yahweh, who gets as followers the tribes of Israelites descended from Jacob. However, the fabricated alteration replaced "sons (or children) of God/El" with "sons of Israel," a change intended to appropriate God to the Israelites and to erase any suggestion of polytheism from the original text:

> In place of the reference to the "sons of Israel" the Greek witnesses read "angels of God" or "sons of God" (the latter is found in the most ancient tradition), a reading presupposed in several early sources and referred to as late as the medieval period ... The *Vorlage* of the Greek is now confirmed by Deuteronomy, which preserves the phrase "sons of Elohim" (cf. Psalm 82.1 for a similar reference to divine beings). This is in all likelihood the original reading, as it is more probable that a reference to divine beings was later suppressed for theological reasons than that it was substituted for the reading "sons of Israel."[19]

Yet, other commentators who seem to be aware of the text in the Dead Sea Scrolls still want to insist on the implications of the later altered text.[20]

This key passage from Qumran's first- or second-century BCE Dead Sea Scrolls shows that some change was made later, reflected afterward in the Hebrew text protected by the Masoretes, which was adopted for the most common translations made during the fifteenth, sixteenth, and seventeenth centuries and is today still used by most readers in "revised" versions. In that changed text, the Old Testament god Yahweh, a son of the chief deity Il / El, is made to assume an exclusive role in a manner similar to what happened in other regional pantheons and in the Greek pantheon. (In fact, the Greek pantheon is, with natural modifications, directly derived from the Cana'anite pantheon: Il / El = Kronos, Ba'al = Zeus, and so on.)[21]

Just as with the original biblical text, the Ugaritic cycles (see Chapter 4 and note 5 there) also speak of *yw* (Yahweh) as a son of Il (El). The qur'anic Allah is most likely a return to the Abrahamic Il (El), a link emphasized in the Qur'an itself. An early fifteenth-century Arabic dictionary, based on earlier sources, incredibly, still defined "Il," under the letter "lam," as "Allah [God] the Almighty."[22] While traditional translations continue to confuse Il (El) and Yahweh, using "God" and "Lord," the fact remains that the monotheistic sacred texts still contain polytheistic leftovers and pantheon gods, even after attempts at priestly removal.

OLD AND NEW TESTAMENTS

Typology is a theological exercise in connecting the Old and New Testaments, such as the parallel between the tree in Paradise whose fruit caused Original Sin and the cross on which Jesus provides the means to erase that sin. It helps this typology that the gospel of Matthew was placed first in the New Testament although it is not the oldest gospel. For one, Matthew starts with a genealogy (which differs from Luke's) that connects Jesus through his non-father Joseph to David and all the way up to Abraham.[23] As a result, a kind of false impression of continuity is generated between the Old Testament and the New Testament.

However, the coupling of the two Testaments is more incongruous than typologically minded theologians assume. Investments in old thinking derived from the Old Testament are not at all consistent with New Testament principles of love and forgiveness. With few exceptions, such as the Book of Job/Ayyūb (which is atypical and most likely derived from an Arabic source[24]), the Old Testament is a book that is generally filled with violence and hatred toward other peoples—a book that has been used to support all sorts of colonial projects and exclusivist ideologies. The gap between violence and exclusivity on the one hand and charity and love on the other is simply too wide and contradictory to be bridged with niceties (or with theological typology). This conclusion was reached by writers as various as William Blake, Herman Melville, Friedrich Nietzsche, and Freya Stark, among others.

In "The Marriage of Heaven and Hell," Blake makes the poet-prophet Ezekiel (note that his name ends with -el) comment on how Jews had used God (Yahweh/Jehovah) to curse the deities of the neighboring people and so came to think that all nations would be subject to them. Now, adds Ezekiel, "all the nations" believe in the Jewish code and worship the Jewish god, and "what greater subjection can be." Friedrich Nietzsche states emphatically: "To have bound up this New Testament (a kind of ROCOCO of taste in every respect [the book of mercy?]) along with the Old Testament into one book, as the 'Bible,' as 'The Book in Itself,' is perhaps the greatest audacity and 'sin against the Spirit' which literary Europe has upon its conscience."[25] Both Melville and Twain in their works (see Chapter 3) point to the need for the U.S. to revise its potentially destructive identification with the Old Testament models, which it used during its colonial beginnings to construct a national myth. The British traveler Freya Stark expressed her horror upon seeing missionaries in Damascus teaching children to read the "gruesome massacres in Kings": "I decided on the spot that I should leave the Old Testament out of the curriculum if I were a missionary, and stick to Christian charity and the new."[26]

Hume, Blake, Melville, Twain, and Nietzsche were of course all unaware of much that has been discovered since they wrote; they spoke philosophically or poetically or out of concern. Now, in addition to what is discussed above, the new translations of passages in the Old Testament have removed any possibility of keeping a sense of monopoly over the idea of the one god.

PAGAN CHRISTS

Tammuz, Horus (or Iusa), Osir(is), Ba'al, Adon(is)—these are earlier prototypes of the Christ figure, sons of God, some the product of virgin births (or immaculate conception),[27] who suffer, sacrifice, die, and are resurrected.

The question is not only whether Jesus was a historical figure. Rather, it is the extent to which his story embodies an older messianic tradition, which the early Church wanted people to believe to be literally true. Tom Harpur's *The Pagan Christ* begins the chapter "Christianity Before Christianity: Where It All Began" with a quotation from Augustine that suggests that metaphoric possibility:

> The very thing which is now called the Christian religion existed among the ancients also, nor was it wanting from the inception of the human race until the coming of Christ in the flesh, at which point the true religion [,] which was already in existence [,] began to be called Christian.

Harpur traces the origins of the savior story in earlier Eastern mythology, particularly the similarity to ancient Egyptian and Oriental gods. As a follower of Gerald Massey and Alvin Boyd Kuhn, Harpur narrows down his identification to the Egyptian god Horus (also called Iusu or Iusa): "Egypt was truly the cradle of the Jesus figure of the Gospels." Generally, Harpur's effort is to be commended. As an ex-priest he is trying to understand his past, and he eventually advocates what he calls a "cosmic Christianity" that recovers the spiritual light that was lost when the Jesus myth fell prey to "historicization and literalization" by the early Christian church in the fourth and fifth centuries CE, as it plagiarized, then denied, the pre-Christian, Pagan past.[28]

As others do, however, Harpur overestimates Egyptian influences at the expense of closer origins in the immediate region. Like King David before him, the Jesus of the Bible is an amalgamation of themes from "Near Eastern" mythology and traditions of kingship and divinity.[29] Though they may have some similarities to Egyptian and Babylonian ideology and mythology, these two figures have particular ancestry in the intermediate region of Cana'an. Christ in particular inherits the characteristics of virgin birth, "son of God," death and resurrection that existed in earlier Cana'anite fertility and savior gods, whether in the themes of Ugaritic mythology,[30] or in the story of the birth of Salem, god of Ur-Salem (Jerusalem), son of the goddess 'Ashtar (Ishtar) who is immaculately impregnated by the old chief god Īl (El). Harpur also does not offer other possible explanations of the Christ phenomenon, such as one suggested by J. M. Robertson, who published *Pagan Christs* in 1903: the crucifixion could be a ceremonial remnant, a "mystery-drama," of an old practice of sacrificing a savior-god at a time when cannibalism started to become taboo, or (as usual with other fertility gods) it represents the death of vegetation.[31]

It seems at any rate that the Jesus figure reflects a popular subculture in Palestine that went against the religious establishment of that time, at least of the Jewish priests, though he also relates to older primal beliefs common in other religions. It is equally likely that Jesus may have looked up to God in the figure of the pantheon chief, the Supreme God Īl (El), rather than to one of his sons (namely the tribal god of the Israelites, Yahweh). This would seem to be indicated by his call on the cross in the only Aramaic sentence quoted in the gospels and other indirect evidence, such as in John 1, that show Jesus is not to be associated with Israelites or with traditional Judaism of the time.[32]

The claim that the Jesus of the gospels never existed is less fundamental than the fact that the theme of a messiah is more ancient than any possible historical figure—which emphasizes an inherent and basically human appeal in the Christ-phenomenon. Stories in Old Testament mythology, the idea of the god, and the New Testament story of Jesus all point to continuities with pre-existing polytheism, though they ended up being the record transmitted in the two-tiered bible which the West accepted on faith in the absence of knowledge. What became definite beliefs were accumulations that emerged as catalysts in altered form at a particular time of maturation, or were selected survivors in the only written record available for a time, later enshrined as tradition that priests or powers wanted people to assume to be historical. We have recovered more now.

3
Sacred Sites, Pagan Roots

In the region given the oft-repeated appellation "Holy Land," secular and sacred geographies are so intertwined it is virtually impossible to separate pure invention from genuine fact. This "Holy Land" is a dramatic example of how geography is not only what has been drawn in contours on maps but also what has been rigidly fixed in people's minds. Today we are better able to understand the evolution of such topographies and see the extent to which the geography of holy places has been invented. In fact, most of this geography has its roots in the previous, now-condemned or maligned polytheism.

The truth or falsity of what is written in sacred books is not the issue here. Most historians and archaeologists today find little or no evidence of any trace of history in what have come to be accepted as sacred narratives, although many people still cling to faith in them and some try their best to press any evidence into their service. Popular belief and religious scholarship assume that figures like Abraham and David are historical, whereas historians and archaeologists have shown that they are legendary or literary characters, or in the case of Jesus a synthesis of previous notions available in relation to earlier gods.[1]

As I explained in the previous two chapters, many new discoveries have shattered the old certainties. But even if we want to assume that the religious accounts, or some aspect of them, are historical, the question remains: are the sites now associated with them the real locations? This chapter shows that many famous places of pilgrimage have nothing to do with the events ascribed to them by religious authorities.

PRIESTS OF BA'AL

In one of the ironies of religious history, fundamentalist missionaries worldwide presented (and still present) the Old Testament as the word of the one and only true God, against the pagan religions they once were, or still are, striving to replace. Both Nathaniel

Figure 3.1 Stele of the God Ba'al, Ugarit,
fifteenth–thirteenth century BCE

Hawthorne and Chinua Achebe, about 120 years apart and on two different continents, refer in their literary works to how puritanical priests accuse the joyful maypole worshippers in North American forests and the happy idolatrous natives in African jungles of being followers of the "priests of Baal." [2] In this allusion to the biblical account in I Kings 18–19, the priests of Yahweh defeat the priests of Ba'al ("bꜥl"). The assumption has been that Ba'al is a corrupt pagan god whose worship should be stamped out, while Yahweh (otherwise erroneously transcribed as "Jehovah") is the true god, the monotheistic god, who possesses the only real power and is able to prove it by being victorious.

Little do these missionary zealots realize that, as I point out in the chapter on Ugarit, the biblical story in Kings is a recycled copy (with a reversed outcome) of the battle between the gods Baʿal and Yam (Yaw/Yau, probably the prototype of Yahweh). Yahweh, as I show in Chapter 2, is one of the son gods in a council of gods, whose status as "God" in the West was the outcome of a tradition (and mis-translation) previously unaware of—and now generally unwilling to accept—certain findings.

Curiously, William Golding's popular novel *Lord of the Flies* plays on a mistranslated phrase from the Old Testament intended to demean the god Baʿal as part of the theme of an unpleasant return to primitivism, whereas the phrase "Baal-zebul" denotes princely status rather than filth associated with flies. In contrast, Bertolt Brecht's first play, entitled *Baal*, is a comment on how misplaced this figure of fertility would be in the modernist wasteland. A vast sea-change from Golding's sensibility, *Baal* is a more nuanced work framed in the harsh times of Europe in 1918–20 that tells of a god half-paralyzed in the exploitative environment of industry, anti-social in a rapacious world, both child and pervert, whose tortured idiosyncrasies come from a complex inability to help that world.[3] Brecht is reported to have proudly displayed a huge reproduction of the god Baʿal in his residence.

Obviously, the different responses to this god of thunder, rain, and fertility (later duplicated in Zeus) are a measure of the perceiver's eye and show how various writers respond to a common religious and cultural outlook, then as now.

PALIMPSEST

Identifying the real nature of ancient sites by looking at present-day locations is like trying to decipher a palimpsest, to extract an erased or scratched out text by searching for it through or underneath what has been overwritten. Just as gods and texts were sanctified out of pagan ancestry to privilege monotheism, so the sites of pilgrimage associated with monotheistic narratives were invariably overlaid on pagan locations. While simple pilgrims still flock to worship as before, other holy places are being exploited for political and real-estate gains—a process that occurred many times in earlier historical periods.

It has always been profitable for religious institutions, churches, or political powers to create places of pilgrimage and to erase or incorporate previous belief systems in a process that encourages invented remembering through a process of forgetting. Today, political Zionism wants to keep alive certain aspects of the monotheistic narratives and other ingrained misconceptions on which its self-interested claim system is based. It exploits the places invented by the monotheistic traditions. In a situation of what should have been diminished credibility (one would expect evolution, not regression), especially in an age that purports to be knowledge-driven, the geography of Palestine and Israel, built up by the religious topographic imagination over the past two millennia, takes on surreal proportions in today's maps. The real history of Palestine has been rubbed out, invisibilized. Instead, old imaginaries and new inventions have congealed into unwieldy realities. In normal circumstances, the creation of mental landscapes is a natural human activity, recognized as an idealization. However, in this case the process has resulted in a forced transformation of the imaginary into "real" maps whose consequences continue to affect masses of people in drastic ways.

PAGAN ANCESTRY

The simple unadulterated fact is that all the places purported to relate to biblical characters and sites have pagan origins, converted to Christian use in the fourth century CE by the Byzantine Empire, some later to Muslim uses, and more recently given an Old Testament adaptation by modern Zionism. In addition to the fact that the sites have no original connection to the biblical accounts to which they were attached, the likelihood is that some concepts (such as "temple") were transferred from locations elsewhere to ones in Palestine. The events associated with monotheistic narratives have been shown to be fictionalized (or appropriated or misdated or exaggerated or adapted), so the locations are doubtful or uncertain at best. Even if the stories are to be believed, the passage of time is unlikely to have allowed the retention of either a popular or official memory of any location. How could humans know or have remembered where Noah and Joseph were buried, or where the bush of Moses is supposed to have burned? Was it really possible to know the exact spot where Christ was born or entombed? Even if Christ is believed to be a historical figure, hundreds of years elapsed before a certain cave was selected as a place for his birthing (the Church of the Nativity) and two others for his possible entombment (the Church of the Holy Sepulcher and the Garden Tomb). Still, some pilgrims are persuaded they have seen the bush that burned, others can follow the tracks of Egyptian chariots which pursued the Israelites in the sands of Egypt, while some worship at this or that place assumed to be Christ's tomb.

More importantly, there is incontrovertible proof that the site locations were arbitrarily assigned by the newly Christianized Byzantine Empire, upon instruction by the emperor Constantine (see below), and with one specific intention: *to suppress or supplant the polytheistic religion of the common people.*[4] This motive, along with later inventions, determined all the major sites such as the Ibrahimi Mosque in Hebron (the supposed burial place of Abraham, Sarah, etc.), the Nativity Church, the Holy Sepulcher, the Western/ Wailing Wall, Rachel's Tomb, and all the other presumed biblical or religious locations.

It should be noted that the paganism that existed in the eastern Mediterranean at the beginning of the fourth century CE was a redeployed, Hellenized or Romanized form of more ancient local polytheisms. When Emperor Constantine converted to Christianity, Palestine was largely pagan, as was the rest of the world. This paganism, which descended from the older religions, had been deeply rooted in the region. In fact, Greek and later Roman religions were oriented toward the East, their mythologies being largely derivative of, adapted from, or heavily influenced by earlier eastern Mediterranean mythologies.[5] Such cross-Mediterranean influences enhanced people's readiness to accept the new associations and belief systems.

HELENA

A defining moment for fixing the major sites occurred with the visit of Constantine's mother Helena to the "Holy Land" in 323 CE, as well as with the work of his bishops at the juncture when the Byzantine Empire was converted to Christianity. The Emperor wanted to spread his authority by using the new religion, and his subjects had to worship accordingly.

Discrediting Helena's allocation of biblical sites is not difficult. Even pilgrims and clergy who visited the sites in the last 17 centuries, especially later Protestant visitors, expressed reservations about the arbitrary nature of Helena's selections and the convenient proximity of some of the sites. Tombs are particularly convenient to assign because no one can discover anything to the contrary—except in cases where someone has more than one place of burial. Her decisions were accepted as based on "divine inspiration," though the stories used by her show Helena as incredulously inventive. It was impossible to retrieve any memory or knowledge of locations that go back hundreds and thousands of years, yet Helena and her bishops made it work. Where possible, the most effective strategy was to choose pagan sites that could somehow be appealingly related to the biblical story (e.g., a birthplace associated with a previous messianic god, or a sacred, more ancient burial cave). It was as if the earlier identifications were cases of mistaken identity.

Mark Twain had uproarious fun with Helena's outrageous methods and the gullibility of believers, as much as he did in satirizing the location of all those tombs: "She traveled all over Palestine and was always fortunate ... she would go and search ... and never stop until she found it." The influential sacred geographer Edward Robinson concluded in 1841 that the "alleged discovery" of sites associated with the Church of the Holy Sepulcher (which he notes had a temple of Venus and Jupiter) "may not improbably have been the work of pious fraud."[6] While Protestant clergy were keen to discredit the traditional sites associated with Catholic and Eastern sects, they developed their own brand of literal topography (discussed under "Sacred Geography" below and in Chapter 1). For example, it was more typical of them to affirm their faith by tracing the purported route of the Israelites in the desert, or guessing biblical places from supposed echoes in Arabic place names, or making other such nebulous determinations.

HEBRON

There is definite historical proof that pagan sites were appropriated for entrenching biblical purposes, with the intention of superseding previous beliefs and enforcing the new religion. It is only possible to provide evidence for a few places today, since obviously the sites have been claimed to be real for so long and contrary evidence has been suppressed through erasure or methodical repetition.

E. D. Hunt's *Holy Pilgrimage in the Late Roman Empire* documents how Constantine gave explicit directions to Eusebius, Bishop of Palestine, to implement plans for the "destruction of every vestige of paganism and the building of an appropriate Christian basilica." In this case, he was referring to the site in Hebron—important for its professed connection to the ultimate patriarchal figure, Abraham, a suitable model for Constantine and his empire to appropriate.[7] There a basilica was built, on a site where previously Herod had built a structure. What the site's associations were before Herod is impossible to determine, shadowed as it is by biblical mythology and time. After the coming of Islam, a mosque was built on the remains of the basilica, and more members of Abraham's family were added to the list of those buried there. Similarly, other pagan places were converted to sites that served the purposes of the new religion and the state, such as that assigned as the birthplace of Jesus. What is now called the Milk Grotto, next to the Nativity Church in Bethlehem, was earlier a place of worship to Adon(is). As Jerome mentions, local women wept there for the fertility god Adon, who like Tammuz and Ba'al, dies and is resurrected.

In Hebron, as elsewhere, pagan practices were hard to erase. Both contemporaneous and later writers tell us that the people continued to remember and offer pagan sacrifice for more than a hundred years after the Christianization of the sites. One is the eyewitness report of Sozomen, a fifth-century ecclesiastical historian and native of Gaza, which is corroborated by earlier descriptions of polytheists celebrating around a tree and a spring at Mamre given in Eusebius' *Onomasticon*:

> Here the inhabitants of the country and of the regions round Palestine, the Phoenicians, and the Arabians, assemble annually during the summer season to keep a brilliant feast; and many others, both buyers and sellers, resort there on account of the fair. Indeed, this feast is diligently frequented by all the nations: by the Jews, because they boast of their descent from the patriarch Abraham; by the Pagans, because angels there appeared to men; and by Christians, because He who for the salvation of mankind was born of a virgin, afterwards manifested himself there to a godly man. ... Once while these customs were being celebrated by the Pagans, after the aforesaid manner, and as was the established usage with hilarity, the mother-in-law of Constantine was present for prayer, and apprised the emperor of what was being done. ... He [the emperor] commanded these bishops to hold a conference on this subject with the Phoenician bishops, and issue directions for the demolition, from the foundations, of the alter formerly erected there, the destruction of the carved images by fire, and the erection of a church worthy of so ancient and so holy a place ..., and if any attempt should be made to restore the former rites, the bishops were to inform against the delinquent, in order that he might be subjected to the greatest punishment.[8]

Some would argue that such important sites were paganized by the Romans in order to wipe out traces of Christian events (an unconvincing defense and of course inapplicable to Old Testament sites). Such evidence as Sozomen's description (which also has implications with regard to the diverse ethnic and religious composition of Palestine's population) points to the contrary: namely, the continuity between polytheism and monotheism that the authorities were eager to suppress and discontinue, using the effective strategy of appropriating and attaching to revered sites whatever served the newly adopted religious narratives.

Meron Benvenisti's *Sacred Landscape*, after describing the Zionist fabrication of a "Hebrew map" intended to eradicate the Palestinian character of the landscape, gives several instances of other actions where a variety of excuses and strategies were used to Judaize sites and buildings even when they had no previous Jewish tradition associated with them at all. Such excuses were used to ensure control of a number of major sites belonging to the monotheistic tradition that had been preserved in Muslim sacred geography. This applies of course to El-Khalil/Hebron, at the place where tradition says Abraham and other members of his clan were buried, now a mosque called Al Haram el Ibrahīmi. After the occupation of the West Bank in 1967 and then infiltration by Jewish extremists in the 1980s, supported by the Israeli army, the mosque was forcibly divided and eventually more than two-thirds of it turned into a synagogue. This in effect repeats the process of the site's previous forced transformations.

Thus, association with a name (Ibrahīm/Abraham)—presumably dating back to the second millennium BCE—not with a fact, was manipulated to generate a claim and so create an unwieldy kind of reality and a point of contentious attachment. That Muslims incorporated other burials into this site, such as Sarah's, adding many exaggerated stories about Abraham well beyond the qur'anic account, does not of course explain or excuse Israeli actions. However, the religious pretext has made it easier for the Zionists to dupe and intimidate local Muslim authorities and believers into grudging acquiescence in accepting the site's authenticity on their terms.[9] Israeli actions to appropriate the site seem to be motivated by the intent to control through colonial presence rather than by sincere religious devotion. It is not new in history that one power would use a previous tradition to supplant that tradition itself and to exploit a site for its own uses. Nevertheless, it is ironic that the imaginings of Muslims served as pretexts for their being supplanted by Jewish extremists, for the benefit of new Israeli claims.

WESTERN WALL

"In the geonic period the place of assembly and prayer for Jews was on the Mount of Olives. The Western Wall became a permanent feature in Jewish tradition about 1520 [CE], either as a result of the immigration of the Spanish exiles or in the wake of the Turkish conquest of 1518." This is taken from none other than *The Encyclopaedia Judaica* (1971 edition). Despite its claim-language elsewhere, here it admits something hardly ever mentioned: the Western or Wailing Wall became a place of sanctity only about 500 years ago. Jews expelled along with the Muslims from Spain came to Jerusalem, saw the huge stones next to the Dome of the Rock, and decided to worship there in assumed memory of the "Temple." Archaeology tells us that the large stones that make up the wall, called "Judaism's most sacred place," are what remains of Roman towers, while the cave under the Muslim Dome of the Rock is a Bronze Age burial site.

A religious scholar, Ernest L. Martin, basing his evidence on Josephus and some "archaeology," has argued that the ex-Temple could not have been located on the site of *El Haram esh Sharīf* (Al-Aqsa Mosque and the Dome of the Rock) and that the ancient stones on its periphery (including the Western or Wailing Wall) are remnants of the Roman Fortress Antonia. Rather, Martin believes, the Temple site should be hundreds of meters away on the "Ophel" mound near the "Gihon" spring area.[10] This argument alerts us to the fact that the Western Wall is a fortress wall, although there is the danger that accepting the premise of a presumed temple could lead to a proposal to have a new one built elsewhere nearby.

Other evidence throws even more doubt on the idea of equating the Muslim site and its tradition, as a template, with the idea of either a "First Temple" or "Second Temple." Conveniently, the impression is given that the "second" temple is the same as the "first" temple. The "first" temple is assumed to be Solomon's and is also variously associated with the Ark of the Covenant and Abraham's sacrifice of Isaac—all incredulous associations. Even Adam's skull was, until the nineteenth century, thought to be in that vicinity. Yet it is impossible to assume any reliable recollection of such a location over thousands of years of absence or neglect. Further, a first temple (if it existed) cannot possibly be the same as the second temple associated with the time of Herod.

When the Muslims tried to establish the location in the seventh century CE, they were thinking of Solomon. They asked for the consulting opinion of a Jewish convert to Islam from the Arabian Peninsula, called Ka'b, who worked with the then available legends.[11] But centuries of destruction and neglect, as well as the intervening periods of other pagan religions, would have made any recollection improbable. The chosen site was reportedly so neglected that it was being used as a garbage dump. On the other hand, the "second" temple, built by Herod (whose affiliation with Judaism is often questioned, and was certainly ambivalent), was later utterly destroyed by the Romans, and Jews were forbidden to enter Jerusalem for about six centuries thereafter. More importantly, there is evidence that Herod's temple was a shared temple for all local religions.[12]

The whole idea of a "first" temple is questionable on other counts. How could the "first" temple (Solomon's, from the tenth century BCE) have been Jewish when Judaism had not begun as a religion until several centuries after the presumed time of Solomon? (This is aside from severe doubts many historians now have about the reality or actual existence of the David/Solomon kingdom.) The rock and cave of the Dome of the Rock itself, the major signpost of the complex now embedded in some minds as the "Temple," is a Bronze Age burial site that has bequeathed its mystery of sacredness to later generations. Further, "temple" and "mount" could have been notions transferred from other geographical locations, most likely the godly mountain in Ugaritic mythology located in northwest Syria. ("Saphon" or more likely "Safan" sounds close to "Zion"; see Chapter 4 on Ugarit for the allusions to "temple" and "mount.") "Mount Zion" and "temple" are not dissimilar from "flood," "exodus," "virgin birth," and "resurrection," which have been shown to have come from other chronological or mythological contexts, and then projected onto new locations with new prerogatives by the carriers of beliefs to serve their local purpose.[13] These beliefs, isolated or removed from their original environs, have become major traditions in monotheistic accounts, especially in the West, attributed through insistent repetition or ignorance to people and areas other than the actual sources.

The voracious process undertaken in relation to the mosque in Hebron is also being planned for the Old City of Jerusalem, although the Zionists have to be somewhat more careful how to maneuver there, given the more international atmosphere of Jerusalem. But confiscation of land has already occurred with the expansion of the area around the Western or Wailing Wall, as well as in the vicinity of what is mis-called the "City of David," at the cost of destroying

Palestinian residential neighborhoods. For a number of years, there have been frequent reports in the Israeli media about a movement to build a "third temple" and blatant calls by extremists to destroy the Dome of the Rock in order to build such a temple in its place. Israeli tour guides regularly point to posters of the Dome of the Rock outside Palestinian shops inside the Old City and inquire rhetorically why the Dome is there instead of a temple. In this madness, there is no thought of the apocalyptic consequences of destroying the Dome.

In the obsession with this presumed remnant of a temple, all the historical facts and reasoning mentioned above are conveniently avoided. Zionism and Zionist academia seem to be preparing for the eventuality that the *Haram esh Sharīf* or Dome of the Rock site (what is referred to by them and in Western tradition as "Temple Mount") will receive the same treatment as the mosque in Hebron—that is, become "shared." Even when Israeli scholars are aware of all the details that would debunk Zionist claims, they still employ the same old misleading terminology ("first temple period," "City of David," "second temple period," and such like) and promote the notion that Jews are entitled to this architectural site built by others, which they want to be shared or divided between Muslims and Jews.[14] It is a slow, creeping process.

How the Al-Aqsa Mosque and the Dome of the Rock and later the Western or Wailing Wall became established traditions only emphasizes that people's search for convenient, useful sacredness is not necessarily based on actual locations or historical grounds. In fact, the current locations are the result of what has been transferred from the imagination to what seemed to fit on the ground. In this case, it is, once again, the Muslim tradition established in the seventh century and associated with Solomon's Temple that drove devout Jews coming to Jerusalem in the sixteenth century to latch on to the idea that the huge stones nearby on the periphery of the Muslim site mark the remains of a "temple."

MUSLIM TRADITION

After the Byzantine period, which succeeded in eradicating evidence of pagan precursors, and aside from contact during the Crusades, Western ideas about Palestine developed from the seventh to the nineteenth centuries almost entirely in the imagination and in religious doctrine. Traditional churches left some monasteries and other institutions in the "Holy Land," some of which remain almost intact to this day. Meanwhile, Islam constructed its own sacred history and geography, based both on its own regional context (Mecca was an earlier pagan place of pilgrimage) and the other two monolatries. It incorporated Jerusalem (described as Beit El Maqdis, thus Al-Quds, as the descriptive name for the holy city) as well as Hebron and other places. In addition, over time, Islam developed its own additional places, such as *maqams* associated with holy men and other tomb locations (some coincidentally called by the names of biblical characters, such as "Yousef's/Joseph's Tomb," either in local appropriation of that figure or perhaps because a holy man called Yousef was entombed there).

One such *maqam* is *en Nabi Musa* ("the Prophet Moses"), which is located in the wilderness on the road from Jerusalem to Jericho, several kilometers *west* of the Jordan River. It was reportedly built at the behest of Al-Dhaher Baybers, a Mamluk Sultan, in 1269 CE, and remained a place of annual pilgrimage for the last few hundred years, until 1948. Luckily, this location so contradicts the biblical account—because Moses is mythologized to have died after viewing the Promised Land from the Moab Mountains far east of the Jordan River, and his burial place is reportedly unknown—that fundamentalist Jews and Christians are uninterested in this location.

Perhaps the difference in this respect between Islam and the two other religions is that Islam officially considers the two other faiths as revealed religions, though it wanted also to include and incorporate them. This Muslim attitude usually diminished instances where Muslim power resulted in site appropriation. Such takeover did occur in the major cities of central government (as with the Umayyad Mosque in Damascus and Hagia Sophia in Istanbul) and in the place associated with Ibrahīm/Abraham in Hebron, where the site of a church was later supplanted by a mosque.[15] But, as a general rule, Islam respected the integrity of other sites.

The dubious history of holy places in Palestine has led to unfortunate entrapments in today's contentious political situation. In many ways, what is happening is the eventual outcome not only of Byzantine-imposed traditions and the Muslim continuation of traditions, but also of the crucial developments of fundamentalist sacred geography in the nineteenth century and its exploitation by Zionism. I will discuss this development as it forms an essential link in Zionist implementations.

THE NINETEENTH CENTURY

The phenomenon called sacred geography—which, as I detail in Chapter 1, intensified during the nineteenth century—had more alien roots in a theological typology most fully expressed by fundamentalist forms of Protestantism, and Puritanism in particular, which drew heavily on the Old Testament. In colonial America, this typology was transferred to the practical, lived experience of the colonists, who saw themselves with biblical eyes and thus justified their conquest. One could say the same kind of theological-colonial transfer happened in the nineteenth century with regard to the geography of Palestine. As is still occurring in different forms, there was a concerted fundamentalist reaction and a counter-battle waged to reaffirm the old certainties in the face of the discoveries of new sciences. Many religious writers, for example, tried to defend the biblical creation story against the geological evidence of fossils millions of years old.

Palestine became the natural location where many sacred geographers searched for literal verification of their faith in "the land of the Bible" itself. This explains in part the increase in religious tourism to the eastern Mediterranean during that period. The advent of sacred geography as a movement transformed earlier imaginings about the "Holy Land" from theoretical typologies into literal, physically oriented applications of biblical accounts. While that nineteenth-century doubt-belief crisis eventually resolved itself as a passing stage in Western thought (though it continues to recur in cycles), the resulting fundamentalist geography was a turning point of long-term consequence to the "Holy Land." It laid the foundation and established the models of an imagined topography and various appropriative complexes that assisted—both geographically and politically—Zionist claims and implementations that still rely on them. In fact, it is possible to view the Western "rediscovery" of Palestine in the nineteenth century as "Israeli prehistory."[16] It is a field—what could be called biblical orientalism—to which Edward Said's *Orientalism* (1978) pays no attention, especially its U.S. variety. Two of the severest critics of sacred geography (Herman Melville and Mark Twain, to be discussed below) are given scant, even dismissive, reference in Said's influential book.

As a result of continued religious, ideological, and political investments in this sacred geography, the implications of scholarly discoveries over the past 150 years have been avoided, muffled, or cumulatively modified to fit into pre-existing patterns. Nineteenth-century religious applications differ from those of fourth-century site sanctification, in that they involved the methods of Protestant fundamentalism, and were less relic-oriented and more literally intractable, obsessive, and vaguely perceptual (such as tracing the desert route of the Israelites or the presumed location of battles). However, as with the older crusading sentiments, they laid the groundwork for claims to the land and a colonial presence within it. The situation on the ground today, following British colonization and Zionist incursion, has come about as a result of an intersection of literal religious thinking with colonial ambitions that fully developed the practical consequences of nineteenth-century sacred geography and its Western crusading precedents.

So today does not seem to have more light than yesterday, since most people still seem disinclined to avail themselves of the opportunity to be more informed and less literal than in the past about religious traditions. An article published in 1854 entitled "Sacred Geography," intended to cover this religious movement from the period's perspective, had to admit that "those who visit or who describe the scenes of sacred history expressly for the sake of finding confirmations of Scripture are often tempted to mislead themselves and others by involuntary exaggeration or invention."[17] Imagine, then, what can or should be said today about these exaggerations and inventions as they have become more firmly enshrined as apparent truths and accepted realities.

ZIONIST EXPLOITATION

Israeli writer Meron Benvenisti includes a section in *Sacred Landscape*, "Reconsecration by Conquerors," that details a phenomenon he finds incredible in our time. The last time it had happened was in Spain after the eviction of Muslims and Jews and in Istanbul/Constantinople upon its conquest by the Ottomans.

After the conquest of parts of Palestine and the creation of Israel in 1948, several Muslim holy places of pilgrimage that then fell into Israeli hands were transformed into Jewish sites. The list of presumed burial sites and places of pilgrimage is long: Nabi Rubin, Nabi Judah, Nabi Dan, Nabi Benjamin, and others. ("Nabi" means "prophet" in Arabic.) The Jewish pretext was misleadingly simple: the names are biblical or Jewish, so Jews have a right to control them, although as Benvenisti emphasizes these sites "were not a component in Jewish tradition." The Jews merely took over Muslim sacred geography and appropriated the "pantheon" of Muslim saints and prophets.[18] In an ungrateful process of erasure and the creation of a "Hebrew map," sites whose sanctity was the outcome of Palestinian village heritage were turned into synagogues or to other Jewish uses after 1948.

Figure 3.2   Rachel's Tomb: then and now[19]

Exploitation of sites for political purposes by Israel is so transparent it is beyond comprehension how most people are blind to it or seem not to know what is happening or avoid the issue. Relying on traditions invented in the fourth century and by Islam in later centuries, the Zionist movement bases its claims for control of the sites mostly on associations established by earlier Christian and Muslim sacred geography. The Zionists cannot of course touch strictly Christian places, for obvious reasons, except in cases where properties can be acquired by convincing or coercing church officials. They target Muslim sites, as shown above with Hebron's Ibrahīmi/Abraham Mosque, with their designs on the *Haram esh Sharīf*, and the takeover of smaller locations. This pattern of historical transformation has been repeated with the so-called "City of David" in Silwan just outside the Old City walls, as well as the misnamed "David's Citadel" inside the Old City of Jerusalem, and "Rachel's Tomb" in Bethlehem (located inside the Bilal ben Rabāḥ Mosque). Until 1967, all travelers noted that Rachel's Tomb and Joseph's Tomb are Muslim or "Turkish" structures, and being mere traditions they have no substantiated claim to authenticity. Yet today, Joseph's Tomb near Nablus is a flash point and Rachel's Tomb has already been transformed to conform to a new appearance as Jewish.[20]

Thus, Muslim place names have become excuses for Jewish ownership. Wholesale takeover of what was built by others has been implemented through imitative applications that depend largely on Islam's incorporation of the other two traditions in its narratives and its local development of pilgrimage rituals. The clarity of this understanding is blinded by immediacy and confusion. Willing adherents blissfully repeat a mantra passed on to them, which they are admonished to accept on faith. Previous metaphoric or emotive associations acquire intense literal value and strong emotive power for action, and are then manipulated to control sites and lands.

MELVILLE AND TWAIN

Until the early nineteenth century, both East and West generally accepted biblical geography and biblical historicity, along with its site allocations, without much questioning. However, things started to change in the latter half of the nineteenth century. Figures like Herman Melville and Mark Twain are significant in this respect, although now their insights seem to have been lost in the wave of the most recent fundamentalism and Zionism.

Zionism wants to use (or rather misuse) famous writers for its purposes, to wield their opinions to its service by quoting passages out of context that may appear to support certain contentions. This was illustrated recently when a rumor broke out to the effect that Prime Minister Netanyahu was planning to give a special copy of Twain's *Innocents Abroad* to President Obama, with the intention of trying to bolster claims that Palestine was a neglected and barren land until the Zionists came to improve it.[21] And because Zionists misuse Twain or Melville (and others) by citing their words out of context, Arab and Palestinian writers often are misled into attacking these two writers for that reason, instead of examining more carefully whether what they say in fact refutes Zionism.[22]

It is totally misguided and intentionally deceptive to adhere to this common tactic of using isolated quotations from Twain, Melville or others to support Zionist claims about Palestine being desolate and barren until the Zionists came to plant and make it green. Some ill-intentioned travelers were indeed biblically obsessed and pre-disposed to hate "Arabs." But that does not apply to Melville and Twain, nor can their views about the land or the people be employed that way except by distorting them and placing them out of context.

On the question of anti-Arab bias, it is crucial to note that Twain's narrator in *Innocents Abroad* (1869) makes fun of many other people: the Portuguese, the Italians, and others, but most of all he disparages and disavows the actions of his own compatriots, that is U.S. "pilgrims," including himself. In other words, Twain's irony extends to everyone, including self-ridicule by his narrator. Melville, on the other hand, admired nomadic life (Bedouins, Polynesians, and native North Americans included) and thought of missionaries both in Polynesia and in Palestine as monomaniacal and destructive.[23]

"All who cultivate the soil in Palestine are Arabs." This is a statement from Herman Melville's journal of his visit to Palestine in 1857 that we should all consider and keep in front of us as a corrective testimony.[24]

Second, Melville and Twain are two of the greatest debunkers of biblical narratives. Both questioned the authenticity of holy sites in Palestine (part of which became Israel in 1948) and satirized the efforts of Christian fundamentalists and Adventists in the nineteenth century, whose thinking has been inherited, exploited and applied by the Zionist movement. Both writers, through this biblical criticism, also highlighted the need to subvert the U.S. national myth which based its entitlement on the story of a new "Promised Land"

and other convenient biblical narratives. One of Twain's satirical targets is Joshua, whom he calls "The Genius of Destruction," and Melville's narratives in *Moby Dick* and *Clarel* illustrate the destructiveness of fundamentalist monomania.

Third, Melville and Twain describe other places across the Mediterranean as equally "barren" (such as parts of Greece). Melville in particular saw barrenness as an aesthetic, abstract quality, which in various minds produces contradictory reactions—fear or peacefulness. Melville eventually developed an aesthetic of barrenness that is relevant to the evolution of artistic expression, as a precursor to modernism and abstract art. Further, in the context of the "Holy Land," Melville theorized that the barren desert was the essence of humanity, emptiness, out of which all systems, religions, and civilized accumulations were created. "Man sprang from deserts" is one of his profound conclusions.[25] For many thinkers today the synergy of desert and spiritual reflection is axiomatic. Melville looked at natives in Polynesia and Bedouins in the Levant as people who were blessed with an unconscious ability to live at peace with nature, to accept it rather than challenge or exploit it, or try to tame and conquer it. (It is not a coincidence that the narrator of *Moby Dick* begins by declaring "Call me Ishmael," or that the Pequod and all its crew are destroyed.)

Finally, certain places in Palestine have always been and will always remain "barren." Other places are green or fertile (such as Hebron, or sections around Gaza, Jericho and Jaffa, or the north). Just because more orchards have been planted in suitable places and now genetically enhanced produce is prepared for profitable export does not mean the land has been "improved," or that the Palestinians were not farmers, or that the land is no longer "barren" in the same places it was before. In fact, what the Israelis have created is an exploitative situation where traditional (healthier) Palestinian agriculture has been effectively killed off by the use of genetic enhancement, other controls (such as modified seeds), and marketing strategies, while denying Palestinians sustainable access to fresh water for their agricultural needs.

"Like Homer, he [Nimrod and other ancient characters] is said to be buried in many other places," comments the narrator in Mark Twain's *Innocents Abroad*.[26] Twain satirizes all the holy sites, particularly the numerous tombs of patriarchs and other biblical personalities like Noah and Joseph. To him, tombs are particularly likely to be invented because it is difficult to disprove that a holy or biblical character was buried there anyway. That such burial places exist and people believe in them despite their ridiculous impossibility, however, illustrates the need humans have to usurp sacredness and bring it closer into their midst. Twain's self-ironic satire of modern tourism, a kind of anti-pilgrimage when it comes to the "Holy Land," exposes all the conventions of sacred geography. Biblical accounts are also criticized for the sentimentality that religious readers attach to what are essentially stories containing racist, cruel, and violent actions. *Innocents Abroad* mercilessly deflates these holy associations and all the clichés and emotional crassness in the observations made by sacred geographers.

Similarly, in the journal of his Levant visit in 1856–57, Melville satirizes the missionaries and millenarians at work in Palestine (as he did in his first novels *Typee* and *Omoo*). His neglected great work based on that visit, *Clarel: A Poem and Pilgrimage in the Holy Land* (1876), dramatizes the tensions between belief and doubt in the story of a divinity student whose "pilgrimage," or reverse pilgrimage, like that of Twain's narrator, becomes a process that involves the necessity for unlearning previous certainties rather than one of confirming received knowledge. Serendipitously, both Twain and Melville emphasize this need for "unlearning" all that has been given people to know about Palestine and the "Holy Land." Twain's narrator, faced with the crudely sentimentalized rhetoric of "Promised Land" conquest, declares: "I must studiously and faithfully unlearn a great many things I have somehow absorbed about Palestine."[27] The process is crucial to the plot and movement of *Clarel* as the protagonist graduates into experiences whereby he grows out of all the old notions, and is constantly "Learning, unlearning, word by word" (II.xiv.54).[28]

In different styles, Melville and Twain overturn the obsessive associations of sacred geographers and the acts of geographic imposition that are driven by their topomania. Instead of affirming the holiness associated with Palestine's land, both writers question whether the "holiness" is not a product of the landscape's peculiar nature and people's response to it. Just as he asked questions about the holy associations of the sea in *Moby Dick*, in *Clarel* (as in the canto "Of Deserts"), Melville draws a parallel between pagan sanctification of a site ("Deemed hallowed by the thunder-clap [Jove's]") and the causes of religious developments in "a land / Direful yet holy." In *Clarel* Melville amplifies the thinking which was clear in the journal of his visit: the desert is the essential landscape out of which emerges a human response in the idea of God (which, incidentally, he suggests has an Egyptian source). Subsequently what he saw as the "diabolical" landscape in parts of Palestine produced a "ghastly" kind of theology similar to the effect of Radcliff's gothic architecture.[29]

Such writers as Melville and Twain are rare: they run against the accepted norm. But the same associational complexes they satirize are still rampant in the multiplying connections that continue to accumulate in the monotheistic traditions, in the media and the public mind, as well as in some scholarship. In converting Palestine into a location of faith, all sorts of associations and terminologies have been invented, gaps elided, distances abridged, periods shortened or misleadingly named, nomenclature backdated, and claims amplified. The routes and sites of legendary ancient events are charted out with surprising claims of accuracy, regardless of uncertainties about whether they ever happened.

PERSISTENCE OF THE OLD

All the complexes that characterize previous sacred geographies stubbornly persist. A by-product was a pseudo-archaeology that continues in the guise of archaeological research, to which many Western institutions and much Israeli archaeology are still dedicated. It is not just that history and geography are invented to duplicate an imaginary past. The inventions are sanctified, made credible, and reinforced by support through propagation of nineteenth-century and earlier sources and present constructions. Consider the religion industry and the investments made over many centuries just in terms of religious buildings, personnel, related literature, promotional activities, and in art objects and paraphernalia. Such investments lend credibility by virtue of the resulting massive productions, so that to doubt the veracity of these creations appears daunting.

Through dedicated repetition, the whole tourist industry in Israel and Palestine is geared to reinforce the traditional assumptions of the three monotheistic religions, the paradigm of their convenient sequencing, their privileging, and their invented sites. In 1869, in Chapter 42 of *Innocents Abroad*, the narrator ridicules the "colossal" bunches of grapes lifted by the two spies who, in the biblical account, are sent out to prospect a promised land inhabited and cultivated by other people. Today, a stylized form of that scene is the logo of the Israeli Ministry of Tourism.[30]

I have outlined a range of phenomena that represent journeys in the "landscape of belief." An original cosmic journey first emerged in natural response to a unique landscape. From it later developed the more exclusive monotheistic religions, which in turn gave rise to a systematic institutionalization of faith, a commodification of fixed sites, and finally, especially starting in the nineteenth century, the colonization of religion in sacred geography. What we see today, generally, is an industrialization of both secular and religious knowledge and tourism, the colonization of faith by dogged certainties and obsessions. In the West, the nineteenth century experienced an awakening and a blinding at the same time, an existential recognition that was countered by religious fixations: a dichotomy of existential barrenness and conformist reaffirmation. This was later expressed differently in the modernist period, and eludes naming or definition in the postmodernist, "post-historical" condition with its globalizing trends. At the same time, some of the inventions and falsifications of reality have established their effective hegemony.

On the ground in Palestine a constructed geography has become "real," and the various investments in it make for an aggressive resistance to its devolution. Such investments and attentiveness to this invented geography affect all forms of knowledge about the region and make any future change difficult. Not only has it concretized what was only imagined, it has also made the genuinely concrete effectively invisible. A landscape of belief has colonized the mind, such that both public understanding and the knowledge industry are largely subservient to these constructions and their elaboration. It is a wonder that today the awareness often still escapes us of what has been elided and buried by the hegemony of prevailing narratives and the imperatives of power. Yet humanity now has unprecedented opportunities for uncovering buried or erased knowledge of the past and can choose to be wiser in its beliefs and self-understanding not underwritten by information others have winnowed in order to draw in compliant adherents.

4
Ugaritic Revelations:
What an Ancient City Tells Us

One day in 1928 a farmer digging in a field near the coast in northwest Syria uncovered an archaeological site that turned out to be the ruins of Ugarit, a city that flourished in the second millennium BCE from about 3600 to 3200 years ago. As it was excavated and some of its tablets began to be deciphered, the face of historical and religious development in the region was irreversibly altered.

It is strange that many earth-shattering discoveries have been made accidentally by simple local people: the Al-'Amarna letters (by an Egyptian woman in 1885), Ugarit/Ras Shamra (a Syrian farmer), the Gnostic gospels at Naj Hammādī (by an Egyptian peasant, Muhammad 'Ali as-Sammān, in 1945), the Dead Sea Scrolls (a Bedouin shepherd boy, Muhammad ad-Dīb, in 1947). These people are not always credited as "discoverers" and their names are not usually recorded for posterity, though this should be righted.[1]

There must be something serendipitous, perhaps prophetic, about some of these findings by farmers or Bedouins that relate to old cultures and religions in the East Mediterranean. It is almost as if history is hinting to us that, though forgotten, these people are what matters most: they are speaking in their own way. Nature is avenging unremembered truths, and history is giving itself back to its people. Western scholarship examines how best to deal with another field of research and new knowledge; it begins to try to adjust and re-collect, often ambivalently, its previous knowledge system.

Ugarit yielded many tablets relating to the daily life and customs of its inhabitants that showed it as a typical city in the region. More important were the mythological stories recovered from that period, more than a thousand years after Gilgamesh and nearly a thousand years before the biblical texts were put together. The tablets were written in a 30-sign alphabet (27 consonants + 3 alephs, $\bar{a}$, $\bar{u}$, $\bar{\imath}$), a Cana'anite alphabet adapted to cuneiform technology. Above all, the myth cycles made it possible to clarify and amplify religious developments in the region.

Figure 4.1 Entrance to the city of Ugarit

IMPORTANCE TO PALESTINE

Though located in northern Syria, Ugarit is just as significant for Palestine and Israel as it is for Syria and the region. The tablets found there have changed the traditional approaches to evaluating the region's religions and its history for at least three reasons.

First, the tablets tell mythic stories that give a more detailed, particular picture of ancient Palestinian-Syrian religions, at the same time that they betray close parallels to later biblical accounts. The composition of the Cana'anite pantheon has become more amplified than was previously known and more inter-regional connections were uncovered. The titles of the chief god Īl (El) give additional context for the names of God in the Bible and in the Qur'an, and (as I suggest in Chapter 11) have implications for expressions in popular language today. Added to previously known antecedents from Mesopotamia and Egypt, these parallels further emphasize the mythological and literary character (rather than historicity) of biblical narratives and reveal the debt the latter owe to these antecedents.

In confirming the polytheistic roots of "monotheism," Ugaritic texts undermine many earlier assumptions embedded in biblical scholarship. In addition, they show that some stories and sacred notions may have been transferred from one location to another (in this case, from northern Syria to Palestine). Well-known religious concepts of the past traveled the region unrestricted by the recently imposed boundaries that were unilaterally drawn to impede human contact and to stifle normal development. Now invented information is dispersed to fragment an integrated region and attribute to only a small fraction of the whole knowledge that was once dispersed, shared, and developed throughout the whole region.

Second, the Ugaritic writing system, an alphabetic cuneiform, completes the landscape of the alphabet's development, while the language used is shown to be very close to ancient Cana'anite and, also, to present Arabic. Thus, Ugaritic dispels many misconceptions about Arabic and other ancient languages that are common in popular thinking and in scholarly agendas. It tells us, for example, that the earlier bias of thinking of Ugaritic words as "cognates" of Hebrew is merely an expression of misguided scholarly habits and ignorance about Arabic. It is true that Ugaritic has helped to solve puzzles in the biblical text, such as mis-transcribed expressions whose meanings have become clear by drawing on parallels in Ugaritic. However, Arabic remains the closest language to Ugaritic, as I will explain.

Finally, Ugarit tells us that history is never final, in that such a chance discovery has enabled us to change and deepen our perceptions and understanding so drastically, especially in relation to cultural history, continuities, and previous religious certainties.

'ANAT AND BA'AL

In a story involving the goddess 'Anat and the god Ba'al ("bʕl"), 'Anat intercedes with her father, the supreme old fatherly god Īl (El), on behalf of Ba'al. Earlier, Ba'al conquers Yam/Yaw (Sea) in a fight where he is helped by his consort the goddess 'Anat, sister-in-law of the people: "*ym.lmt.b'lm ymlk*," "Yam is indeed dead! Ba'al shall be king!" This battle has a reverse outcome in the redacted biblical account in I Kings 18–19, which tells a story about the priests of Yahweh defeating the priests of Ba'al. In another Ugaritic story, 'Anat has a powerful role in defeating the god Mōt (Death). Ba'al's victories express a desire for the opportune coming of rain, the essential progress and rhythm of a living cycle, just as summer's rainless heat is needed and feared. At 'Anat's request a dream by Īl (El) anticipates the return of Ba'al, who had been thought consumed by Mōt:

> *bhlm.ltpn.il.dpid* In the dream of Beneficent El the Benign,
> *bdrt.bny.bnwt* In the vision of the Creator of Creatures,

smm.smn.tmtrn	Let the heavens rain oil,
nhlm.tlk.nbtm	The wadis run with honey,
wid^c.khy.aliyn.b^cl	Then I will know that Mightiest Ba'al lives,
kit.zbl.b^cl.ars	The Prince, Lord of the Earth, is alive.[2]

Here the word *"ltpn"* (*-n* is an accented emphasis ending) as a title for Īl (El) has the same form and meaning as Arabic *latīf* (Western scholarly practice always uses only *p* to transcribe the *f/p* sign), which is one of the 99 names of Allah—*al latīf*.[3] There are other appellations for Īl (El) in Ugaritic narratives that are echoed also in the later ones used in the Qur'an.

Chapter 2 related the connections between monotheism and the Cana'anite pantheon. The links include the choice of one chief god out of the pantheon, continuities in the Christ story (the son of God, *Eli/Elahi* as Christ calls him on the cross, immaculate conception, death, and resurrection),[4] and the preservation of Īl (El) the supreme father god in parts of the Old Testament (as in *El Shaddai*). As shown in the Dead Sea Scrolls text of Deuteronomy 32: 8–9, Yahweh is one of the sons of the Most High Īl (El), who upon distributing the earth and its people to his children gives Yahweh as god to Jacob's descendents (that is, the Israelites). Indeed, one Ugaritic text (KTU 1.1 IV 14) refers to *yw* (Yahweh) as one of the sons of Īl (El).[5]

In the Old Testament, the role and titles of Īl (El), as well as the attributes of Ba'al, are eventually appropriated by Yahweh, in a process that is not unusual in other mythologies.[6] The title of Ba'al (Rider on the Clouds) in the Ugaritic cycle is given to Yahweh in Psalm 68, and the Mother Goddess 'Asherah, Īl's (El's) wife and mother of humans and gods, later becomes the consort of Yahweh. As indicated in Kuntilet 'Ajrud (eighth century BCE) and the Elephantine Papyri (third century BCE), the goddess 'Asherah continued to be worshipped and associated with Yahweh. The incorporating of old associations, in a different environment to the south, created an offshoot set of beliefs (specifically in the Old Testament text), which then accidentally became the major tradition in the West. However, the Muslim tradition, reflected in the Qur'an, seems to have gone back to the name of the chief god of Ibrahīm/ Abraham, Īl / El (*Allah*). Ugaritic characteristics and names for Īl / El (old father of men and beneficent creator of creation) are similar to those used for the Bible god and later in the Qur'an. Islam beautified further the appellations of God, his nature and his powers, giving Allah 99 attributes, each reflecting a special quality.

Other narratives and allusions suggest the transfer of notions and stories adopted by the Bible from Ugaritic mythology. In Isaiah 27: 1, for example, Yahweh ("Lord" in most translations) kills the dragon called "Leviathan," who is instead smitten by Ba'al in the much earlier Ugaritic cycle. The more accurate name for the "wriggling serpent" or dragon is Ugaritic *ltn* (a word close to *al tannīn* in Arabic). In Psalm 48, "the city of our God, his holy mountain ... in the far recesses of the north" is usually read as "Mount Zion" by apologists, who scurry to comment that this is in Jerusalem—a location that obviously does not fit. This is more likely the same as the mountain called *Saphon* (more accurately, *Safan*) associated with the gods in Ugarit. Many other psalms either echo Ugaritic poetry or, as some scholars believe, are copied from Ugaritic hymns to serve again in the Old Testament. Much of the poetic "beauty," even "morality," people bestow on some Bible passages could be assigned to the earlier Ugaritic tradition.[7]

MUFFLING

Even those who recognize Ugarit's singular importance often overemphasize biblical applications. They want to use Ugaritic merely to "understand" or "enlighten" the Bible. At first, scholars were reticent to cite biblical comparisons, a reaction continued in the tendency "to overlook or suppress continuities between the early religion of Israel and the Canaanite (or Northwest Semitic) culture from which it emerged."[8] Dissemblers of habituated beliefs find such demonstrated source material difficult to consider, even to tolerate in discussion. An article on "Ugaritic" adopts the view that Ugarit is helpful for "understanding" the Bible.[9] As in other instances, this represents a kind of skewed perspective where the original sources on hard clay become less worthy or believable than the redacted derivative.

Another strategy to minimize Ugaritic connections uses euphemisms such as "contacts" and "cognate" to explain linguistic or other links, misleading because they elide the huge time distance between Ugarit and the Hebrew Bible. To maintain a notion of Israelite special distinction or an exclusionary "uniqueness," Ugaritic texts are said to show an epic or mythic tradition "assimilated" to express the imagery of God. An allied strategy appropriates recent discoveries into the confines of the faith, arguing for "transformations": "the Bible intentionally employed words and images from these mythological stories. ... The strangeness of the Bible will remain."[10]

Fortunately, corrections are beginning to be made to such evasions and misguided attempts that try to keep the Bible as superior rather than see it as an intermediary reference. An introduction by Adrian Curtis to the recent *Handbook of Ugaritic Studies* acknowledges that "the issue of the relevance of the discoveries at Ugarit for the study of the Hebrew Bible ... has been unduly dominant, at the expense of an appreciation of Ugarit and its texts in their own right." Curtis mentions the common illusion that "the newly discovered language was seen as akin to Hebrew." However, this impression is corrected in a chapter by two of the best experts in the field, Manfried Dietrich and Oswald Loretz, who note that: "The language they [the 30 signs] represented could be described as an idiom which in terms of content seemed to be comparable to Canaanite texts, but from a phonological perspective, however, was more like Arabic." Moreover, the discovery at Ugarit of an abecedary arranged in the same order as the "South Semitic" alphabet has led to the suggestion that people from the south, whether the Arabian Peninsula or southeastern Palestine, migrated to Ugarit or otherwise influenced it in the middle of the second millennium BCE.[11]

UGARITIC AND ARABIC

The Ugaritic alphabet contains signs representing sounds that are exactly the same as the 28-letter Cana'anite alphabet and the 28-letter Arabic alphabet—the only difference being that there are three signs for the *aleph* (*ā*, *ū*, *ē*), instead of one sign, to facilitate differentiation (which is done in Arabic today by using diacritical marks in proximity to the aleph).

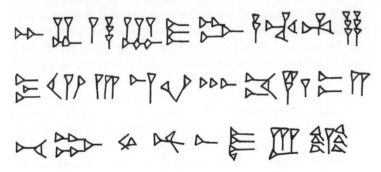

Figure 4.2   Ugaritic alphabet (left to right)

While some scholars are moving away from previous biases and prejudices to study the obvious similarities to Arabic, there is a still-prevalent tendency to relate Ugaritic to Hebrew. Of course, it always remains possible to indicate Hebrew cognates since many Hebrew words come from the same source. But when Arabic words are exactly the same as Ugaritic, it would seem a matter of ignorance or habit to point out a linguistically distant Hebrew cognate and neglect the Arabic similarity. Perhaps it is simply that most scholars of ancient languages in the West have grown up having learned Hebrew (as well as Latin and Greek) but not Arabic. With transcription, the same biases occur. A respectable reference, *The World's Writing Systems*, tells us that the wedge-shaped script records an inventory of sounds that is closer to that found in Classical Arabic (ca. 28 sounds) than to that found in biblical Hebrew (ca. 22 sounds). Still, it continues to transcribe Ugaritic using Hebrew "equivalents."[12] "Phoenician" inscriptions are similarly rendered in square Hebrew.[13] One result of such biased and inaccurate transcription, giving preference to Hebrew and Latin scripts, is that the Arabic language is sidelined and underestimated in its usefulness or degree of equivalence to Ugaritic, not to mention its actual importance as a language. Ignoring its study validates the spread of misinformation and disinformation.

In a count I made of a glossary of Ugaritic words compiled by J. C. L. Gibson, close to 70 percent of the words have exactly the same form as Arabic, although scholars unfamiliar with Arabic do not or cannot generally recognize the similarity. The letter "k," for example, has 71 entries, of which seven at least are titles of gods or have other local mythological associations, inapplicable today; out of the remaining 64, more than 37 are readily identifiable by an average speaker of Arabic (and a classical Arabic dictionary could account for other ancestral possibilities not immediately apparent). Still, the list under "k" supplied by Gibson notes only four cognates from Arabic, as opposed to twelve from Hebrew (some very distant, or with different stipulated pronunciation). With the letter "b," the percentage of exact equivalence to Arabic is even higher (out of 72 words listed, at least 49 are exactly like Arabic), but in this case Gibson's notes mention Arabic for only six words as opposed to 17 mentions of Hebrew. Throughout the glossary, there is no reference to the exact Ugaritic-Arabic equivalence of many words, like *brq* (meaning "lightning"), *krm* ("vineyard"), *kf* (transcribed as *kp*, "palm of the hand"), *mlk* ("king"), *mzn* ("scale"), *snnt* ("swallows"), and *'br* ("crossed"). For Ugaritic *brd* ("carved"), Gibson cites only Hebrew *parad*, whereas in Arabic the word is also *brd*. For *ktr* ("prosperity" or "plenty") the Hebrew Gibson cites is too distant (*kóšárót*), whereas the Arabic *ktr* (كَثَر katar) is exactly the same as Ugaritic. With the words listed under the letter "p," the equivalence to Arabic is equally high if one keeps in mind that "p" should be "f."[14] When a majority of words in the list are exactly the same as Arabic, to cite a small fraction of them and triple the citations for Hebrew says much about the orientation of Western scholarship in this area of study. Another scholar hardly mentions Arabic as a possibility in his introduction to a translation of Ugaritic texts.[15]

One major contribution to the study of Ugaritic literature is a book by Mark S. Smith on the origins of biblical monotheism. It has a comprehensive introduction, a bit too cautious in tone in places, about the effect of Ugarit on our understanding of biblical narratives—saying in effect that it disrupts previous notions about biblical "monotheism." Despite being lodged safely in mainstream scholarship, Smith seems nevertheless frustrated with the scholarly/ theological agendas that want to retain the "uniqueness" of the biblical god and the Israelites: "The religious posture of interpreters is in itself no argument against their views. However, there is little or no basis for these contrasts distinguishing monotheism from polytheism, nor is there a firm basis for the theological weight attached to biblical monotheism itself, a weight that the Bible itself hardly reflects."[16]

Yet Smith's scholarly background also leads to his failure to see Arabic as a possibility in interpreting key Ugaritic terms, for which there is really no other better tool. In one instance, Smith is translating Ugaritic expressions about the chief god Il (El). Most of the expressions would be transparently clear and accurate for anyone with average knowledge of Arabic (especially if that *p* is transcribed as an *f*). But when Smith guesses the phrase *bšrp 'il* as "By the incandescence (?) of El" (the question mark is his), he does not see that the Arabic *bšrf 'il* would have given him a more definitive and logical "By the honor of Il (El)."[17]

A few scholars are beginning to recognize how Ugaritic, as a language, correlates to Arabic. Manfried Dietrich mentions that the people in Ugarit may have originated from northwest Arabia. In a more recent discussion in *Handbook of Ugaritic Studies* (see above and note 11), Dietrich and Loretz have no hesitation in stating that Ugaritic is phonologically the same as Arabic.[18]

As a result of this now clear equation of Arabic and Ugaritic sounds and words, it becomes more difficult to maintain or propagate the assumption that Arabic entered the region of Palestine and Syria with the Arab-Muslim conquest in 638 CE (an assumption especially convenient for the Zionist claim system), and that somehow it can be distanced from its influencing contact or connection in earlier periods. Rather, more accurately, not only is Arabic connected to the other "languages" in the more northern regions from the most ancient periods, but it is, by virtue of its long continuity and existence, the living storehouse and present reincarnation of all the other ancient languages in a now Arabized region. It is perhaps time to revise some entrenched theories.

IMPLICATIONS FOR SCHOLARSHIP

These shocks to general understanding, such as the revelation that Arabic can no longer be predominantly associated only with the Arabian Peninsula in more recent periods rather than with more ancient times and with Ugarit (fifteenth to twelfth century BCE), are hard to accept for some scholars in the West or for Zionist scholarship. What has been transmitted and what is not transmitted, what is dominant and what was buried, dissembled, or scraped away, and what happens in the popular mind now and in scholarship—these show contradictions too hard to reconcile with what has been discovered to be closer to the truth. Such contradictions reveal how high is the investment in maintaining and nurturing an erroneous past understanding. Human consciousness tends to resist new knowledge that shakes habitual certainties to the core, especially when there is a keen interest in continuing to fit new knowledge into old receptacles, adding new water to already stagnant pools.

What Ugarit reveals has multiple implications for the old paradigms of scholarship and for the religious and cultural assumptions implicit in them. Just as with antecedents discovered earlier in Egypt and Mesopotamia, scholarly interpretations tended at first (as some still do) to incorporate Ugarit into previous understandings, in effect to perpetuate dominant thinking and subvert the discoveries by repeating ideas about "parallels" in a "biblical world." These are skewed perspectives inclined to meander over well-worn terrain and to insist on considering the originals on stone or clay tablets as somehow less important or less reliable than the subsequent overwritten or "redacted" (sometimes faked) copies. They arise from misguided thinking that has exaggerated the biblical tradition in the Western imagination, at the expense of the much larger (in dimension and historical reality) cultures and civilizations of the ancient world that started the great civilizational advances people rely on today.

In the end it is impossible to maintain these self-deceptive strategies and insistent duplicities of justifying the old certainties while still giving the appearance of dealing with the new discoveries. It is no longer possible to depend merely on a comparative approach and to neglect all the evidence for direct derivation and copying. The details of the pantheon, the dismantling of monotheistic monopolies and notions of "uniqueness," the evidence for transfer of stories, and the linguistic implications—all these should make it impossible to maintain the agenda of subverting the evidence. It is time for knowledge to be used to expand our perceptions, backward and forward, to correct the view of religious development as inherited through monotheistic telescopes and to restore the importance of Arabic to the study of ancient languages and literatures.

If Ugarit had not been discovered, how much less would we know today, how much less would we be aware of the ways in which human perception can continue to be shaped? To see the same regional gods present thousands of years earlier should suffice to reveal a major blindness in the monotheistic tradition. Rather than providing more excuses for notions about "parallels," Ugarit offers more definite clues about the process of reconstructing how the monotheistic religions relate to the older root sources of religious beliefs. To see a language so close to Arabic in use 3500 years ago changes many assumptions. What Ugarit and other discoveries teach us today should be sources of humbling reflection. If people still want to continue insisting on their exclusive ideas and inherited beliefs, then they will have opted for the comforts of unknowing or a willed ignorance.

5
Wheels of Fortune: The Alphabet

It may be a surprise to realize that the letters I am using now, in fact the letters people use and teach their children to use, or the ones they guess on the TV show "Wheel of Fortune," originated in the East Mediterranean region more than 3500 years ago at a time when the people living there were Cana'anites.

Yet, as I explain in Chapter 1, while Cana'an is idealized as a land of great bounty, the Cana'anites themselves (generalized as the Other) are demonized as a people—a prerequisite for justifying why they (and others) could be slaughtered and dispossessed of their lands. Given such rapacious attitudes toward them, it is no wonder that they are not given the full credit for a great invention such as the alphabet. A reader might say: "But I am told the alphabet was introduced to ancient Greece by the Phoenicians." This is true if one accepts the usual terminology, or euphemism. "Phoenician," however, whether a term assigned by the Greeks or a local identification that became widespread, applies to coastal Cana'anites who were culturally indistinguishable from people living inland.[1] The coast is the home of Cadmus (or Kadmos), who is said to have traveled from Ṣūr/Tyre to found the city state of Thebes and introduce the alphabet to Greece, and whose name is really *qdm* if we take out the Greek ending *-us*. It is the same larger region where people lived in city states between Egypt and Mesopotamia and the region from which the Carthaginians also emerged to found Carthage (now in Tunis) and other settlements across the whole Mediterranean.

There are other distracting ascriptions, biases, and credit-taking which relate to the alphabet's beginnings and the cultural environment that resulted in its transmission across the Mediterranean. To dispel them is to understand the role of writing in a historical context as well as to go beyond its current limitations in order to discover its promises.

PRIMAL ORIGINS

By virtue of its medial position, Cana'anite culture was a crucial creative force in the development of the phonetic alphabet. Being a non-empire and an outward-looking, migratory society helped it to take this step of logical abstraction and communicative economy based on the neighboring accomplishments of cuneiform and hieroglyphic. The earlier writing systems of Mesopotamia and Egypt were indeed the first, the basis of the advance to follow. Those two systems contained hundreds of signs based on pictorial representation in the case of hieroglyphic and a syllabic principle in the case of cuneiform—somewhat cumbersome and limited in use to specialized scribes. The novel idea was to find a sort of sound shorthand, just the right number of signs to represent the spoken language efficiently.

We don't know where exactly in Cana'an the alphabet first originated—though Jubayl in Lebanon (ancient *Jubla*; Greek *Byblos*) or a location in southern Palestine is most likely. Southern Palestine, near the borders of Egypt, seems the more probable geography, in view of the discovery of a proto-alphabet at Serabit el Khadim, a turquoise mine in Sinai dating to the Middle Bronze period. For its inception, the alphabet benefited from this intermediary point of interaction by adapting the idea of pictographs. (Its somewhat later implementation at Ugarit shows how the same alphabet was adapted to cuneiform technology at a location closer to Mesopotamia.) It began to take form, using pictures of common objects and their initial sounds for 28 letters sufficient to represent the language in writing. The signs were derived from essential shapes and aspects fundamental to the development of civilization, natural forces, and parts of the human body.

If one looks at the original signs of the alphabet, the current forms of letters used in European and other scripts are already evident and conform to what they now signify in most cases, especially in capital letters. The first letter reproduced the head of a bull, an animal associated with godly power. What better place to start than with the connection to the holy and one's chief god? Thus "aleph," which comes from *alīf* (meaning a tamed animal) denoted the process of domestication that is essential for cultivation of land and plants and the gathering of livestock, thus settlement and civilization. This first sign stood for the three long vowels *ā-ū-ē*. The capital letter A in Greek and Latin scripts is an evolution from that first shape, rotated first sideways then upside down. The next basic letter, B, comes from *beit*, which meant "house" in Cana'anite (and still means "house" in Arabic), and so took the shape of a basic place of habitation, which stood more or less like a square first, then acquired stylization with time, dictated by the medium and direction of writing. The sign for L has not really changed much, except in direction of writing, and is very similar to the current *lam* in Arabic. The letter K (from *kf*, palm) was derived from a shape that has four fingers, later stylized into a three-fingered palm, and further simplified and rotated so as to produce the close "k" of today. The letter M started by using marks that typified sea waves (related to *ym*, meaning sea), while R originally had the shape of a human head in profile (from *rās*, head), evidenced by the fact that Greek *rho* is shaped like a P.

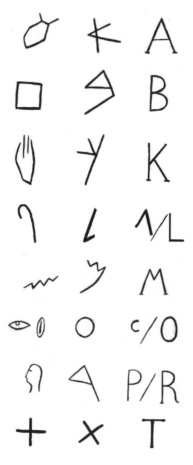

Figure 5.1 Evolution of the alphabet signs
ABKLMORT

NON-RECOGNIZING BIASES

No doubt the alphabet is one of the greatest intellectual inventions in history, which is why it is subject to many claims. Without it, there would be none of the systematic recording that has accumulated over the past three millennia. In fact, without a simple alphabet there would probably be no such thing as organized history and no extensive libraries of expanding knowledge—also none of the dependent advances as we know them today. It was, as Marshal McLuhan said, a "most radical technology," whose later "extensions" enabled the "West" to harness "aggregate uniform power," the processing of data, classification, literacy, and systematic science.

Yet McLuhan wants to identify the alphabet as "Graeco-Roman."[2] This hyphenated conclusion is based partly on the assumption that Greek script has the distinction of including "vowels," making Greek and then Latin rather than "Phoenician" the first "true" alphabet.[3] Of course, the original alphabet had the basic long vowels ($\bar{a}$-$\bar{u}$-$\bar{e}$), and the short vowels were understood (or can, now, be indicated by diacritical marks in Arabic). The Greeks adapted the Cana'anite system to enable them to write *their* language. Since not all the available consonants were needed for their sounds they turned some of them into vowels, as in the sign for *'ayn*, an eye (see Figure 5.1), which became the omicron (other adjustments occurred, such as *h* ultimately representing the *E* while the sign for the guttural ḥ was used for *H*). As we have already seen, "Phoenician" as a euphemism itself displays a complex of biases: it is another name for Cana'anite (as *rasna* became Etruscans), a designation also useful to biblicists who want to demean them; whether as a localized name or an appellation used for coastal Cana'anites by the Greeks, it is equivalent to the Roman *Poenicus* (Carthaginians), hence the insulting sense of the word "punic" in English dictionaries (see Chapter 1, note 21). The Romans vilified the Carthaginians, as they did the Etruscans; and the Bible degrades the Cana'anites as pagans destined to become slaves or be exterminated; later in the New Testament "Phoenicia" appears as a more limited geographic area in northern Palestine and southern Lebanon.

So, use of the term "Phoenician" only serves to cloud the issue, preventing the recognition that would give full credit to the Cana'anites. It is an elision that avoids contradicting the preferential model of Western civilization and the select elements of its Judeo-Christian-Greek-Roman construct, which (as I detailed in Chapter 1) contains, in each and all the elements combined, entrenched biases against other civilizations and people, including the Babylonians, Cana'anites, Egyptians, and Philistines. In much scholarship, in traversable tropes, ancient civilizations placed outside the sanctioned model are appropriated for their advances but nevertheless also labeled as decadent, money-oriented, imperialistic, or pagan. Biblicist William Foxwell Albright, while unable to neglect Cana'anite contributions, nevertheless maintains that the decimation of these pagans (much like that of the native "Indians" in North America) was inevitable and "fortunate," since it replaced "gross mythology" with "lofty monotheism." Then, inconsistently (or consistently with such supremacist thinking), Albright admires the "superior Romans" and their "singularly elevated paganism."[4]

Another allied prejudice relates to the direction of writing (right to left or left to right), as if this represented something other than a difference in habit or convenience. Latin was borrowed from the Etruscan script, which was borrowed (like the Greek) from the Cana'anite invention. The Romans had taken over use of the Etruscan alphabet, which was made into Latin by merely changing the direction of writing. So, to lend Latin more distinction, the notion was devised of deeming left-to-right to be more advanced, while viewing Etruscan as "retrograde" because of its right-to-left orientation.[5] In reality, in its beginnings about 4000 years ago, the alphabet showed no right/left preferences, but was written in all directions. Epigraphists puzzled over ancient Greek inscriptions until they deciphered that, like proto-Cana'anite, they were written boustrophedon. This not only suggests an earlier date for Greek borrowing from Cana'anite (around 1500 BCE), rather than from the later period when the Cana'anite script took a more fixed right-left direction, but also the ridiculousness of the notion that left-right is somehow a more refined stage. The eventual shift in Greek to the left-right direction was not unprecedented. At Ugarit in northern Syria, around 1400 BCE, scribes adapted figuration by using a reed stylus, the cuneiform printing technology, for the 30 signs representing the same alphabet sounds. Contrary to other "Semitic" scripts, Ugaritic was imprinted from left to right on the tablets, probably to avoid smudging the clay.

Martin Bernal writes that "language is the *sanctum sanctorum* of the Aryan Model."[6] On the subject of the alphabet, some scholarship wants to make the distinction between a consonantal alphabet and a "true" alphabet as a way of "privileging the distinctive role of Greek consciousness."[7] Other attempts have been made to wield the alphabet's evolution and characteristics to fit into the appropriative complex and amalgam called "Western civilization." Often, the biases implicit or explicit in one of the constituents of this construction aim to privilege and sanctify Greek or Roman or Judeo-Christian traditions.

OTHER CLAIMS

Grammatology (the linguistic study of script), like biblical scholarship, is therefore often characterized by approaches designed to take advantage and to interpret by agenda. While the agenda is diminishment of the real inventors in the case of "Graeco-Roman" credit-giving, it is appropriation by subscribers to biblical credit-taking. It is not uncommon to see in scholarship various claims that backdate Hebrew as a language or a script in order to place it in a position of ascendancy, not dissimilar to what Bernal describes. One extreme example is a book by Leonard Shlain who, in order to invent a theory about how Yahweh gave the alphabet to his chosen males first in the world, has to dismiss the "Phoenicians" as ethnically and culturally incapable of devising such a great system and to bypass Ugarit as if it never existed.[8]

Even in encyclopedia accounts (where more accuracy might be expected), occasional hedging, invention, and euphemism seem intended to establish particular claims or to create uncertainties. The *Britannica* article on "Writing" and *Collier's Encyclopedia* entry on "Alphabet" backdate an early "Hebrew" alphabet to the "period of Saul and David" in the eleventh century BCE. Thus they sideline the overwhelming doubts about David's historicity, neglect to mention that the "Israelites" were "preliterate," or that Hebrew cannot be that old, or that the "Gezer calendar," which both articles cite as proof, is "Phoenician" (that is, Cana'anite) with some of its letter characteristics being close to Moabite.[9] The older edition of *Encyclopaedia Judaica* (1971) clarifies that the "Hebrews" adopted the Cana'anite alphabet and "followed the current Phoenician script until the ninth century," then adopted a variety of Aramaic. Even if one doubts the equation of "Hebrew" with "Israelite" and with the much later religion Judaism, this hypothetical explanation of the descent of Hebrew as a script at least avoids moving branches and burying other branches in the alphabet tree.

The tree in Daniels and Bright's *The World's Writing Systems* is generally accepted: from proto-Cana'anite, the 28-letter linear script developed around 2000 BCE and wedge-shaped Ugaritic around 1500 BCE. From linear Cana'anite developed Old Arabian scripts and

"Phoenician" around 1200 BCE. The reduced "Phoenician" 22-letter alphabet dominated northern and western regions of Greater Syria until about 850 BCE, with various "script varieties" deriving from it, such as Aramaic. From Aramaic (an international language from about 700 BCE) developed later "Semitic" scripts, including square Hebrew. Arabic more likely developed from a pre-1300 BCE South Semitic group, since it retained a 28-letter alphabet.[10] In a side development that has become major, all Western alphabets later evolved from the Cana'anite. "About 1700 BCE, someone in Canaan ... created the alphabet. This brilliant achievement would revolutionize the development of writing and literacy throughout the Western world."[11] Despite any doubts about language classification related to this region, perhaps we should try at least to let *this* tree stand.

SOUND

Languages are best related through sound rather than script. It is fallacious to note only similarities in script form, or to rely on such similarities to create connections, especially when looking at ancient languages. The connection to Arabic of the original Cana'anite, Southern Arabic and Ugaritic is more demonstrable if sounds are examined rather than merely the shapes of letters, which are different from each other. What the signs represent and their number are the more important considerations. Yet, it is a very common bias in scholarship to think of the later, more abridged 22 signs as the original alphabet, to use the term "Phoenician," and to transcribe "Phoenician" and other ancient languages using the much later 22-letter square Hebrew (which is really unacknowledged square Aramaic).[12]

The original Cana'anite had 28 signs and sounds. Similarly, Ugaritic had basically 28 sounds, although it used cuneiform technology to etch 30 signs on clay tablets and wanted to distinguish the three alephs, $\bar{a}$-$\bar{u}$-$\bar{e}$. Arabic today has 28 sounds. Thus, the sound systems of Arabic, proto-Cana'anite, South Arabian, and Ugaritic are basically identical.

What distorts the evidence of this fact is that Arabic letters evolved differently and eventually the writing used the cursive joining of letters to form words. While the sign for *lam* ل did not change much, the other sounds are the same though the script is distant. In Arabic, joining letters (a later development) resulted in certain evolutions intended to achieve economy and ease of writing.

Economy is further achieved by using the same sign for two or three sounds (as in ح ج خ ğ ḥ ẖ and ﺭ ﺯ r z), somewhat adapting their shapes when they are placed in initial, medial or terminal positions, and making sound distinctions by using dots and diacritical marks. That the order of the present Arabic alphabet is somewhat different from, say, Ugaritic was simply the result of later scholarly ordering, so that sounds represented by similar signs are placed next to each other. This is proof of evolution in Arabic, a positive development that (in contrast to fossilized languages) evidences constant use and inventiveness.

WRITING WRITING

"The certitude that everything has been written negates us or turns us into phantoms." The disorder made order by infinite alphabetary arrangements Borges imagines in his mixed trope "The Library of Babel" is yet to come—though one hopes not. In an ontological void, the space of language is defined by the library, "a monotonous line of language left to its own devices," where a book—because it cannot be all books and is no longer where speech adopts a form—will be shelved among other "endless murmuring."[13]

Our contemporary predicament, however, is that all conditions of language apply at once: literature and interpretation are self-perpetuating, but there are also single books that many consider the last word, about which commentary multiplies. Assuming the finality of any writing only leads to an endless reshaping of it (often perversely) in ever-changing psyches and times. When that happens, minds monomaniacally fixate on a point spinning on itself. But why can't writing and its materiality be employed, instead, to call into question all claims of totality and to challenge systems, making the very limitations of writing as hitherto employed an advantage by allowing "the unveiling of the silences, conflicts, and power realities in all religious and cultural traditions"?[14] This materiality itself, in probing criticism and insightful analysis of material cultures, in its exposure of hierarchies and repressions, can avoid the weight of a writing tradition, or its futile fate.

So, paradoxically, it is in writing that we must generate models of how to transmit knowledge, how to avoid a fate of writing. Just as in the historic abuse of writing there are traces of its gaps, so in the origin of our writing systems we might find the prospect of its future.

Recognition here is paramount because it is an irony of ironies that the originators of the alphabet so central to the globalization of knowledge should be subjected to the tropes of civilizational hate and cultural appropriation. There are lessons in this language history that should annul any Babel bias. The alphabet seems to have developed in a climate of cultural openness and exchange where all participants were willing to offer and to accept debt. Otherwise, it might not have evolved to become the varied alphabets of East and West. This accommodative nature at its source could be a model for cultural globalization and for how people might live together, though the history of the alphabet's inventors highlights the dangers in such openness if not everyone participates in it and acknowledges the participation of others.

Writing in the materiality of signs need not be a *terminus ad quem*. Beyond its practical applications, it has been, like the art in caves, a means to express the silences of the self, the loneliness of existence, the charm against death that comes every moment and at the end. Poet or scribe, alone or in concert, Ilimilku notched in clay this episode of the Baʻal cycle in the city of Ugarit about 3400 years ago. As he withholds the rains, Baʻal recalls ʻAnat from her ritualistic autumnal violence so she can relay a plea to Īl (El) to build a palace that will acknowledge his victory over Mōt (Death) and Yam (Sea). He calls her from *her* warring, albeit on behalf of the people and of him:

qryy.bars / mlhmt	"Bury war in the earth;
st.bʻprt.ddym	set strife in the dust;
sk.slm.lkbd.ars	pour a libation into the midst of the earth,
ar bdd.lkbd.sdm	honey from a jar into the midst of the steppe.
hsk.ʻsk.ʻbsk	Grasp your spear (and) your mace:
ʻmy.pʻnk.tlsmn	let your feet hasten towards me,
ʻmy / twth.isdk.	let your legs hurry to me!
dm.rgm / it.ly.w.argmk	For I have a word that I would say to you,
hwt.w.atnyk.	a message that I would repeat to you:
rgm / ʻs.w.lhst.abn	a word of tree and whisper of stone,
tant.smm.ʻm.ars	the sighing of the heavens to the earth,
thmt.ʻmn.kbkbm	of the deep to the stars,
abn.brq.dl.tdʻ.smm	I understand the thunder which the heavens do not know,
rgm ltdʻ.nsm	a word unknown to men
wltbn / hmlt.ars	and which the multitudes of the earth do not understand."[15]

Ilimilku and his consorts labored in the profession of recording the drama and movement of forces. Though their world was also troubled with struggle and weariness, they reflected on its delicate balance and retained its wonder.

It is no longer possible to retrieve this fusion of oral and written, primal and civilized sensibilities. Nothing, though, should prevent learning of this past and unearthing its wisdom, or including it in our consciousness and priorities—much as we revise theories and epistemologies. By contrast, a life devoted to appropriation, accumulation of wealth, and abuse of others through willed ignorance or stereotyping unleashes ever more predatory and calculating acts. Even charity is then deceptive. Cultural connectivity is not realized merely through mechanical, economic, electronic globality. And exclusivist ideologies will only continue to transfer identities into claims for innovations, gods, or lands. "A life without joy—what advantage does it have over death?" asks an Ugaritic school text.[16] Absence of recognition is another form of death, the death of culture as a wholesome sustaining force. Instead, it is possible to realize that we hold much in common if we see history together rather than use it for our special purposes. An inclusive model that globalizes recognitions, that breaks old molds, and that unshackles knowledge, is more compelling now than before. It might reconcile us to what has been unjustly devalued—but has been part of us from the beginning.

Part Two
Modern Myths and (De)Colonized History

6
"Last of the Phoenicians": Identity Questions

Some real traces of the past are forgotten or neglected, while invented or false links acquire an obsessive reality all their own. It is a strange thing indeed that, in the construction of identity, the imaginary often has a stronger effect than do real connections. This applies particularly to the use of ancient history. Those who have a right to that history may be unaware of it, and instead of being able to appreciate its depth they live under its weight and are disabled by it. But the past is distant and therefore exploitable by those who have the tools to wield for the purposes of power.

PHOENICIANS VERSUS ISRAELITES

A U.S. scholar recently delivered a lecture in west Jerusalem entitled "In Search of the 'Last' of the Phoenicians." Rather than the significance of seals found in "northern Israel," what struck me about the lecture was the intriguing echo of James Fenimore Cooper's novel, *The Last of the Mohicans*, suggesting that the "Phoenicians" (or, more accurately, coastal Cana'anites), like the Mohicans, are now similarly extinct.[1] Was this a kind of nostalgia, a sense of humor, an academic preconception, or a wish for extinction? Other scholars now study the Philistines, in effect accepting their reality beyond the prejudices of the biblical accounts, though at the same time appropriating them in another way into a pre-ordained system. It is the same with the Cana'anites. Their material remains are all that can be found as real objects over the millennia, so they become the target of appropriation. Some scholars now theorize (contrary to debunked biblical accounts about conquest, slaughter, and enslavement) that the "Israelites" were really "Canaanites" who merely, and peacefully, changed their ideology and religion. But such a theory only fabricates another legitimating claim to replace the discredited assumptions. (See the section "Old-New Scholarly Agendas" and note 41 in Chapter 1).

111

Regardless of how far the biblical stories have been deprived of their credibility as history, the public and much scholarship still operate within the old notions. Even when it appears that biblical history is being debunked, what scholars often do is to generate theories that result yet again in appropriating other cultures, adapting or recycling old claim systems, and attempting to acquire more cultural legitimacy.[2]

It is particularly odd to hear, in Jerusalem, that the "Phoenicians" or Philistines or other ancient peoples have disappeared into thin air. On the other hand, the ancient legendary designations "Hebrew" and "Israelite" are not only considered valid but are somehow reincarnated in the present identities of Jews or Israelis. Even if there is a shade of connection between some Jews today and the Judaism of 2000 years ago, or even if one can vaguely, though fallaciously, link contemporary Jews to the so-called "Hebrews" or "Israelites" mentioned in the religious tradition, the fact of separation from Palestine and the region for millennia should have been enough to remove any traces. It is now a matter of some embarrassment to the old thinking that there is mounting evidence, as I detail below, to show the extent of conversions to Judaism in Eastern Europe and North Africa in recent, as in older, periods that have nothing to do with "exile" or "Diaspora."

Is it not transparent that ancient peoples like the Cana'anites/"Phoenicians," Philistines, Babylonians, Egyptians, Moabites, and others remained on the land and could not have disappeared from existence? They changed identities, adopted different religious beliefs, and moved about, but for the most part they had no place else to go! However, this perverse assumption of invisibility evaporates when it becomes useful to cite them or to use engrained biases to collapse them onto present people, namely "Arabs." While a Zionist-inclined writer concedes this obvious continuity (that the population of "Lebanon, Syria, Jordan, and Egypt ... descend directly from their ancient predecessors"), he is quick to add, to preserve his argument about "ancient Israel," that the "ancestors of the Palestinians are more difficult to identify."[3] He would like to preserve the idea that the people of Palestine do not follow the rule he has just established, and that Palestinians should be dismissed as recent arrivals from the Arabian Peninsula, so as to vacate the space for Zionist claims. It is unconvincing for anyone to make a distinction between the Palestinians and the people in their immediate proximity since they are all basically indistinguishable from each other, in a region which has experienced the same historical events, and now lies divided by artificial, colonially created boundaries.

Biblical historiography and the claims based on it as they relate to ancient periods and peoples therefore assume all sorts of ethnic monopolies, convenient groupings, and many other monolithic notions, regardless of whether these can be supported by actual history, archaeology, or common sense.

ISRAELITES ARE NOT JEWS

Though it remains unacknowledged by almost everyone, Hebrews and Israelites, two idealized communities associated with biblical narratives, cannot by any stretch of the imagination be related to Jews, even the Jews of 2000 years ago. The Zionist claim system posits the most unlikely links among these disparate idealized ancient entities, both in terms of ethnicity and religious affiliation, and then declares their relation to present-day Jews.[4] These imagined links are supposed to establish an identity stretching continuously over almost 4000 years—despite all the fallacies and historical twists involved in linking such entities. Misleading narratives and connections are designed to delude people into this oft-repeated design. Even the most liberal Jews and pro-Palestinian critics of Zionism (not to mention the Palestinians themselves) fail to examine or deconstruct this tactic, and so sometimes confuse Jews or Israelis with "Israelites." It is not uncommon to read or hear a Palestinian or an Israeli say "Israeli" when "Israelite" is intended.[5]

Chronologically and in terms of nomenclature, the distinctions are enormous. These disparate groups (Hebrews, Israelites, Jews 2000 years ago) are nebulous and far removed from each other. "Israelite" refers to the tribes that presumably descend from Ya'qūb (Jacob) and whose stories are told in the Bible. It is unfortunate that "Hebrew" has become associated with "Jewish" and with the language that Judaism uses (some languages in Europe even use "Hebrew" as a replacement for "Jew"). "Hebrew" is a more ancient designation than "Israelite" that derives from 'abiru, suggesting generally people who lived a nomadic or Bedouin life and crossed borders. How this nomadic life interacts with settlement has been a permanent feature of this region, and still has substantial remnants today. The "Israelites" themselves, if they existed in that idealized form, could not have been "Jews" (a term that derives from "Judean" in much later periods), nor is the mere acceptance of the biblical narrative tradition enough to establish such a hazy identity. "Israelites" are the product of biblical narratives redacted to produce a particular line of descent that excludes presumed relatives in a well-designed family tree.

At the time it is purported that the "first temple" was built (tenth century BCE), the people living in Palestine were pagan in their religious practices. "Judaism" did not develop until at least 500 years later. Still, Solomon's "temple" is deemed to be "Jewish" at a time when Judaism did not exist as a religion. Palestine remained largely pagan until the fourth or fifth century CE, and it was then and has been ever since characterized by a multiplicity of religious practices and ethnicities. In terms of religion (rather than ethnicity), the most likely scenario is that a percentage of the people who stayed on the land (now "Palestinians") merely changed their religious affiliation over time (pagan, pagan and Jewish, pagan and Christian, finally Muslim, Jewish and Christian). Such conclusions are supported by historical research and by the results of DNA studies conducted by Jewish scholars during the peace process in the late 1990s (see Chapter 11). Even over the last couple of centuries Jewish families in Palestinian towns and villages, among the minority of Jews in Palestine before the 1920s, changed their religion, notably in places like Hebron and Nablus. Additionally, as we have seen, scholarship has now established the general lack of historicity in biblical narratives: myths such as the Kingdom of David or "Exodus" are products of invention, literary construction or copying from others, having no archaeological or historical corroboration.[6]

For present-day Jews to claim these sorts of connections would be like Muslims from Indonesia, 2000 years from now, saying they descend from the prophet's line and claiming Mecca and Medina as their ancestral homeland.

Such calculated confusion among terms and fallacious assumptions of historicity become entrapments. They disable the distinction between fact and tradition, between Judaism as a religion in which people believed and the idealized entities called "Hebrews" or "Israelites."

PRESENT JEWS ARE NOT ANCIENT JEWS

Evidence is mounting that most Jews today who had been assumed to be "Semites" (or the result of a "Diaspora" or "exile") are instead the product of more recent conversions and hence have nothing but belief in Judaism to connect them to ancient Jews (among whom conversion was also normal). Yet, the Zionist movement and the State of Israel have constructed a national identity based on "return" to the land of "ancestors" that many Jews still believe in blindly.

Arthur Koestler angered the Zionists when in 1976 he wrote *The Thirteenth Tribe*, a book about the wholesale conversion in the eighth century CE of the Khazarite tribes in Eastern Europe. One of his points is that since eastern European Jewry is the result of conversion in later periods, the term "Semites" does not apply to them, and so the ascription of "anti-Semitism" is nonsensical in that context. Recently, Shlomo Sand's *The Invention of the Jewish People* (2009) recovered (in addition to the Khazarites) another chapter of conversion relating to Berber tribes and other populations, which produced North African and Spanish Jewry. All older reports by Arab and Jewish historians point to the strength of the conversions, in contrast to the more recent Zionist historiography about a "nation-race." Proselytization of the Berbers and Punics in North Africa as well as the Iberian populations began in the early centuries CE. The conversions were encouraged in Romanized areas by the fact that Judaism was a recognized religion whereas Christianity was prohibited. Rabbinical authorities had expressed their anxiety about proselytes. By the time the Muslims arrived at the end of the seventh century they had to defeat a proselytized Jewish tribal queen, Dihya al-Kahina, in 693 CE. Many Berber Jews joined the Muslim conquest of the Iberian Peninsula in 711 CE, while Spanish Jews also helped the conquerors. For evidence of the non-exilic origin of North African and Sephardic Jews, Sand also cites the work of Paul Wexler, which points to the lack of any linguistic traces of an exilic nature: the proselytes spoke their own languages, while Aramaic and Hebrew appeared in Jewish texts only in the tenth century CE. For Sand, as for others (even for early Zionists) the myth of Jewish populations being deported does not make historical sense; populations had remained in place, overall, with maybe some of the elite being deported. The conclusion (inevitably) Sand suggests is that present-day Palestinians are more likely to be the "descendents" of earlier ancient populations. Another Israeli writer, Uri Avnery, has added his voice to questioning the myth of a Jewish "people" descending from the ancients. Thus, generally, East European, North African, and Spanish Jews have no "Semitic" descent and are not the result of some "Diaspora" or "exile" or a "race," but are converts.

Moreover, the same applies to earlier Judaism in the region, a religion to which people converted just like any other faith. The

Hellenized Hasmoneans imposed Judaism on some of their neighbors (such as the Edomites) during the last two centuries BCE, and Judaism continued to be a relatively popular religion for converts more specifically until the fourth century CE, when Christianity was accepted by the Byzantine Empire, and even beyond as in the case of the Khazarites.[7]

Until the recent importation of European and North American Jews, as well as Jews from the Arab World, into Palestine (part of which became Israel) in the twentieth century, the region contained a majority of "Arab" Muslims, a strong minority of "Arab" Christians (15 to 50 percent depending on the "country"), and a minority of "Arab" Jews, in addition to small sects. In terms of identity and affiliation, what is described for the time of Herod has continued to pertain in the region until recently (with some variation in terms): "A person could be *Phoenician* by descent, *Hellenized* by culture, *Idumaean* by place of birth, *Jewish* by official religion, *Jerusalemite* by residence, and *Roman* by citizenship."[8]

IDENTITY TRAPS

Some Lebanese are doing something similar to the Israelis with respect to their identity, except that they have a grain of truth to aid them, notwithstanding the deep misunderstanding that makes their attempt a less-than-useful one.[9] Some people in the Lebanese Christian community who want to distance themselves from the "Arab" environment say they can trace their roots to the "Phoenicians." In this case, a curious religious or political motive drives them to affiliate with the pagan past. Little do they realize that "Phoenician," as I explain in Chapter 1 (see notes 18–21) and Chapter 5, is most likely a Greek term applied to coastal Cana'anites, or a limited local designation of people in "Tyre and Sidon" that became more extended with time, or a Greek term that became common as the region was Hellenized for a time. Regardless, the people on the coast were culturally similar to those living inland, and so not that distant from "Arabs" in other parts of the Arabized region, who had earlier connections to the Arabian Peninsula in terms of origin and language.[10] For a Lebanese to use the term that way ("We are Phoenicians, not Arabs!"), regardless of the term's derivation, is to employ a self-colonizing designation that results in discord and divisiveness.

It is an unfortunate characteristic of this region that more recent religious and political identities have obscured identification with the ancient past that is still part of it. In other cases where ancient history is used (as with some Egyptians relating to the Pharaohs, or the Iraqi regime when it tried to look back to the Babylonians), the effect is fragmentary and generally ill-informed rather than constructive.

Figure 6.1   I, Ismaʿīl

Identity traps can be useful or destructive, and they are varied and many. Identity construction, even when based on an invented past, can seem to be successful when it manages to control people's minds for a particular direction and purpose. In one of the greatest confiscations of national heritage, the Israelis have turned an imaginary, "biblical" landscape into an identity with the land by appropriating and exploiting Palestine's environment and resources, as well as aspects of Palestinian heritage—all the elements that Palestinians have lived with for millennia. As Zionist identity has succeeded as an invention, so too "Western civilization" has been a useful and employable construct. Many nations not only nourish affiliation with the ancient past but often invent or embellish it for use in the construction of their own national identity, nations or cultures being "imagined communities" (a notion popularized by Benedict Anderson's book of the same name). As I explain in Chapter 1, the paradigm of "Western civilization" is a fairly recent construct, dating from about the sixteenth century, made up of selected ancient Greek, Roman, and Judeo-Christian elements, conveniently appropriated and amalgamated to acquire historical depth, civil precedent, and serviceable truth. No one prevented the West from using these elements despite the lack of real historical or practical links. Over time, different populations have engaged in building up a romanticized self-subterfuge in order to weave their own identities, and present-day Greeks or Italians and others have little difficulty in associating or being proud of their pre-Christian past.

These issues are more problematic and contradictory in the East Mediterranean region. The identities tend to be layered but their outward signs often reflect the effect of religious and localized identifications. Just as we have seen with respect to the fallacy of equating contemporary Jews with the ancient idealized entity "Israelite," the Zionist claim that Palestinians are to be associated with the "Arabs" and Muslims who conquered the land in 638 CE (AD) is inaccurate and misleading. It is a more recent adaptation in Zionist rationalization, as I explain in Chapter 11. Yet, while it is to be expected that Zionists will theorize this way, it is quite another thing for Palestinians or other people in the region to fall into the trap of thinking along the same lines. A prominent literary critic once declared in defense of Palestinian historic rights: "We have been here for 1300 years." A long time indeed—good enough in other cases to confirm property rights! He (and he was of Christian background) did not realize that saying this was not only historically inaccurate, bypassing the continuity of the population over millennia, but also an inadvertent concession to Zionist claims. Such a statement assumes that the presence of Palestinian "Arabs" is to be associated with the Muslim conquest in the seventh century CE—exactly what the Zionists now argue to establish their claim for prior possession based on mythic connections. Similarly, a Christian student from Bethlehem proclaimed in front of an international audience that she was descended from the Crusaders (and she looked perfectly dark-eyed and black-haired, totally un-Crusader like). A Palestinian Christian professor dates his ancestry to the time of Byzantine emperor Constantine. He assumes that since Christianity came to Palestine as a dominant religion in the time of Constantine, some Christian Palestinians can say "We have been here for 1700 years." Historical records point to systematic efforts by Constantine to suppress paganism among the local population, which policy his mother Helena helped implement by fixing the presumed locations of biblical events by using pagan sites and having churches built on them (see Chapter 3). The same applies to Islam, which came to a region whose population was already Christianized. It required several centuries for the population to become mostly Muslim. In other contexts, as I outline in Chapter 1 and Chapter 11, the present Palestinian population has often been confusedly associated with all sorts of ancient and modern peoples, from the ancient "Canaanites" or Philistines to Ishmael and the modern Arabs.

PALESTINIAN IDENTITY

The legitimacy of Palestinian identity is not to be seen as a reply to Zionist disinheriting and devaluing strategies or as a reaction to the injection into Palestine of an imported Zionist nationalism. Palestinian identity has passed through periods of latency and diversity. It was often related to a sense of belonging to a village or town, or to a religion or sect in the narrow sense, or of being part of the region of Greater Syria, or of being associated with Arab nationalism. Especially after the Nakba of 1948, it has become more definitely oriented toward Palestine as a country to which both Christian and Muslim Palestinians belong.[11]

Identity formation relates to issues of "consciousness" and "memory"—and questions about whether these elements somehow lend more legitimacy to an identity. Israelis often argue that they have a strong identity because they are more "conscious" of the past. Is identity to be conceived as a conscious and calculated act (something of an obsession), or is it more genuine when its cultural attributes have evolved naturally in a geographic region and so does not need to be justified? A regional, more nuanced, culturally oriented identity—transcending narrow nationalistic or religious lines, or anything similarly limited and problematic—would be the best for everyone. It would be more inclusive and would incorporate the various periods of history in the region. The Palestinians and other people in the region had this identity more implicitly available in the past, until they were divided along arbitrary geographical lines designed by colonial powers.

But such a regional identity does not seem possible anymore, at least not in the short term. The Palestinians have been singled out for invasion and dispossession. They cannot be blamed, or their rights diminished, because in earlier centuries they had not developed a strong, particular Palestine-related consciousness, or for having seen themselves as belonging to a particular village or town or sect, or for having thought of themselves more as "Arabs." The idea of national "consciousness" itself is largely misguided; it is often more the result of blinding obsession or indoctrination than of positive awareness.

Unfortunately, some writers on aspects related to identity seem to suggest that Palestinian "national consciousness" (which existed in nascent form all along) is to be compared to Israeli national "consciousness" or that it emerged as a response to Zionist ideology. It is further assumed that interest in the archaeological past (generally much less passionate among "Arabs" and Palestinians), an obsessive digging for "heritage," is somehow legitimating. Does being a collector then mean one can be assumed to have a "culture"? Palestinians are criticized for lack of interest in their archaeology, at the same time as they are instructed to stick to "Arab" or Muslim remains and are discouraged if they try to establish connections outside that limit. There is concern and even fear among some Israeli archaeologists of the potential implications for ancient history when they excavate Philistine or Cana'anite or other ancient remains.[12]

If Palestinians should concentrate on their connections to the ancient past, it is not out of choice or need, but as a critical response to what has been taken from them. Palestinians and other people in the region have a more layered, latent, and less consciously constructed relation to ancient history, expressed through an enduring relation to the land itself. But Palestine and the Palestinians have not yet found a total narrative, partly because of lack of "knowledge," partly due to the effect of a colonized incubus under which they have suffered, and mostly because they are being prevented from doing so. National "consciousness" (more often a less complimentary word applies) and the obsessive, exclusivist narratives of national origin seem in some eyes to be positive or legitimate constructions. For Palestinians it is a necessity both to recover their own history and to overcome their self-colonization.

A question remains as to how "useful" various models and constructions have been with respect to the inclusiveness of humanity. Though recent communication advances promise new possibilities for greater understanding of the human story, they can also become tools for standardization and indoctrination. In the modern globalized world, the result of national or ideological constructions could be either "disaster" or "success" in terms of how people relate to each other and identify themselves, and how some might find the justice and recognition they deserve. Amin Maalouf advocates diversity and a "composite" identity that is "the sum of all our allegiances"—whether to nation, language, ethnicity, religion, region, village, or other grouping—though he seems to avoid the past. Diversity nourishes a universality that does not deny other elements of individual identity, on condition that the various allegiances are not employed at the expense of other people's dignity or their human rights. Maalouf believes that religion, which can become an ultimate identity (like somewhat narrower traditional allegiances to nation or race or ethnicity or other affiliation) can also become lethal, or nourish fanaticism, terror, and ethnic wars, in the absence of a greater allegiance to a humanity based on equality and respect. He is wary of claims to ideals that are built on strife and cause harm to others, and implies that it is every individual's responsibility to learn, become more aware, and live the values that build a better world for every child, woman, and man.[13] Maalouf was born and raised in Lebanon, a son of the East Mediterranean, but he now lives and writes in France and has become comfortable in his various affiliations..

Yet can the Palestinians, faced as they are with ever increasing dispossession and the constant threat to their very existence as a people, afford to remain fractured in their identity, or to rely on others, or to advocate the kind of composite and diverse self they implicitly had before and are now being forced to abandon? The universalism Maalouf wants, a desirable end, would for Palestinians now mean enduring injustice and ultimately forgetting about their basic national and human rights. There is a route to diversity, a positive mixture of identifications, a healthy acceptance of the other, and a truthful education about the past and for the future. But such diversity has as its preconditions: the removal of monolithic narratives of exclusivity and the establishment instead of a mood of mutuality.

The question that arises from this discussion concerns the very legitimacy of national identity construction. In an atmosphere of pervasive nationalist inventions with their potentially dehumanizing effects on others, what can be said that is legitimate about national sentiments? Are there genuine claims to national identity? As the postcolonial critic R. Radhakrishnan has noted there is a contradiction in the world today: nationalisms are on the rise worldwide, while the idea of nationalism has been thoroughly discredited in theory. This situation only highlights the centrality, authenticity, and urgency of the Palestinian situation: "How does the political need for nationalism coexist with the intellectual deconstruction of nationalism? I would argue that the only, and the inescapably compelling, rationale for the legitimacy of nationalism is the plight of the Palestinian people: a people without a sovereign home. For the rest of the world both to enjoy nationalism and at the same time to spout a deconstructive rhetoric about nationalism in the face of Palestinian homelessness is downright perfidious and unconscionable."[14] Much needs to be done to realize this thought.

7
Appropriation:
Zionist Cultural Takeover

One of the gurus of the East Indian subaltern group, Ranajit Guha, in advocating a historiography of the silent and poor that would disentangle it from hegemonic and colonial-leftover-elite-state history, opens one of his essays by stating: "There was one Indian battle that Britain never won. It was a battle for appropriation of the Indian past."[1] In the case of Palestine, however, with the passage of years, consolidated efforts by Zionist practices, politics, and affiliated scholarship, a national public relations campaign, as well as inadequate responses, have succeeded in appropriating the history and culture of Palestine and the Palestinians, often with collaboration by reputable scholarly establishments in the West.

WHO IS "NATIVE"?

The colonization of Palestine has some parallels to other historical situations such as the conquest of North and South America, Australia, South Africa, or the Indian subcontinent. Some of the colonizing patterns of justification are therefore similar, as are the coping strategies of the oppressed, and the effects of the colonizer's activities on the minds of both colonized and colonizer. Palestine is special in that, while it collapses and subsumes almost all varieties and layers of colonization, it has some unprecedented peculiarities in terms of cultural and historical assumptions to which it has been victim. In the conquest of America, for example, because the colonizing paradigm had claims of being more advanced or superior, or had other notions of "progress," it did not intend to absorb native culture and knowledge into its own (although it did so nevertheless without acknowledgement). The intention was at first only to tame, to dispossess, or to exterminate. What the settler society discovered, belatedly, whether among the Romantics in the nineteenth century or environmentalists today, is that some native values related to the treatment of nature are superior in the long term.

In Palestine, there is of course a Zionist posture of superiority and a condescending racist attitude toward the native Palestinians (insistently called "Arabs"). But the Zionists are also stuck in a paradox, for how can they possibly exterminate the local traditions and customs they need and that are so entangled in their own claims of nativity? The life of the Palestinian villages and the manners of the Bedouins, the shepherds, the landscape itself, are the only things that are reminiscent of what was and continues to be presumed "biblical," as travelers and early Zionists had to admit. For many travelers (see Chapter 11), the strategy was to use the Palestinian people and the land for the purpose of illustration, at the same time to render them invisible as human beings. For the Zionists, this "native land" they want to be theirs, which in fact was not theirs, and their presumed "return" to it, premised on invented connections, led to a process that pretends and behaves as if real past events of history did not really occur while imaginary ones did, at the same time that it had to do what other colonizing projects did and so moved history along.

The appropriation and confiscation with which Israel has plagued Palestine illustrate a set of complexes in the Zionist claim system. They are shown in a range of areas I deal with here and elsewhere in this book—history, religion, landscape, language, heritage, and other aspects. Zionism as a colonial project is impelled by an imperative to disinherit and disperse the Palestinians, and to control those who have not yet been forced to leave. Simultaneously, it wants to make the Palestinians disappear, or be as invisible and as valueless as possible. It robs them of the native status which Zionists see as competing with their assumed entitlement and pretended nativity.

WHAT IS YOURS IS NOW MINE

Appropriation here involves the taking of cultural products, ideas or inventions from others and calling them one's own. Throughout the history of cultural development, borrowing and exchange were normal and necessary. Often the process was benign, part of the evolution of humanity, essential in periods when inventions and borrowings facilitated life and mobility and opened the world to interconnected growth.

It becomes an unhealthy practice when the taking hides the source or fails to give implicit or explicit credit, when power and self-interest prevent recognition of the other from which one takes— even, often necessarily, to the point of demeaning and demonizing the source so as to deflect attention from the act. Appropriation in this context is a form of plagiarism or theft applied to ideas, culture, and history. In what Zionism and Israel have done in Palestine and to Palestinians, the appropriative complexes are insidious in their intent and unhealthy in their psychology.

Primarily, Zionist appropriation is inherently marked by ingratitude because the Jewish assumption of native status necessarily implies denying the reality of Palestinian nativity. And it is not the first time this has happened in history. The same kind of disinheriting devaluation of other cultures occurred, for example, in the biblical stories when the Israelites reportedly conquered Cana'an or later fought with the Philistines; or when the Romans took over the Etruscan city states in the Italian peninsula; or, more recently, in the Americas as the indigenous First Nations were systematically dispossessed and decimated.

Neither is it the first time that Palestine has been subjected to claims of ownership. The latest pre-Zionist crusading claim came from fundamentalists in Britain and the U.S. during the nineteenth century, typified in the call pronounced at the first public meeting of the Palestine Exploration Fund in 1865 by William Thomson, Archbishop of York and the PEF's first president:

> This country of Palestine belongs to *you* and to *me*, it is essentially ours. It was given to the Father of Israel in the words: "Walk through the land in the length of it, and in the breadth of it, for I will give it unto thee". *We* mean to walk through Palestine in the length and in the breadth of it, because that land has been given unto us. It is the land from which comes news of our Redemption. It is the land towards which we turn as the fountain of all our hopes; it is the land to which we may look with as true a patriotism as we do to this dear old England, which we love so much. (Cheers).[2]

The Christian Zionist interest in Palestine needed tools to demonstrate its claim, tools which fixated on "biblical illustration" requiring the Palestinian population to be used as evidence of "biblical life" and, simultaneously, to be invisibilized because their presence contradicts the claim. What characterizes Jewish Zionism, in contrast, is the claim of nativity for itself, an urge that is forced. It hinges on, and tries to concretize, past imaginaries (negated by recent findings), while also relying on the inability of native Palestinians to construct a useful past and to realize the depth of their culture in the present chaos. By their nature, ungrateful appropriative models are adaptive, in the sense that they change with time, and are ultimately ill-intentioned in their designs and practices. In the decades before 1948, it was not unusual for Zionists to acknowledge native Palestinian culture or to want to emulate it (see Chapter 11). In time, to achieve some consistency, the Zionist system gradually appropriated almost everything that is Palestinian: foods, popular heritage, dress, customs, landscape, architecture, language, religious heritage, and history. Now the Palestinians are left almost completely unacknowledged.

HUNGER FOR FOODS AND ROOTS

Once local dishes are now for everyone. The Japanese eat hamburgers, Canadians eat Chinese dumpling soup and Japanese sushi, British people like Indian curries and Turkish kebabs, modified Italian pizza and pasta are popular in the U.S., and almost everyone now samples ḥumus.

Israelis, however, eat Palestinian and Lebanese food and call it Israeli. They have learned about and gradually taken over local and regional foods and plants as their own. These include the foods that are typical of Greater Syria like falafel, ḥumus, kabab, and shawerma, sweets like baklawa, and local plants and trees—such as olives, figs, and Jaffa oranges. When "Middle Eastern" foods started to become popular in North America and Europe, aggressive sales campaigns declared the dishes to be Israeli national food, in the hunger for such things. Tabouleh, ḥumus, taḥinah (pronounced "takhina" by most Israelis), and local flat bread (Arabic "khubez," called "pita")—these "Middle Eastern" foods are still presented as national Israeli "home-grown" specialties.[3]

One can perhaps understand this kind of appropriation. The Israelis, in search of local flavor and in need of eating well too, recognize these foods for their indigenous character and appropriateness to the land, and so take them for their own use. These foods and plants are part of the environment and the region's character. After all, a high percentage of Israelis are Arab Jews, or Palestinian Arab Israelis who remained after 1948. They have some reason to claim the food as part of their culture, though Israelis of European or U.S. origin are happy to make that claim too. But perhaps a little acknowledgment and humility would be in order.

SNITCHING EMBROIDERY

Presenting Palestinian embroidery and other popular arts as Israeli is just too much. Palestinians are rightly proud of their embroidery. It involves varied, intricate, and colorful needlework—one of the most beautiful in the world. It is an imaginative expression of cultural elements in a hand-crafted art that has been handed down by generations of women in the villages of Palestine. Each village has its unique patterns and colors for dresses as well as items such as cushions and shawls.

Figure 7.1   Palestinian woman's village dress, Ramallah, 1880s

In finely stitched multi-colored threads on hand-loomed cotton or linen, this art reproduces familiar patterns available in nature—cypresses, palms, birds, wheat ears, grapes, stars, landscape features, and geometric shapes. Some artists now create designs that incorporate significant social or cultural events into the more traditional patterns. This art connects people to a long tradition and to the land, out of which its designs grew.

That's why Israelis have not only bought much of the old embroidery but tried to appropriate this art as a national characteristic. A not uncommon sight is an Israeli collector or a North American professional haggling over a few dollars for a dress or other embroidered item that probably took hundreds of work hours by a woman who had hoped to pass the dress on to her daughters. The poverty forced on the people since 1948 has resulted in the sale of household goods, jewelry, embroidered treasures—expressions of a people's history and experience. Now under economic imprisonment and the occupation, an east Jerusalem shop owner can be forced into transactions that will give away original artistry.

An Israeli book on embroidery, *Arabesque: Decorative Needlework from the Holy Land*, starts with "biblical times" and ends with photographs showing Israeli adults and children wearing the embroidered clothing of Palestinian villagers (many from the villages from which Palestinians were forced to flee in 1948). These Israelis have put on an act for the photographs. The book not only takes over a Palestinian art form; it impersonates it. The euphemistic allusion to the "Holy Land" helps to camouflage the real, Palestinian source of this unique form of village art.[4]

For a number of years, the *World Book Encyclopedia* listed under the heading "Clothing" the traditional costume of various countries, mostly the more exotic dresses of Africa and parts of Asia. For "Israel" it showed a woman wearing a traditional Palestinian embroidered dress. Obvious to anyone familiar with Palestinian heritage is that the dress happens to be the traditional attire of women in Bethlehem, for millennia a Palestinian town and until recently mostly Christian. That encyclopedia entry (only recently dropped by the publisher) made Maha Saca furious because in her personal collection at a workshop in Bethlehem she has her grandmother's dress, which looks exactly the same.[5] Ms Saca has also pointed out in her illustrations how close some of the Palestinian village dresses are to those worn by women several millennia ago.[6] The dress patterns and colors have evolved differently in the various parts of Palestine, incorporating particular local meanings and land signifiers.

In Israeli or "international" sources (not to mention some fashion shows) there has been no mention of Palestine and no suggestion of how much embroidery is deeply rooted in ordinary Palestinian farming customs and the life of towns and villages, more than 450 of which were decimated by the Israelis in 1948.[7] In addition to the villages, the people's natural heritage and their buildings have been confiscated. In human interaction terms, what has been done smacks of something pathological or worse.

And in a few of the villages that were not destroyed, a trend has emerged of using these Palestinian villages as Israeli art colonies, as has happened in the village of 'Ein Ḥoud and in the old city of Yāfa/Jaffa.[8]

APPROPRIATIVE PSYCHOLOGY

When Kurtz in Joseph Conrad's *Heart of Darkness*, in the depth of the Congo jungles, utters the haunted expressions of his possessive mania, "My Intended, my ivory, my station, my river," he is representing a mind divided within itself between the rapacious greed of colonial exploitative practices and the deceptive idealism of convenient justifying principles. Kurtz is Conrad's image of all that is horrible about such contradictions and the convoluted logic in which humans engage. Most manage to find calming ways to maintain an unexamined conscience, for how else would they be able to live with themselves? Kurtz, to his credit, recognizes the "horror" he has fallen into, from his own perspective. He grapples with his own savagery, the savagery of Western "civilized" conduct that is much worse than any "savagery" in the natives. We are, after all, not just in the world: we are in what we do to each other what the world has done to us and what we have done to the world.

A Jewish-American journalist writing in the food section of *The Jerusalem Post* claims that her "ancestors" enjoyed figs.[9] Israeli contractors pull out old stones from Palestinian areas to use in their building, or employ Palestinian stonemasons, to lend local authenticity or age to their presence. They live in old (and desirable) "Arab" houses, from which Israel evicted the Palestinian inhabitants in 1948, and don't seem to feel any guilt. Many books on the land written by Israelis or Western Jews have pictures of Palestinian towns and landscapes, without noting of course the implications of who the builders or original inhabitants were. Instead, the animals, the trees, the plants, the zoos, the terraces are all "biblical." That applies to all the fauna and flora of Palestine. In one description, flax is made, anachronistically, to date back to "5000 BC in the Land of Israel," and all the other plants are couched in the context of the biblical "Promised Land." When there is a need to explain "native" (Palestinian) use of certain plants, the reference is vague and does not mention Palestinians. In pictures where Palestinian houses or Palestinians themselves appear, the invisibility is complete. Among others, a book entitled *Daily Life in Biblical Times* has a cover photo of a Palestinian shepherd with his flock, though the book is careful to void any mention of Palestinians within its covers, even when their customs or foods are described. Instead, the author uses vague allusions to "some present-day societies" and "the locals."[10]

Meanwhile, Israeli colonists on the West Bank continue to attack Palestinian farmers and regularly uproot Palestinian olive trees, while the Israeli army has maintained a similar policy in Gaza. In areas affected by the building of the Separation Wall, the army protects and participates with those engaged in uprooting both people and trees. It is part of a longstanding strategy practiced by Israeli authorities over the past decades: to suffocate Palestinian agriculture and starve it of water, to disrupt the Palestinian social fabric and daily life. Israeli colonists desire to be "native" so much that they take over whatever they want of local resources and land, to which they themselves are not natural. At the same time, they destroy what Palestinians have and how they live—perhaps because they are, unconsciously, reminded that the Palestinians are the owners of real nativity. In an age that is supposedly more enlightened, their excuse for such robbery and cruelty is still that their god gave them the land. This disregard for others is understood from the perspective of a monotheism out of which some of its believers have yet to evolve contemporary notions of justice and ethics in their behaviour toward the Other, whose land and resources they covet. Pretence at originality or greatness has underneath it the pretender's feeling of inadequacy, a lack of real cultural depth, which is why there is compulsive cruelty, often maliciousness, and a pathological withholding of any acknowledgment. The very elements that Zionists crave to appropriate have their source and reality built into the historic presence and accumulated living of the local Palestinian and regional populations.

An irony arises in the Israeli metaphor of "sabra." It comes from the Arabic word ṣabr (meaning "cactus" and "patience"). Palestinians now associate the prickly pear cactus with their perseverance against Zionist aggression, and they eat its fruit in summer. Locally born Israelis like to assume the character of this plant, to suggest how they are rough and tough on the outside but sweet on the inside. Tourist promotions also like to describe Israelis as "hospitable," a quality that (in a sense unfortunately) belongs historically to the Arabs and Palestinians. Cactus fences had been used by Palestinian farmers as plot dividers for decades. Israelis have more recently adopted the practice to "remind" themselves of their "ancestors" and to give their hedges a local flavor they observe but do not understand. However, this cactus plant was imported into the region only in the eighteenth century, having originated in Mexico and been brought over after the colonization of the New World by Europeans.

REGIONAL TAKEOVER

Zionist scholars, along with some Western scholars who still suffer from biblical biases and inventions, tailor regional ancient history to old assumptions and the claim system of specially reconfigured myths. Despite antecedent discoveries (discussed particularly in Chapters 2 and 4), there is still insufficient recognition that the Bible is largely an amalgam of literary and religious production in the region over millennia—exaggerated into believability by centuries of ignorance. Cultural material to support the Bible's historicity is non-existent compared to the demonstrable material culture of other sources from which much of it was copied or adapted. The antecedents were themselves appropriated, and are now being re-appropriated for political and cultural gains.

The Zionist claim system hangs on certain old religious traditions: the historicity of biblical narratives, profitable privileged notions, the myth of Diaspora, the religious importance of Hebrew, and claims of Judaism as the first monotheism. I show in this book how much such traditions are misguided. However, most scholarship, even when it tries to digest the new findings, still works to maintain the old claim system and its monopolies. The notion of the first monotheism bypasses earlier attempts at "monotheism," such as in Egypt and Babylon, and neglects recent findings about the continuity between monotheistic beliefs and the preceding polytheism. Primary among the tools in the Zionist claim system are the biblical narratives— stories of an "exodus," a covenant involving a "Promised Land," then a "Diaspora," and now "return," which have continued to underlie the entitlement logic of a purportedly secular Zionist movement since its establishment more than 100 years ago.

Many of these stories are themselves appropriations and reconstructions, and they assume ownership of a tradition that only later was associated with what became Judaism after the sixth–fifth century BCE. For example, the exodus narrative (arbitrarily dated to about the fourteenth century BCE), for which there is no historical corroboration, has been shown to be modified and redacted from earlier legendary narratives belonging to other people. In fact, as several scholars have argued, not only was there no such "exodus," but the Israelites were never in Egypt, the patriarchs are legendary, and there was no conquest of the Promised Land and no great united monarchy of David and Solomon.[11] Past ignorance and now circumlocution make it possible to exploit the sacred geography common in the West until the nineteenth century as well as the fundamentalist Christian Zionism that preceded (and in many ways prepared for) the Jewish Zionist movement.

The complexes of appropriation are powerfully ingrained because these old assumed-to-be-historical narratives have come down through monolithic transmission and are invested with monotheistic notions that are very hard to erase from the minds of believers who have relied on them so faithfully and for so long. As a result, when the region is described or illustrated, the catch-all phrase "Bible Lands" is often used. Some, though not all, of these works have clearly Zionist-inspired agendas. When one looks inside such works, there is little if anything material that derives from the Bible itself. All the cultural products referred to are Egyptian or Mesopotamian or Cana'anite. Yet the inclusive tags are "Bible Lands," "Bible Times," and "Biblical World," far more extended than "Holy Land."[12]

Ancient languages are rife with takeovers. Whereas some ancient cultures are demonized (including the Cana'anite, Philistine, Assyrian, and "Phoenician"), their languages are useful for confiscation. Since "square Hebrew" script is nothing but late square Aramaic, and descended originally from Cana'anite, it becomes easy to try to elide the differences, to exaggerate the importance of Hebrew in ancient times, and to backdate its existence. Hebrew is made to look more ancient than it is because the intention is to make it go back to the times of at least a Moses and then a David (though the historical existence of both figures has been questioned by scholars), which necessitates strategies of circumvention and appropriation. Since square Hebrew (or rather square Aramaic) cannot go that far back, the need arises to use the terms "Paleo-Hebrew" and "ancient Hebrew."[13]

Ancient inscriptions classified as "ancient Hebrew," once examined, show clearly they are not different from "Phoenician." In fact, they are "Phoenician." It is an intended confusion of scripts to identify the two. One such inscription is the "Gezer calendar," which dates to the tenth or eleventh century BCE. Zionist scholars (see the example in note 16), and now some standard encyclopedias (working within Zionist agendas or old assumptions), classify this text as "ancient Hebrew." Other authorities and any impartial observer would notice that the calendar is written in signs that are "Phoenician," similar to other inscriptions in the whole region in that period; in this case, the letters show some demonstrable affinities to Moabite (see Chapter 5 and note 9 there). The claims can become ridiculous. As mentioned in Chapter 5, one Jewish writer provides a most ingenious theory of how Yahweh gave the alphabet to his chosen males first, in the process bypassing Ugarit and demeaning the "Phoenicians" as incapable of such an invention. An article on a Philistine inscription appropriates the "enemy" by speaking of "Hebreo-Philistine."[14]

While Arabic is the only surviving, continuous, live regional language, a storehouse and inventory of ancient languages, it is diminished in its importance, as I discuss in Chapters 1, 4, 5 and 10. That applies to how it is made to relate (or not) to ancient languages like Cana'anite/"Phoenician," Ugaritic, and Aramaic. Instead, scholars attempt to establish less convincing similarities to Hebrew. For example, Ugaritic words from about 3400 years ago, exactly the same as Arabic, are thought of in terms of distant Hebrew cognates (see Chapter 4). Only recently are more scholars realizing that Ugaritic is closer to Arabic than to any other language.

The implications affect the perspectives taken on other regional ancient languages. While impressions and theories about ancient languages were the outcome of old scholarly habits, today they are used to strengthen Zionist claims for links to ancient history. Arabic is underestimated in range and age, whereas Hebrew's importance is magnified. Hebrew is made to look more ancient than it actually is and to have stronger links to other ancient languages. Assumptions about Hebrew's importance or its age, however, are a backdating of current feelings or old scholarly assumptions, and could not have been the case in ancient times. To give an unjustified ascendancy to Hebrew, scholars employ two annoying practices: using square Hebrew to transcribe ancient languages and hyphenating languages (such as "Hebrew-Aramaic") and always placing "Hebrew" first. (For more on this, see Chapters 1 and 10.)

Such traditional practices are not always unintentional and are often manipulated in the misinformation that accompanies the promotion of political or religious agendas. For example, as noted in Chapter 1, in the case of a special stone plaque erected in 1985 within the premises of the Pater Noster Church on the Mount of Olives, in east Jerusalem, Aramaic and Hebrew are placed next to each other (needlessly so since the languages are available among the older ceramic plaques lining the courtyard). The plaque is placed prominently with the intention of showing that the scripts look the same (see Figure 7.2). The trick is made easier because the original Aramaic text of the Lord's Prayer, which had been especially carved on the floor of a niche long before, was accidentally sanded down to almost nothing by a worker who had misunderstood instructions. That "square Hebrew" looks similar to square Aramaic has nothing to do with whether Hebrew was ever a spoken language, nor does the same script mean the same sound. Why highlight the similarity in script? Israeli tour guides are eager to point out to visitors: "Look, Hebrew and Aramaic are exactly the same, and so there is no difference if it is said that Christ spoke Aramaic."

Equally dangerous are other adaptive and appropriative trends. In one recent twist in Israeli and Zionist scholarship, it has become

Figure 7.2   Special plaque, Pater Noster Church, Mount of Olives, Jerusalem

more convincing (given the current consensus that Joshua's conquest of the "Promised Land" is unhistorical) for some scholars like Jonathan Tubb and Israel Finkelstein to develop further the theory of a "peaceful" religious or ideological transition. They say that there is really no difference between "Israelites" and "Canaanites" (see Chapter 1, note 41; Chapters 6 and 11). In effect, however, such a theory is an adaptation that takes over Cana'anite culture, for which alone is there any material evidence on the ground.

MONEY

Appropriation extends to aspects related to "enemy" languages and empires as well. The name of Israel's currency, the shekel, is ancient Babylonian, both in terms of etymology and the invention of currency. Recent dictionaries and encyclopedias, however, reflecting Zionist influence, are either misleading or contradictory about its origin. *Merriam-Webster* identifies the shekel only with Hebrew and the State of Israel, as does the online *Encyclopaedia Britannica.* The older *Oxford English Dictionary* (1933), the *Shorter Oxford Dictionary* (1973), and even the older *Encyclopaedia Judaica* (1971 edition), give the correct origin as Babylonian, and tell us that it became a common currency in the region. But a more recent edition of the *Concise Oxford* has the word "shekel" as "Hebrew." The 2002 *Shorter Oxford English Dictionary* makes it a "unit of weight and silver coin used in ancient Israel," while *The Oxford Advanced Learner's Dictionary of Current English* (seventh edition, 2004) defines shekel as: "1. The unit of money in Israel 2. an ancient silver coin used by the Jews."

It is not only that the facts have been changed in making both the word and the currency assume a "Jewish" origin. In the definitions, there is confusion in the use of the different terms "Hebrew" and "Jewish," making them appear to be the same. In disregarding Babylonian advances, the claim deprives Babylon of the privilege of inventing such financial trappings of civilization. Meanwhile, Babylon is still condemned, via biblical prejudices, as the epitome of "decadence," and is subjected to contempt for its money practices and supposed profligacy.

TERRACE FARMING

Much myth is circulated about the late second millennium (the "Iron Age") by Zionists always keen to support legitimizing claims.

One invention concerns the construction of agricultural terraces, or cultivated steps on hills. This ancient feature was developed long before the "Iron Age" by various peoples and used in locations across the East Mediterranean, such as Cyprus, Syria, and Turkey. In Zionist history writing, terraces are said to have been developed by the ancient Israelites. In addition to false credit-taking, this story is an attempt to use the argument of human labor as a justification for the modern colonization of Palestine. A promotional book *The Holy Land: A Unique Perspective* provides the following text in connection with the photograph of a terrace: "Because the Canaanites were largely successful in keeping the Israelites out of the plains and the valleys (see Joshua 17: 16–18; Judges 1: 34), the Israelites had to become economically self-sufficient by mastering terrace agriculture."[15] Even the redacted biblical accounts thrown in for support actually present a different view: Joshua and company, a preliterate nomadic group if it existed, first defeated the Cana'anites in the cultivated plains and then moved on to cultivated towns in the hills. The book of Judges reflects a somewhat different cultural diversity in that period—that is, according to such versions. At any rate, there is no logic that would reconcile a conquest or any other historical periodization with this claim of Israelite invention of terraces.

Contradiction: another appropriator writing about land use in the Iron Age lists several scholars who point out that terraces were invented during the Bronze Age by the "early Phoenicians," or Cana'anites, and "Jebusites," much earlier than the ancient Israelites given in the biblical accounts. In fact, hill terracing is known to have been used in the whole East Mediterranean region from at least the fourth millennium BCE. One page later, however, this writer states that "terracing in the hill-country has been practiced continuously from its introduction by the Israelites at the beginning of the Iron Age till the present day."[16] It is left unclear who has continued the practicing, when the Israelites obviously did not remain in the region. Hence one can add the question: who has maintained the terraces and planted over the last three or four thousand years? In fact, there is a Palestinian farmer actually working the terrace in the photograph in *The Holy Land: A Unique Perspective* (Figure 7.3), though the farmer is of course made invisible in the text. The appropriation and confiscation thus works to its own advantage in any way it finds suitable, regardless of any historical considerations or appreciation of or sensitivity to others.

Thus modern labor and ancient labor too are denied, confiscated, even as property and culture are taken.

Figure 7.3   Terraces in Palestine, with invisible Palestinian farmer plowing

As noted in Chapter 3, the official logo of the Israeli Ministry of Tourism shows two men (the spies of the Old Testament) carrying a huge cluster of grapes back from the "Promised Land." Did not the spies take the grapes from someone else's vine, probably grown on a Canaʿanite terrace? One wonders why the ministry is not at all embarrassed to advertise this kind of association. As I explain in Chapter 3, Mark Twain (whose account is often misused in Zionist writing) makes glorious fun of the indoctrinating appeal of sacred geography and in particular the exaggerated image of this bunch of grapes.[17]

In a contemporary re-creation of this presumed ancient labor, at Sataf and other locations Israelis are invited to pay a fee to explore the landscape and to farm their own terrace "as their ancestors did before them." What a way to concretize an ideological invention. Sataf happens to be a deserted Palestinian village, one among the hundreds whose population was evicted in the ethnic cleansing implemented by Zionist forces in 1948.[18] The terraces may be ancient, but the people who really continued to cultivate them until recently were the Palestinian farmers of Sataf—now refugees.

Additionally, the Zionist claim to the land is more easily argued (adapting a common colonizing logic) by neglecting to record that most Palestinians are/were villagers who tilled the land and tended the orchards in Jaffa and Hebron and all over the country, as well as on terraces, long before the Zionist project started. Instead it is customary, in line with the colonizer's worldview, to say that the Palestinians are "Arabs" and therefore (a) have neglected the land and left it barren, and (b) should now go to other "Arab" countries or to the Arabian Desert. This strategy of dismissing Palestinian labor is a particular blending of the biblical paradigm with other colonizing justifications: the land-use argument, the savagery or nomadism of the locals, as opposed to the colonizers' self-description of being chosen by a god to improve the land, which leads to all sorts of inventions and credit-taking.

LEGAL ASSUMPTIONS

Appropriators can be brazen in their claims. In Israel, the appropriative-assumptive paradigm is both inventive and contradictory. This applies also to the Israeli legal system, which is eclectic in the sense that it conveniently employs a mix of older pre-1948 and newly enacted laws to serve its purposes. Its legal system gives an impression of democracy and equality at the same time that it institutionalizes discriminatory practices. The very law on who is eligible for citizenship (Jews, automatically) depends on a primary discrimination. Palestinians who were forced to leave or moved for fear of massacres in 1948 are not allowed to claim their properties or return to them because Israel enacted an "Absentee Property Law" in 1950 to disallow that possibility, contrary to the most basic rules of international law. Other than the hundreds of villages vacated or destroyed by the Israelis, there are examples of complete sites that were purged of their Palestinian owners, all personal belongings and family heirlooms confiscated, and their stone houses repopulated with Jews—as in 'Ein Houd or towns like old Jaffa (both now turned into artist colonies) and 'Ein Karem.

On the whole, no trace of guilt exists about such confiscations and the resultant reduction of a whole population to impoverishment. In claiming one's destiny according to the will of a god, one convinces oneself of innocence. Most Israelis seem to enjoy the antiqueness of the stone houses in such villages and cities and are not concerned that these houses and lands were stolen from Palestinians. One sees advertisements in Israeli newspapers for the sale of an "old Arab house." Many have even deluded themselves into thinking these houses are actually theirs as a god-given "heritage," a mode of thinking that elsewhere would be deemed as illegal, racist, and exclusionary. As an example, I think of the many old Palestinian stone houses (including my grandparents' large three-storey house) in West Jerusalem now occupied by Jews without purchase or permission, in addition to the thousands of houses in cities and villages taken over without shame. Do these Israeli Jews not think that the homes, money, and properties in Europe other Jews left during World War II should be claimed back (as they are) and that Jews must be compensated both for their losses and their suffering? Does the same justice not extend to Palestinian properties and Palestinian suffering?

SELF-APPROPRIATION

By not claiming their ancient heritage, most Palestinians seem unaware they are unintentionally allowing its free appropriation. While some Palestinians continue to use emotional rhetoric and others are now resorting to religious fundamentalism as a reaction, most are unaware of the full implications of their own historical situation. These are symptoms that have developed as a result of the long subjection of a native people to colonization, and in reaction to an endless oppression. One marvels that native identity can still persist in some form under such obfuscation and contradiction.

In the Palestinian context, it is ironic that appropriation is not limited to the Israeli colonizers and their attempts to control the land and to seek false nativity. The colonized, from whom everything has been expropriated and who have been massively deprived of opportunities, sometimes turn against themselves. In acts of powerlessness, they sometimes only take from each other in return. This phenomenon would seem to be a human tendency that appears among those who seek some kind of sense of accomplishment in an environment where action for innovation and development is stifled. Likewise with projects and academic programs in such an environment, the generation of ideas is depressed but there is still a hunger by some to accomplish something meaningful. This may lead them to claim the ideas of others as their own. Under conditions of turmoil, dispersal and lack of security, the eventual outcome is an unfortunate diminishment of initiative and cooperation. The lack of appreciation for initiative becomes a disincentive to those able to offer what could be beneficial for the community's progress. Eventually, there is a loss in cumulative development, though some individuals will always attempt to initiate whatever potential for progress might be possible.[19]

REVERSING APPROPRIATION

Systemic antagonism and ideological invention are part and parcel of the effort by Zionism to establish its own claims as it denies and undermines the native Palestinian presence. Implicitly and explicitly, the Zionist claim system's practices and laws are intended to exclude, diminish, disinherit, and harm. In any other context, such exclusionary practices enshrined in taught beliefs would be more clearly identified as racist. At the same time, an indigenous Palestinian narrative that might counter the monolithic Zionist construction is still largely unrealized. Partial knowledge, lack of awareness, historical shortening, and other limitations imposed on Palestinians and other people in the region (those who have the real historical connections) have all helped to allow blatant Zionist and Western confiscation of various items, past and recent—from ancient history, religion, languages, place names, and heritage, to foods, arts, currency, and other cultural phenomena. The dominant agenda continues to deny the memory of the Palestinian people and their long, rich history and to erase them from the narrative of the country, forcing political decisions based on myth rather than history.

The continuing denial of Palestinian nativity and Zionist appro-priations of ancient history are exhibited in information widely circulated and used for the purposes of indoctrination. While present-day Zionist indoctrination violates all the demonstrable evidence and even past Zionist strategies, it simultaneously entraps Zionist thinking in contradictions that require leaps of faith and various degrees of self-blinding. Further, the effort to keep constructing such arguments requires a constant adaptation in the fabrication. Robert Young writes in *White Mythologies*:

> As Cixous suggests, the mode of knowledge as a politics of arrogation pivots at a theoretical level on the dialectic of the same and the other. Such knowledge is always centered in a self even though it is outward looking, searching for power and control of what is other to it. Anthropology has always provided the clearest symptomatic instance, as was foreseen by Rousseau from the outset. History, with a capital H, similarly cannot tolerate otherness or leaves it outside its economy of inclusion. The appropriation of the other as a form of knowledge within a totalizing system can thus be set alongside the history (if not the project) of European imperialism, and the constitution of the other as "other" alongside racism and sexism.[20]

Zionist ideology, which determines the actions of the Israeli state, is built largely on inventions of memory and of ancient history. It should be difficult for a conscientious person to accept such inventions in lieu of the buried truths of history. However, the forces built by political systems do not welcome change and work zealously to preserve the continuity of their established power. It threatens such systems when individuals begin to reverse systemic pseudo-knowledge and replace it with more even-handed recognitions that affect the education of generations and public opinion. Acknowledging past abuses, one-sided claims, acts of dispossession, and other historic injustices are all prerequisites for any possible rapprochement and healing to occur. If there is to be any conciliation among peoples, the injustices inherent in the premises of appropriation cannot continue to remove those very aspects that might form possible means of connection. If disinheritance and denial of another's equality and rights remain profitable aspirations, human enmity will thrive and no amount of public relations effort to redescribe acts of dispossession will bring any hoped for peace or reconciliation of antagonisms.

History cannot, through neglect or selective ignorance, or inattention to truthfulness, permit the normalization of the aberrant and the perpetuation of false cultural hegemonies. History must expose the phenomenon that reveres inventions and moulds narratives into self-interested, opportunistic claims. Appropriation of the culture and history of Palestine must be reversed in the interest of a commitment to seek the "truth." It is then that modern access to accurate information might open up possibilities for an innovative space where individuals and societies can produce new understandings.

8
Self-Colonization:
Symptoms and Outcomes

All monolithic systems are inherently colonizing in that they require acceptance of certain inherited knowledge, cultural values, and constructed ideologies of identity. Colonization of the mind includes any unquestioning acceptance of indoctrination, of what a system wants people to believe for its own ends. In cross-cultural contact, borrowing may exhibit itself in either positive or negative ways, such as in language learning or in exchange of ideas, or in clothing and foods. While such borrowing may be beneficial or benign, it can also be a symptom of shallow pretense or the internalization of another culture's dominance and superiority. Eating ḥumus or sushi in the West is considered a sign of openness and sharing within a multicultural society. On the other hand, eating hamburgers and other junk foods in Saudi Arabia and Jordan may be an attempt to signify a belated "modernity," though such fast foods are now recognized in the West as unhealthy. When Lebanese or Algerian youth mix French or English phrases in daily conversation this can project a superficial show of sophistication.

In the case of an active colonizing situation, self-colonization becomes a severe danger to the integrity and existence of those suffering under domination, as has been shown in various forms in past colonized nations across the world. With the Zionist occupation of Palestine, however, the stakes are particularly high because the claims of the colonizers negate the existential legitimacy of the colonized. Consequently, history and identity are in the balance. This is not merely a situation where resources are exploited and the oppressed made to value the oppressor's culture. Zionism aims to dispossess and uproot the native Palestinians completely—in which it has succeeded in part—and to install itself as the native culture instead. In the process, it wants to displace Palestinian culture, to make the Palestinians feel they have no land rights at all, and to imprint images and histories on the ground and in the mind. It may be possible to liberate the land, but it is much more difficult to free the mind where history has been falsely constructed and natural identity is being systemically annulled.

EMBROIDERED CITIES

Particularly since 1948, it has been customary to embroider the names of cities either in calligraphy or on a map of geographic Palestine—the Palestine that was lost. Embroidery is a hand-crafted art form that is characteristic of Palestinian villages. Each village and town has special patterns, colors, and themes for women's dresses, shawls, and household and ceremonial articles. Today, Palestinian women in refugee camps in the West Bank and Gaza as well as

Figure 8.1 Palestinian cities embroidered in Arabic calligraphy

in Jordan, Syria, and Lebanon continue the tradition. Palestinian embroidery, uniquely creative, has become quite popular, with old dresses and other artifacts snapped up by collectors, whether within the "country" or outside it. And much of this work, being the only source of, or a meager supplement to, family income, has now become oriented toward the tourist.

The names of cities are most often embroidered in Arabic in beautiful calligraphic forms. Important cities are graphically designed on maps or decorative hangings: 'Akka, Yāfa, Haifa, Safad, 'Asqalan, Al-Quds, Beit Lahm, Beit Jala, Ramallah.

When trying to think of a present to give to a friend who did not read Arabic, I decided to look for a map with the cities embroidered in Latin script. I finally found one, intended for sale to tourists. It translated the names, so Yāfa was Jaffa, Al-Quds Jerusalem, Beit Lahm Bethlehem.[1] To my shock, one of the cities on the coast was carefully embroidered as "Acco," which is the Israeli usage ("Acre" in Western sources). This is a city that has not changed its original Cana'anite and Arabic name, 'Akka, for more than 4000 years (see Chapter 10). The woman who had stitched the threads most likely did not know the difference, indeed probably could not even read the Western script. Someone else, presumably an educated Palestinian, had written this down for her to copy.

COLONIZING TRAPS

Palestinian construction workers supervised by Israelis build the colonies on the West Bank; Palestinian tractor drivers move concrete blocks for the Separation Wall; Palestinian stone masons are employed to give the illusion of local authenticity to Israeli houses. These workers need jobs and money to support their families. But what are they doing to themselves and to their nation? What does this forced labor do to the personal conscience and to the collective consciousness as it tries to meet the constant demands of the colonizer for labor that disinherits the laborers? And why isn't the Palestinian Authority doing anything to offer alternatives and to prevent this drain on the Palestinian psyche?

A young Palestinian from Jerusalem working at an information desk for David's Citadel distributes brochures in Arabic that are mostly translations of what the Israeli Ministry of Tourism has prepared. She does not feel she is doing anything wrong; it's a job and she needs one. She has no idea about the quality or reliability of the information given in the brochures. She does not quite know that the place has nothing to do with "David," or that "David" is a legend rather than a historical figure, or that the whole myth around David serves the Zionist claim for Jerusalem as the "City of David." More seriously, she does not seem to realize that what she is distributing denies her identity, undermines her existence, disinherits her, and even absolves her of an interior struggle over how she is being used to legitimate the distribution of false information.

Figure 8.2   Wall in the Head

As I pointed out in Chapter 6, Palestinians often only aid Zionist rationalizations by falling into the trap of religious sequencing and associating themselves historically with the Muslim conquest in the seventh century (if they are Muslim) or the Christianization of Palestine in the fourth century (if they are Christian). Since Muslims believe in Da'oud (David) as a prophet, it is less difficult for the Israelis to rely on that familiarity to promote their own version of David and use him to justify all sorts of constructions. Some elite Palestinian Muslim families proudly display a nicely constructed family tree that goes back to one of the noble families in Mecca. A broadcaster on Al-Jazeera, obviously with anti-Zionist tendencies, mentioned in passing that "Jews" lived in Palestine more than 3000 years ago, not realizing that Jews are not the same as the idealized "Israelites" or "Hebrews" of biblical stories. A Dubai TV channel celebrates the career of Stephen Spielberg, failing to recognize how much he promotes the Zionist cause or maligns native people in the region (as in his insidious adaptation of the Exodus story in the child-targeted animated film *Prince of Egypt*).[2]

Palestinians and "Arabs" in the region would not do or say such things if they knew more about their ancient history, or had developed better arguments for a critical consciousness, or were able to see themselves more as the total cultural unit that they are, or were able to recognize their own obliviousness to what is in their own best interest. Instead, they are prone to accept mainstream historical narratives, or are led into the assumption that what the religious books say is historical, or confuse the qur'anic heritage with the biblical one. Much of the present book is intended to dissuade Palestinians and others from falling into such notional traps, which inadvertently only prop up the Zionist claim system.[3] Such instances of misconception illustrate how the colonizer exploits the very narratives of the colonized, which in the case of the Zionization of Palestine has been made possible by apparent similarities and misinterpreted connections (though essentially fallacious) among the three monotheistic religious narratives. In this regard, there is a compelling need, as I show in the other chapters of this book, for de-mythologizing and de-indoctrination.[4]

COLONIZER AND COLONIZED

Self-colonization is a phenomenon that plagues the colonized and the colonizer alike, in various forms. The colonizer holds the power, monopolizes all forms of debilitating control, and manipulates knowledge. In the case of oppressed and subjugated colonized people, self-colonization means that they internalize facts and values that run counter to their own national or cultural interest. Unaware of this, they do worse harm to their identity and culture by believing what the enemy wants, by accepting what is othering them, by absorbing the culture that is smothering their integrity and the information that disinherits them. In self-colonization, one accepts as superior values, as genuine information, as real history what is against one's identity and group interest. The outcome is a cultural vacuum and lack of counter-knowledge and historical consciousness, which also leads to a diminishment of political will and a constant sense of discord within one's self.

Of course, the colonizers are also self-colonized in terms of their ideas and history—the difference being that the process benefits their own interests and sense of a desired national identity. One wonders whether they have some degree of recognition of what they are doing, and if so why they remain blind or half-blind to the consequences, to the disturbance in identity consciousness on both sides, to the existential damage that is occurring in their minds and consciences. J. M. Coetzee suggests, in his *Waiting for the Barbarians*, that the colonizer knows somewhere in his or her mind or heart what is being done. That is how the narrator's consciousness evolves. However, with a few exceptions, self-interest and systemic investments are too strong to bring conscience or consciousness into play. Instead, more colonizers contribute to the destructive effort of forcing the colonized to adopt their ideas even as they go about oppressing and dispossessing them.

As for most of the colonized, even as they resist, they cannot help being overwhelmed and frustrated by strategies calculated to numb their sense of integrity and prevent their exercise of independent thinking and action. Such strategies are ultimately intended to mute or nullify or de-legitimate resistance, since a strong determination generated by an opposing ideology is the only answer to colonization—though that still does not necessarily free the mind.

The great danger to the colonial system is an informed population, with a national education and supportive knowledge, capable of resistance on all fronts. In order to succeed, the colonizers need to instill in the colonized their version of history and to distort their sense of human rights, to pen them in. And they do so not only with those who are less aware or less educated, and who do not therefore have all the tools to resist mental control. They also cultivate, directly or indirectly, certain other segments of the colonized population, either the traditional leadership or the so-called elite, who do not need much prompting to realize that colluding with the colonizer helps them to keep at bay any challenge to whatever privilege or prestige they may have acquired. As Frantz Fanon suggested, the greatest threat to national consciousness and a positive mobilization of the people is the "spiritual penury" and "intellectual laziness" of the middle class and the elite who inherit positions of power and end up serving the previous or current colonizers.[5]

In the case of Palestine, this situation is much more acute than in other previously colonized countries like India or Nigeria. Not only does it suffer from the postcolonial ailments and mutilation caused by the previous British and Ottoman colonizations, but layered on top of all that are the debilitating effects of present colonization by Israel, the unmitigated U.S. support for Israel's colonizing policies, and the general silence of most European nations. All these countries prefer to patronize the safer, traditional elite leadership.

ACADEMIC COLONIZATION

It is only to be expected that most of the academics in a colonizing country would support the system that feeds them. However, for some members of a colonized academia to help further the colonizers' agenda is more perverse. This phenomenon stems from an educational and political history that has made collaboration with enemy institutions an option. Among some of the colonized elite, it comes out of their descent from a land-owning or titular leadership, appointed to collect colonial taxes, implement orders, and generally help keep the population under control. Partly because native institutions are inadequately resourced, the few who are given the opportunity are happy to be affiliated with well-funded foreign and colonial institutions that, to varying degrees, serve objectives that are part of a colonial system designed to work against their national interest.

In most cases, colonized academics simply lack the resources, institutional or national, to develop approaches or works likely to provide direction and vision to future generations. So, from a sense of inadequacy or incompetence, some of them may find some small personal benefit, a sense of high-brow belonging, or some nominal recognition in such institutional affiliation. Foreign or colonial institutions often welcome nominal native involvement, as long as they themselves retain control and the natives do not affect anything much. The result is predictable: foreign political and educational notions and models designed for others are implemented, while the native population fails to develop its own organizational skills or create appropriate materials or concepts that would adequately respond to their needs, or to develop their own independent thinking, or to nourish ambitions for a vibrant culture.

As I explain in Chapter 1 and elsewhere, the attention given to Palestine by missionary organs and by colonial ambitions was accompanied by much "research" on the "Holy Land." In the middle of the nineteenth century especially, this was done by the religiously minded, mostly fundamentalist Protestant and Anglican, whether clergy or lay people. Edward Robinson started the whole practice of trying to guess the locations of biblical events based on current Arabic names, a practice inflated and further distorted by the Zionists (see Chapter 10). William Thomson produced a model of how to appropriate the land and connect "the book" to it, while ensuring the real local people remained invisible. To varying degrees, others who followed (even apparent secularists) stayed on the same track. Many expeditions of "discovery" were commissioned by the Palestine Exploration Fund, established in 1865 under the patronage of the British queen and the presidency of the Archbishop of Canterbury, with the objective of securing "biblical illustrations."[6]

These and other such efforts have left behind many research and various other institutions in Palestine that represent the interests of and investments by British, French, U.S., Russian, German, Swedish, and other foreign countries. I mention here only a few of those based in Jerusalem, not so much for what they are as for how they relate to Palestinians. One descendent of the Palestine Exploration Fund is the British School of Archaeology, now called the Kenyon Institute (after a renowned archaeologist). It has been weakened over the past few decades, particularly as a result of the creation of the "Israel Exploration Fund," though it has been trying to revive itself more recently. Its institutional structure is still largely controlled by the old formulas, though it has become more progressive and helpful in its Palestinian environment in east Jerusalem. In terms of research priorities, it seems to prefer projects that would not imply anything political in the new context (after the creation of the State of Israel in 1948 and the occupation of east Jerusalem in 1967). Still, the Kenyon has the potential to advance some alternative research and understanding across the region.

Another such body is the École Biblique, a French institute established in 1890 by Dominican priests. Its mission is biblical exegesis and the study of "Semitic" languages. Particularly, it has been involved in translating the Qumran or Dead Sea Scrolls. As a result, the École is famous for producing a new translation of the Bible called The New Jerusalem Bible, which is the most accurate translation to date in many respects because it benefits from insights resulting from the Dead Sea Scrolls.[7] It has an excellent specialized library, and does not shy away from acquiring a range of publications. This contrasts to other presumably secular institutions like the Albright, whose library avoids acquiring publications by critics of traditional biblical archaeology. The priestly professors are generally fair-minded, and are more likely to feel some depth of understanding and compassion toward the Palestinians than they are to be pro-Zionist. (This is probably also a Catholic inclination in view of the tension resulting from Israeli attempts to take over Catholic properties in Palestine and Zionist irritation at Catholic statements about the Palestinian situation.) However, like some other religious establishments, the École still tends to be insular in terms of how it relates to its environment.

Two institutions that reflect the peculiarity of the U.S. interest (perhaps the peculiarity of U.S. religion and how it influences identification) are the local campus of Brigham Young University and the Albright Institute. Brigham Young is a Mormon university in Utah, and we know that the Mormons think they are the New Israel. As a result, its campus in Jerusalem, called the Jerusalem Center for Near Eastern Studies, gravitates toward study of the Old Testament, although it seems also to express interest in other subjects. This center has a strange relationship to the State of Israel, a relationship that Israel is of course willing to tolerate and use, on condition the center is not employed in proselytizing. It therefore has a generally dubious role in the Palestinian context. Naturally, it cannot help but reflect what it has inherited, though it has tried recently to give some small symbolic assistance to a few Palestinian students in the way of short-term scholarships to Utah. Should these be about genuine scholarly learning and not indoctrination, it is an indication that even traditional institutions can begin to question unsustainable circumstances.

Incidentally, the chorus from Brigham Young was sponsored to perform in Israel a few years ago. It was also invited to come to Birzeit University in the West Bank. My partner and I found the hall packed when we arrived. We looked at the program of songs: they were all biblically inspired songs and chants. We listened as the Palestinian audience applauded, uncertain if this was out of politeness or genuine enthusiasm. We were relieved by the intermission. One of the songs due to be performed in the second half was about how the "walls of Jericho are falling down" (a reference to the biblical account of Joshua's conquest of the "Promised Land"). We found our way toward a gathering of the resting choir—all dressed the same and with facial expressions almost as similar. We asked them if they knew where they were singing: in a Palestinian university and to a Palestinian audience. We asked if they realized they were going to be chanting in celebration of the very account that forms one of the justifying claims of Zionism and all other colonizing projects elsewhere (such as in North America and South Africa). It was doubtful they were convinced, and the director appeared to admonish the choir for speaking to "outsiders." Nevertheless, that song was not performed after the intermission.

Though it has been debunked, biblical geography is still strongly entrenched in several quarters in the West and within Israel. For Israel it is a necessity: the claims on which the state itself is based are now so taken for granted that to retract them would involve a drastic reorientation in thinking. When the clear objective is biblical research, or when the people involved cannot help being deluded, or need the comfort of unreflective delusion, one could say fine, do what you like and invest as much money as you want in what is really a large industry. But when an institution pretends to be neutral and strictly scientific while pursuing an agenda that is still covertly biblical, colonial or Zionist, then such an institution can only be described as duplicitous.

That applies to the Albright Institute, located in the heart of east Jerusalem at the end of Salah-eddin Street. It was called the Albright in honor of the U.S. archaeologist William Foxwell Albright, one of the "fathers" of biblical archaeology. As I show in Chapter 5, though Albright could not avoid studying Cana'anite cultural remains (the only remains for millennia) he still expressed racist feelings toward the Cana'anites and imperialistic views that privileged the Judeo-Christian tradition, which he thought was the ultimate in moral evolution.[8] It is this kind of supremacist legacy that the Albright Institute perpetuates in its mission and in its structure. Its current director is proud to declare: "The house that Albright built is still going strong." Burke O. Long's study of U.S. imaginings about the "Holy Land" has pointed out the ideologically biblical beginnings of the American School of Oriental Studies, which was renamed after Albright.[9] This house has an organizational structure that ensures colonizing controls: the director is a biblical archaeologist and a U.S. rabbi, his special research assistant is (or was) an Israeli Zionist, the two librarians are Israeli Jews, the research fellows are Western or Israeli, while the only Palestinians are a powerless secretary, the cook, and the cleaner. To lend an image of neutrality or a patina of concern, the institute inducts a number of Palestinians as fellows. But this inclusion remains nominal, intended to fill the quota of "balance," when in effect most of the Palestinian fellows cannot even reach the Albright because of Israeli travel restrictions, and none of them is engaged in any significant research or is enabled by the institute or its associated Israeli organs to participate in any excavations. As a Zionist tool pretending to be neutral, it attracts these Palestinian "fellows," academics or archaeologists, who are willing to have their names on its lists, and to be invited to its luncheons and barbeques, for the apparent prestige of that affiliation. They are either unaware of the implications of such an affiliation, or maintain it perhaps for other reasons or some future hope.

In these circumstances, one wonders how Palestinian archaeology and history can contribute, or have a chance to grow and become independent, or generate a vision and purpose unaffected by the biblical shadow or by colonial agendas. This is hardly possible when Palestinian academics are prevented from realizing their potential and when some of them are willing to be co-opted into schemes that silence their own history.

TOURIST (MIS)INFORMATION

The predicament of Palestinian historical information is most tragically illustrated in the way tourism is conceptualized and presented. While Israeli tourist sites and publications are generously subsidized, attractively packaged, and geared to support Zionist claims, Palestinian official websites and printed materials are still traditional, ill-conceived, and often copied from Western or Israeli sources. Even worse, most Palestinian sources tend to present the tourist sites in the context of monotheism, the Oslo Accords, and the consequent normalization with the Israelis. In other words, "Palestine" is now only the West Bank and Gaza, and this "Palestine" is the land of the three monotheistic religions. Statements made in this connection sound somewhat vacuous, such as: "Jerusalem, known as Beit Makdes in Arabic and Yerushalayim in Hebrew, has been known for centuries as a center for three major religions: Judaism, Christianity and Islam."[10] An *Inventory of Cultural and Natural Heritage Sites of Potential Outstanding Universal Value in Palestine* begins with the city of Bethlehem, "Birthplace of Christ," rather than the much more ancient 'Ariha/Jericho, presumably in an attempt to appeal to Western pilgrims.[11]

This narrow approach to the monotheistic religions is only matched by poorly written and ill-informed texts. The following sample from the Palestinian National Information Center, issued by the Palestinian National Authority, illustrates the ludicrous content put out to readers:

> Every single bookshop in the entire world capitals includes tens of books and editions, in all languages, issued by world publication houses annually, which wrote about Palestine and the civilizations it had witnessed. Even all programs of the study of history, throughout world institutes, manefisted [sic] the history of Palestine and the significant religious events occurred [sic]. Moreover, the heavenly books [sic] recounted several historical events related to West Bank and Gaza strip. This fact has been a solid base on which the developing cultural tourist projects are built [sic].

Under "Cultural Tourism in West Bank and Gaza," the same source provides strikingly incongruous examples of biblical geographers like M. V. Guerin and William M. Thomson. Concerning Thomson's *The Land and the Book* (a model for the appropriation of Palestine within the biblical tradition), which is given as "The Land—of the Book," the source adds: "In this book William Tomson [sic] explained the cultural and social life features in West bank [sic] and Gaza." Needless to say, the problem with such presentations would not be solved by having competent language graduates correct the grammar.

Whether in print or on the internet, in photographic representations, Western guidebooks, or in Israeli and Palestinian publications, the results are not salutary. Generally Western guidebooks fall into the quagmire of the Zionist version of ancient history, as do unfortunately (often for religious reasons) many Palestinian sources. An alternative tourism is gradually emerging in some Palestinian areas, but it concentrates more on the political agenda, such as organizing visits to the Separation Wall and refugee camps. Only recently has a fairly decent guidebook become available in English and French, entitled *Palestine and Palestinians* (published by the Alternative Tourism Group in Beit Sahour in limited circulation), though still the telling of ancient history poses some difficulties.

To liberate Palestinians and tourists alike from the restrictive chains of fictive mainstream and Zionist-constructed history, to break entrenched stereotypes and distortions, it will be necessary to reconstitute the whole informational system about Palestine (the larger Palestine that now includes Gaza, Israel, and the West Bank). Urgently required is the production and dissemination of a coherent total history, and consistent emphasis on cultural continuities that comprehend the full extent of Palestinian presence from prehistoric times to the present. Many fresh discoveries—thus far restricted to specialized journals and unpublicized books—could, if activated, form the elements of a new history to replace the dominant, exclusivist history being circulated today. It is possible to undertake comprehensive studies that synthesize significant new scholarship and inject an objective view of history into the informational system for both educational use and for tourism.

Could it ever be realistic to hope for a single narrative that might be shared between "Israel" and "Palestine" in tourism and education? Apart from the political difficulties, the major problem is that the current approach to tourism remains mostly religious in its orientation. This approach is of course the most profitable on many counts, so there will be resistance to its de-emphasis. It is, however, in Palestine's national interest to promote a multi-dimensional appeal to a variety of trends, such as eco-tourism, informed religious tourism, entertainment, local tourism, and cultural tourism. By not limiting the tourist to religious or ideological sites, there will be opportunities for a progressive enlightenment. Most of all, it would be essential to reverse as much as possible the hegemonic information disseminated by ministries, educational systems, and the media. Otherwise, in the misguided context of normalization under the cover of a "peace" process or a possible agreement, two incompatible narratives would continue to be propagated and the inventions of Zionism would be accepted despite their serious implications for Palestinian history and rights. The best outcome for everyone is a cultural tourism that is informed by a new political vision and a revised understanding of Palestine's history.

CRISIS OF EDUCATION

Most crucial to this process of informing both tourism and the public mind, on both sides, is the evolution of a historical approach based on fair-minded research and a healthy vision for the region. Without such a vision, supported by real knowledge and rethinking, the future looks predetermined and hence extremely bleak. Can this bleak prospect perhaps foster the realization that it is time to begin rewriting the future?

Deconstructive research and teaching in the humanities is common in the West, although it still occurs mostly within a framework that does not altogether threaten the existing system. One would expect critical research to be at least as intense in Palestine and the Arab World. However, that is not the case. Arab scholarship and education are mired in traditionalism and unreflective imitation in all the crucial subjects—history, archaeology, geography, literature, cultural studies, and most other fields of the humanities. The case is particularly acute in archaeology and history, as well as in cultural studies and literature, which are usually taught in a style that is the outcome of legacies of past and present colonization. Generally emaciated, imitative, safe and compliant work in the humanities betrays a lack of vision about the past and the future. Yet it is unrealistic to expect that, under Israel's destructive occupation and current Arab policies, a vibrant, natural re-examination and evolution of all aspects of culture would occur spontaneously, without a strong moral and intellectual commitment.

It is mandatory to develop approaches to teaching history and cultural studies in ways that provide meaningful connections to the region and have a relevance to the existence of its young generations. In order for Palestinian youth to acquire a meaningful identity and solid sense of self-worth, they need to become engaged with their instructors in re-evaluating regional history and the region's many contributions to world civilization—a region still blocked from expressing its true self in this way, and from being freely acknowledged by the world for its marvelous gifts. The youth of the region also need to be given the analytic tools to understand Western civilization and how it affects them. How can they benefit from the West without responding critically to, instead of silently absorbing, its projections of superiority, its perpetuation of prejudicial notions and biases against their culture in both words and actions?

One way to understand Western civilization and the public mind in the West is to become more aware of how scholarship constructs its paradigms and how it applies them to the region, imposing its images. Another method is to locate in Western thought and literature what is not antagonistic to or devoid of relevance to our region (since unlike scholarship, great writing is almost invariably subversive and critical of its system). It is often possible to find points of conjunction where historical situations coincide, where prophetic voices can be heeded here and now as they could have been there and then. For instance, in literature, rather than merely appreciating poetry and prose in the canonical Western fashion, it is more credible to explore what certain works (such as, to cite randomly, those by William Blake, Herman Melville, Emily Brontë, Langston Hughes, C. L. R. James, or William Faulkner) tell us about Western culture and how they might inform us now in our historical context. Otherwise, in the absence of a deeper, more critical understanding of cultural developments and historical situations, the problematic outcome is one of either violent, inflexible antagonism or slavish, self-colonized imitation.

DECOLONIZING THE MIND

Even the impossibly rigid control system described in Huxley's *Brave New World* (1932) leaves some openings for escaping the most severe indoctrinating constraints to reach a state of (in that case, tragic) freedom. The question is how to get to the point of starting a process of decolonizing the mind. How does one begin to get out of one's colonized skin?

In *Black Skin, White Masks*, Frantz Fanon describes the inferiority complex engendered in the minds and actions of black people that drives a wedge between the development of the personality of the oppressed and its imitation of white society. The colonized who imitate the colonizer are as miserable as those who simply hate— Fanon's view, *mutatis mutandis*, is that "the man who adores the Negro is as 'sick' as the man who abominates him"—though in Palestine and Israel, a Palestinian or an Israeli or a Jew, Muslim or Christian who can extricate him or herself from the mental grip of the system, to see the Palestinian predicament and what the system is doing to his or her mind, can be said to have been freed.[12]

Henry David Thoreau's model of leadership and "conscience" in his formative essay "Civil Disobedience" would be useful to study and to implement, focusing as it does on the necessity in historic situations for one or a few to stand up to a misguided majority or a utilitarian and unconscionable government. Ngugi wa Thiong'o advocates in *Decolonizing the Mind* one means to recapture identity through affirmation of the native language and its natural connections. He struggled to resist the English that was forced on him by the British colonials, whose strategy was to make him feel stupid for using his native language.[13] A similar problem occurs to a degree among Israeli Palestinians or young Jerusalem Palestinians who occasionally brandish words in Hebrew, or utter Arabic words with Hebrew pronunciation, using language in a way that negates their identity. However, colonization through language is not overwhelming to the same degree in Palestine—except in the form of Zionist efforts to make Hebrew appear more important than Arabic in street signs and in scholarly practices. In contrast to the imperialistic adventures of previous centuries, when colonial powers imposed their language, religion, values, clothing, or lifestyle on the colonized, Israel attempts to take everything from the native population and systemically to degrade their environment. It does this through confiscation of territory, destruction of agricultural land, uprooting of trees, demolition of homes, denial of building permits, prohibition of free movement, denial of consistent access to education, diversion of water resources, cutting towns and villages off from each other, and other restrictions and policies designed to create a life so intolerable that the natives will be forced to pack up and leave, or at least to make those who stay give up and remain compliant and slavish. The intent is to wash away any trace of the Palestinian people as the most ancient inhabitants of the land. In India, the British may have left a linguistic legacy, but they did not succeed in appropriating the local past as the Zionists have done in Palestine. Native Americans attempt against all odds to do what the Dakota language describes as *ki wasico etanham induhdayapi*—stripping the whiteness from one's self. Paulo Freire suggests provocatively that the oppressed should lead in liberating both themselves and their oppressors.[14] Though seemingly impossible in this context, the step is essential to attempt to take forward for any enfranchisement to be realizable.

These other colonial and postcolonial situations are quite different from the overwhelming incubus under which the Palestinians now find themselves. Upon them is forced an oppressive reality and many challenges to overcome in constantly shifting circumstances. Israel is set on a course intended to exclude and disinherit, not to share. Palestine's predicament is that it combines many of the problematic aspects of other postcolonial and colonial conditions yet has its own intractable peculiarities.

To propose a manifesto for freeing the mind, even before liberating the land, is indeed a hopeful task affirming a vision of human possibilities. Where would it start? Who could be entrusted to initiate it? Would others participate? How can it be implemented and sustained? A Palestinian national plan is required, but how would it be put into practice given all the controls of the colonizer, the pressures to normalize in a "peace process" (reduced to constant talk of a "process"), the internal divisions and tribalism, and the inadequacies of the ruling elites? How is it possible to transmit

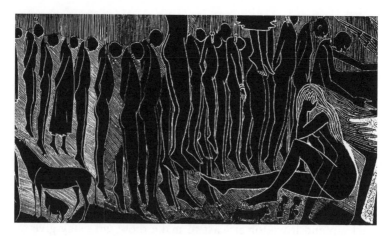

Figure 8.3   Untitled, or How to Be Hanged Alive

enough individual initiative to affect actions at all levels and in all classes of society?

The dedication of a few may be the only means to generate favorable circumstances and to create greater awareness of the historical and cultural preconditions for what is to follow. Education for human liberation should gain from all the deconstructive ideas available elsewhere in order to promote exploratory and liberatory learning and confidence in a knowledge-driven future. Just as critical as it is in Africa and other "postcolonial" situations, reconstruction in Palestinian and Arab education must permeate all fields of knowledge and activity. Educators need to make consolidated efforts to work for a positive survival and self-actualization that will nurture critical consciousness and initiative, rather than unreflectively adopting or rejecting foreign identities and attitudes that inevitably promote loss and self-defeat. Research is crucial, and so is the development of a long-range plan that aims to nourish identity and to protect cultural interests. It is equally fundamental to give young people a sense of purpose and direction, emphasizing the power of both individual and collective voices, the importance of recording the past and the present, and the urgency of cultural reconstruction.

Self-colonization has dangerous and debilitating long-term effects on the minds and souls of the oppressed, and on their future hopes and prospects. The colonizer is happy to see it happen and will encourage all sorts of trends (such as tribalism, division, in-fighting, low self-esteem, and misinformation) that are destructive to the formation of a purposeful identity. Paramount in the work of liberation is to avoid falling into the traps set by what we are told repeatedly about our history and identity, by what the colonizer wants us to perceive, absorbing what we are not, unwittingly internalizing bias in what we learn and teach. What means do we adopt to raise consciousness, to deconstruct and replace rather than absorb the poisonous mix of biased concepts and narratives? Who will take up the challenge when willed ignorance may seem less demanding, or a less painful escape from such abnormality?

Non-monolithic research and writing would provide the material to seed and to nourish a constructive historical perspective, a healthy sense of identity, self- and other-understanding, critical skills, and diversity. Based on such research, long-term national and educational strategies are urgently required in the current predicament, not only for Palestinians and Israelis, who need it most, but for others throughout the region and the world too. Although many around the globe have been taught to look to Palestine or the "Holy Land" as their spiritual homeland, most have yet to be inspired to become students of its actual history. These strategies, however, are difficult to develop and implement since political exigencies are not likely to encourage them. Individual will and independent leadership are therefore required more than ever for the project of decolonizing minds.

9
Cats of Jerusalem

The solitariness of cats in Jerusalem, their scruffiness, their wariness, the mode of their survival in a city that is holy and not holy, how they mirror the old city's insular nature, its current predicament, and the people's life in that situation—all tell us about the city and the particularly peculiar nature of human relations within it. They are also a sign of our time.

What happened with me and the cats in Jerusalem is like nothing I have experienced anywhere else. While it says something about cats in general, it also says much about the specific condition of the city. Society itself is reflected in how it treats animals, and they in turn respond to the humans around them. If a society is under stress, it reacts to animals within it and they parallel that reaction: if it is violent, the violence is revealed in how it affects animals; if a society is decadent, this will manifest itself in its treatment of pets. It is said that cruelty is latent in the human character, even though we usually think of children as innocent. Is civilized brutality, or instinct perverted by socialization, worse than natural cruelty? Cruelty can be diminished by cultural constraints, but if a society is left to its own devices at the same time that it is being strangled by a colonizing power intent on disintegrating it, then it may find outlets in subterranean ways, or even turn on itself.

HISTORICAL AND LITERARY CATS

In ancient Egypt, where some gods were represented in animal form, cats were domesticated and inducted into a symbiotic relationship with human society.[1] They were respected and made sacred, and so a halo of mystery and reverence surrounded them. They were regarded as especially favored by the gods, and while not made into gods themselves they were taken to exhibit particular god-like characteristics. Seen as protective of their young and yet as lovers of a beneficent sun, cats typified motherhood and fertility and were associated with the regenerative powers of the sun's warmth. Reflecting attributes of a mother goddess, cats became favored by the people as well. The cats in Egypt today are the descendants of those honored cats, but live now under degraded conditions that also apply to much of the human population.

In strong contrast, in medieval times in Europe religious beliefs associated cats with evil and with witchcraft. It is a weird thing this association of cats with witchcraft; even Judas is connected to a cat in paintings of the Last Supper. And so it goes. Cats become the displaced objects for people's fears and paranoia—telling us more about the perversions of religion by the clergy and believers than about cats themselves.

All that changed again in a later period. The Romantic poets and writers reminded us that our original nature is to be found in the wilderness. William Blake's "Tiger" captures the mystery of the cat family in the famous lines: "Tiger, Tiger burning bright / In the forests of the night." For him, the tiger is a symbol of primal energy and passion, a form of perfect symmetry. It stands outside convoluted human societies that distort primitive instincts and turn adult experience into a system of repression and injustice.

Wild cats today seem instinctively vengeful of humans for disrupting their habitats, for injecting their self-centered initiatives into the life of all nature and making it impossible for the rare wild animal to survive. In the colonization of America, instead of making a fresh start, humans engaged in wholesale extermination of both wild animals and of other humans they conveniently saw as savages and beasts, thinking that by relegating these humans to animal status they would stamp them with inferiority, make them worthless, and so justify their dispossession. Humanity in general has been unable to keep wild things wild, to be comfortable with ambiguities or uncertainties within or outside societies. So humans have domesticated most animals and turned them into regulated food sources or what they think are harmless pets. As a kind of counterweight perhaps, Edgar Allan Poe's story "The Black Cat" is a catalyst of revenge for what humans have done in projecting onto the natural and the neutral their own insecurities, their perversity, superstitions, and obsessions.

Cats and other animals become entertainers for public consumption in Hollywood and in the Western cultural imagination. There is *Archy and Mehitabel the Cat* (Archy is a cockroach), Morris the Cat, Tom and Jerry, and countless other cartoons. In Looney Toons, there is Sylvester, and also in the Pepe Le Pew series the sleek, coquettish black cat, who becomes the object of a crazy skunk's unshakable desire. Ducks, mice, ants, pigs, cats, and dogs of course are endeared as pets of one kind or another. In fact, insects and animals that have become pests proliferate because of human congestion and human filth, while finer and more delicate things become rare or extinct because they are desired for their obvious exclusivity. Curiously, humans today sentimentalize certain animals, whether a duck or a piglet or a deer or a lamb or a cow, then proceed to slaughter them in meat factories or in the wild or on the roads. And even in caring for and possessing their pets they take them away from a condition that may have been better for them. With some contradiction, in cities we often see a love for pets existing side by side with a lack of care for human neighbors. At a dinner gathering, a guest spoke disparagingly of a hopeless people who had lost a conflict, and concluded that the weak get what they deserve. Later, he described how much he loved his dog, and let him share the bed on cold nights with himself and his wife. Asked about this disparity in his sentiment, he stormed off from the dinner table and left. Little do we consider how such symptoms speak volumes about the extent to which human societies have moved away from a natural state into distraction or decadence.

Then there is the popular musical *Cats*, based on T. S. Eliot's volume of playful poems entitled *Old Possum's Book of Practical Cats*.[2] In "The Naming of Cats," Eliot tells us that cats have three different names: a regular family name, a peculiar name, and a name we can never guess that only the cat knows. His poems portray various cat-human characters, among them: "The Rum Tum Tugger," who always wants the opposite of what he is offered; "Macavity: The Mystery Cat," the "Napoleon of crime"; and "Gus: The Theatre Cat," whose name is really Asparagus.

PET CATS

Rum Tum reminds me of a cat I met on a recent visit to Italy. She lived mostly in the kitchen of my host's city apartment. She was in the way all the time, wanting attention, and so the kitchen had to remain closed to prevent her from taking over the whole apartment. She was later left in my care at my host's country house, out in the relative wild so to speak. The cat was at first conflicted between her habits living in a city apartment and the freedom and sun she was getting on the farm. The first two nights, she meowed at 5 a.m. outside the window to wake me up and to say she wanted food, company, or to sleep inside. Eventually, we agreed on a language—food, affection, likes and dislikes; what her "g-rr" and "g-h-m" meant. She started sniffing in the bushes and the grass. She hunted down a lizard, flipping it up just as I saw feral Jerusalem cats do as they toyed with a mouse, bloodying the steps and door entrance, making an offering of sorts to please me. My guest cat bit off the poor lizard's tail, so I had to free it and put it far away to grow another tail.

One night she definitely refused to stay inside. As the sun had beckoned to her in the day, the moon called at night. The next morning she didn't even eat the gourmet food my hosts provided, probably having hunted something at night. She ran around free, stayed outside at night as she liked, and didn't wake me up at 5 a.m. She still walked wherever I walked, and ran and ran, ahead of me and back, wanting doses of affection, arching her back in joy. She started wanting to run around more, and disappeared into the surroundings for hours. Her whiskers became increasingly decorated with bits of dry vegetation.

I've heard that when they are close to death cats may go off alone to die quietly. (Unless in a city or on a highway the cat—or dog or deer or other animal—is struck by a vehicle, its blood and guts spread over the black asphalt. And who will pick up the dead animal and throw it into the garbage bin or put it to the side to rot away?) I remember this curiosity about cats going off to die because of what happened to an old cat we took from friends in Canada who were leaving to go abroad. She was fat and arthritic. They felt so much for their pet that they had wanted to "put her to sleep"; she couldn't move much, and they felt so responsible. So instead of euthanasia we offered to take her in and let her live a little longer. Though used to an enclosed environment, she now spent time in the garden, often sleeping outside in the sun on a bench. As her pained bones and joints absorbed more sun, she gained strength and ventured to go up steps and other minor obstacles. Then, about three months later she just vanished. We looked and posted notices, but she was gone. When I called our friends overseas to tell them their cat had disappeared, that she either went away to die or was taken in by a charitable neighbor, they were upset about what had happened. I guess they would have preferred to give her a proper funeral, to have decided her fate, to have their own sense of "closure."

THE PARIS CAT MASSACRE

The "great" Paris cat massacre, which occurred in the 1730s, reveals much about the sources of human cruelty. It also relates to what I say here about cats and people, and what meaning there is in other situations, as in the circumstances of habitation and occupation in the Old City of Jerusalem.

The Paris event is discussed in a chapter by Robert Darnton, based on a report by Nicolas Contat, who gives stories of what happened in printers' shops at the time.[3] One anecdote concerns two apprentices, Jerome and Léveillé, who worked at the shop of Jacques Vincent situated on Rue Saint-Séverin. The workers and apprentices had dingy sleeping quarters, endured miserable living conditions, and were kept awake by the constant howling of alley cats at night. While the apprentices suffered from this profusion of alley cats, the master's wife kept as a pet a female cat she called *la grise* (the grey one). In response to such preference for animal over human, Léveillé used his talent for mimicry to torture the masters by going on their roof at night, meowing and howling horribly to make it equally difficult for them to asleep. After several nights of this treatment, the master and mistress charged the apprentices to get rid of the cats. The apprentices collected as many cats as they could and hanged them, including *la grise*.

That the apprentices would openly kill cats in Paris was of course made possible by the cultural accumulation of superstitions and myths about cats. Cats were fair game, although a pet culture had already developed among the bourgeoisie and the aristocracy. There were common cats and luxury cats. In one sense, the apprentices exploited cultural themes that relied on human fear of cats, superstitious associations with witchcraft, the occult, and sexual powers. As Darnton suggests, the cat is "a sexual metaphor or metonym" and the killing of *la grise* is "an oblique attack on the master and his wife": the apprentices were making a subversive statement not only to say that the wife was a witch of sorts but also that the husband was being cuckolded.[4] It is one way to make a statement and go apparently unpunished.

Yet this "metonymic insult" is surpassed by the political implications of the workers' ploy. It highlights bourgeois hypocrisy and moral duplicity, the sharp lines between luxury and poverty, tyranny and oppression. It is thus an act of revolt camouflaged as a cruel joke. In his account, Contat explains: "The masters love cats, so consequently they [the apprentices] must hate them."[5] In the psychology of this incident, it seems that the attack on the cats (making them objects of torture and hate) is subterfuge for hatred of the masters. It is an act of resistance. For often, the oppressed find inverted outlets to escape from their condition as they react to the cruelties and injustices that make them restless. How that restlessness is channeled is not always predictable, though often it is inwardly directed in self-destructive actions. In this case, the resentment took both actual and symbolic forms of violence and persecution projected onto accessible objects, like the easy-to-catch domesticated cats. By contrast in Egypt, where cats were revered, a story survives of an occupying Roman soldier who killed a cat and lost his life at the hands of the enraged people.

CATS OF OLD JERUSALEM

Something similar happens with cats and people in the old streets of Jerusalem. Jerusalem cats stand apart; they are and are not like other cats. What is striking is the absolute non-pet nature of their existence and the feline grace some of them can exhibit, even under conditions of hardship. I am speaking of the many street cats, not the ones owned by west Jerusalem Israelis who have come from the West and imported that pet culture (and sometimes the pets themselves) with them, or the few cats kept by "aristocratic" Palestinian families in east Jerusalem who generally keep their pets locked up inside. That kind of culture comes with luxury. The "non-pets" are the many feral cats on the streets, mostly on the east side of the city or within the confines of the Old City walls.

These street cats are the hardiest variety, having had to survive in an environment in which they are not really welcome but allowed to remain because they are there. Maybe they help to control the mice, though probably not the rats. Mating in this closed cage over the ages, they have become more and more mongrelized. A litter has an unpredictable variety, mixed colors, big heads and small heads, long legs and pigmy legs, and other mixed genetic features— often multi-colored with no particular pattern, mottled, though occasionally one has an odd single color or two colors only; the shape and bone structure, the character, so different among siblings.

Into them has been genetically instilled generations of suspicion, so they rarely let people get close or touch them. In other cities where people feed the cats and are kinder to them, even when not their own pets, one could walk by and the cats won't move. Not these Jerusalem cats: not allowing humans to get close is instinctive. As they grow, the attrition is great. One sees blind cats, lame or otherwise handicapped cats, sick cats dying, and cats with tails cut off. Obviously, the cats here have not benefited much from human advances in medical care.

The ones that remain are tough, with highly developed survival strategies: I am strong so I get the food first; humans are abusive or unhelpful so I run away from them; this person gives me food so I accept her or him; I know where to hide my litter. And the central venue for food is usually the garbage container. One can hardly ever throw a bag into a garbage container without some cats jumping out in panic. And the garbage is also the central point for infighting. Little cats who dare go for food before a strong adult risk being beaten, pounded repeatedly by the larger cat (though occasionally I saw several cats, perhaps relatives, taking turns to share the food). Their nature in the city enclosure is a strange blend of the tame and the feral, a forced and unnatural condition.

Figure 9.1   Cat on Tombstone, Jerusalem

Human adults, other than those who offer them leftovers, don't care much for them, often don't even notice them. But many of the kids are attentive to animals on the street, mostly dogs or cats. More often than not, they abuse them, if they can catch them. They may not be quite aware they are being abusive, and sometimes they just want to "play" with them. Usually the targets are smaller animals that are not sophisticated enough to find ways of escape.

And the children: why do some abuse cats? How could one explain their cruelty to animals? Though Palestinians in general cannot afford to have a pet culture, I didn't see this kind of abuse happening in other Palestinian villages and towns. One still feels there survives a childhood innocence, care, and deference, even more in the refugee camps of Gaza than elsewhere. So it seems to be something more specific to male children in Jerusalem. They are used to talking to tourists, and can be brash on the streets. They even brandish their use of Hebrew by calling out in a silly way a greeting like "Shalom," even when the recipient doesn't want to hear that word. They are exposed to the Israelis more than are people in the West Bank and Gaza, mostly the ever-present soldiers who oversee them, who are figures of power over them. In glimpses, the children also notice Zionist colonists as they pass by on their way to their hideouts in the Old City, where their presence is imposed through force, trickery, or fraud.

In this treatment of cats there are all the signs of a damaged and brutalized environment. The behaviour of the occupier toward the occupied can only be a source of personal humiliation. In east Jerusalem, most of the adults seem to accept such humiliation grudgingly as a matter of necessity. Defenseless and lacking organized resistance, they are unsupported, and some may be more easily bribed with small advantages (such as better health care) over their compatriots in the West Bank and Gaza. At the same time, they are sucked dry by the imposition of Israeli taxes out of which they don't get a reasonable return in services, only a small fraction of what Jewish communities get, and can easily fall under the threat of land confiscation or house demolition. They know the grand design of the Zionists to take over the city completely, to Judaize it, getting rid of Jerusalem Palestinians or minimizing their number to a small minority that has no voice. Gradually, more pressure is exerted on the population, more Palestinians lose their residency in the city, and more areas are turned into Jewish outposts. Yet Palestinian Jerusalemites seem to accept what happens without much resistance (except when the flashpoint is Al-Aqsa Mosque). Often they acquiesce for merely the sake of survival.

The children don't understand all these intricacies, but they internalize their parents' attitudes. Perhaps in claiming power over cats they are exposing the nakedness of the brute show of force that rules their lives in every detail. Instinctively, their cruelty to animals comes from a misplaced persecution—a projection onto the animal of a power over which they will have no control or any opportunity to change. They cannot affect what happens around them, and are unequal, unfree in the city of their birth.

Israel's grand design is even worse. Ultimately it wants to destroy the values inherent in Palestinian society, to degrade the Palestinians and render them purposeless. As they set about their goals, the Israelis neglect the general welfare of Palestinians living in occupied Jerusalem while giving preference to Jewish development. This is not merely casual neglect; it is policy.[6] If there is drug addiction, they look the other way; if there is small crime, they turn a blind eye. When neighborhood conflicts occur, the Israelis either allow them to escalate or permit local leaders to revert to their "tribal" customs to resolve them. Tribal structures don't exist in Jerusalem, so residents sometimes have to call in negotiators from surrounding villages or Bedouin groups. In one instance, when the local Palestinian police wanted to arrest a drug dealer in a West Bank suburb of Jerusalem, the Israeli army came in with jeeps just as the arrest was taking place and carried the drug dealer to safety (making it likely that he was a collaborator). The plan is to increase disintegration and the loss of societal cohesion—enforcing a selfish-cat type of existence on every Palestinian who remains.

When one is self-colonized, identity is subverted and one accepts its destruction, swallows it. It is much more dangerous to be self-colonized than to be merely under occupation. When one is colonized, there is awareness and a desire to be rid of the colonizer. Children sense this, as they are exposed to colonization, become victims of it, seeing fathers unable to provide or protect. What values can they then hold, what pride can there be? Their sense of oppression spills over into their behaviour on the streets, their purpose being to let off steam against something outside their little circle, something easy to persecute, and that poses no danger of reprisal. But this is not, of course, to confront the real enemy, nor what the enemy plans.

PERSONAL CATS

A few of Jerusalem's cats are majestic—a crack in the genetic line from some pure breed, or a less degraded variety. Feline grace and regeneration can appear in a proud, insouciant walk and independence. Like the one who came around to befriend me one day. I had rented a small house just outside the Old City walls, close to the Rockefeller Museum (previously the Palestine Museum).[7] On an early autumn day a cat walked into the garden, golden brown in color with dark and lighter stripes, almost like a tigress, with long legs and amber eyes. She seemed to want more than just something to eat. I scrambled to find some leftover food, only to discover she wanted what was good and fresh, and without too much fat. She had decided this garden would be her home and quiet shelter against a backdrop of danger and confusion. In her manner, she recalled the idea of *ash sha'ab* ("the people" in Arabic), expressed also in the popular chant "El pueblo unido jamas sara vencido" ("The people united never will be vanquished"). One might hope that the people of Jerusalem will similarly show their pride and stand more firmly to claim their rights.

She fulfilled her *nom de guerre* somewhat differently in that she started a line of cats and had two deliveries within a few months. One of her habits was to lie in the garden and turn for me to rub her stomach. I noticed the bulging, and she delivered in March. She didn't want to eat the day she delivered. (I guess cats are not hungry right after delivery because they eat their afterbirth and lick the litter clean.) I couldn't find where she had hidden the kittens until they started walking. None of them looked anything like mother, and one of them was particularly odd, short, and pesky. I returned after a summer break to find none of the litter around, all presumably killed. Mother was still there, and she welcomed me back as if I had left only the day before.

After about two months, I noticed a bulge in her belly again. This seemed impossible, since it is commonly said that cats only mate in late winter or early spring. I wondered whether this pregnancy was her reaction to having lost the first litter. In late October, she delivered a litter of three in a fairly open spot: a cavity in the trunk of an old mulberry tree. More autumn rain was coming, and perhaps she thought the spot was protected from the rain, or maybe she felt safe enough in this garden to leave the babies so open to sight. This time she let me touch them. She later moved the litter twice, for cleanliness perhaps or out of possible danger. One spot was deep into a huge overhanging rosemary bush, a place almost impossible to see or access. She signaled them to come out using a low-pitched sound. Of the two that survived, one kitten was almost totally white, with a small patch of brown, a poor copy of her mother, "beautiful" in appearance but unattractive in character; the other one was bony and shaggy, in various shades of black and brown, a bit of white on the breast, and greenish eyes.

One day mother disappeared, and a second day passed. The two kittens were restless, searching, crying. On the third day, as I was walking to the house, I saw a ten-year-old boy coming up the street. I stopped to ask him. He knew, described her to me, and told me that two or three days before she had been run over by a car at the intersection near the bottom of the hill, and he had taken her and put her in a garbage container. It was then that the two kittens allowed me to get close.

What happened later was a mini-drama. The white kitten was less than five months old when males began chasing her, and she was in heat. I tried to defend her from almost-rape, especially after she was bitten on the neck by a huge brown male. My many efforts were of no avail, and a litter of two males and a female was the result. A child had given birth to smaller children. She couldn't take care of them, hide them well, or defend them. One day the littlest male, who had a large head, was stretched out in the middle of the yard, with the child-mother licking him and trying to revive him. One of the neighborhood kids told me that an older boy had gone into the yard when the kittens were out and kicked the little one with his boot. Obviously, the neck was broken. I buried him in the garden under a pomegranate tree and placed a stone marker there. I know where. The harsh modern environment of cat life in Jerusalem is very different from that found in ancient Egypt where people once developed a custom of mummifying dead cats and burying them in special cat cemeteries. That particular human-animal past has degenerated into our present treatment of cats, both feral and tame.

The bony one, belatedly, was also pregnant. She must have delivered too, but I was not there to see her raise the litter, or what the little ones looked like. I imagined her as a careful mother, resourceful and protective. When I returned months later, within seconds she was on the fence, looking older, shaggier so her boniness did not show, her large, green eyes melting, as she ran after me on the edges, calling.

INSULARITY

The cats seem far removed from the "holy" nature of the city. The city's religious associations have eventually produced, as priests and people practiced their religions, something like an odd type of cat existence.

I don't think a figure like Jesus, prophet of love, could have disliked cats. The gospels refer to dogs and pigs in uncomplimentary ways, that's true, but only in parables that reflect cultural differences. Though cats are not mentioned, it is not hard to imagine Christ favoring them. The Muslim prophet Muhammad is reported to have liked cats, particularly one he called *mu'izza* (the endeared one). Reportedly, a cat (I'm not sure if it was *mu'izza* or another one)

Figure 9.2   Jerusalem cat at the École Biblique, 2009

was sleeping on the sleeve of his robe. It is said that he preferred to tear off the sleeve from the robe rather than disturb the cat.

Yet such concern is not what one finds with respect to cats in the city of monotheistic religions. If one were to walk down the Old City's alleys and look beyond the tourist shops and religious sites, examining instead the structure of the habitation, one would understand its inward and insular nature. Most homes are constructed around central courtyards, with people in small apartments piled on top of each other. No wonder cats are shouted away. Each complex is usually solidly gated and locked. It is not like today's Damascus where the courtyards are more open and welcoming. Many of Jerusalem's old residential complexes are associated with religious sects. Numerous monasteries, nunneries, churches, and other religious compounds (not to mention now the massive Israeli outposts) in and around the Old City are like fortresses, to which entry is strictly controlled. This stems from centuries of self-protective behaviour in response to real or imagined dangers, dangers that now are amplified under occupation by a constructed fear whereby each is taught to survive by being cautious.

People of various religions and ethnicities had lived together peacefully but guardedly in Jerusalem for many centuries. Communities interacted in economic affairs and in more limited social ways. They greeted each other politely on the street; they were neighbors in shops; they did business together; some even were friends and visited each other on occasions. But intermarriage was taboo, and one did not switch sect or religion without consequences. Nothing changed abruptly, but at the same time suspicion grew out of people's wariness.

Even among the Christian sects there was competition and tension, especially over how to divide the sacred places. The Church of the Holy Sepulcher is sliced into sections by traditional Christian sects, and to avoid further conflict the main keys are entrusted to a Muslim family. Often tensions boil over into fist-fights among priests and followers. And then there are the city's quarters: Christian, Muslim, Jewish, Armenian, and so on.

Such a mixture of humanity is positive, normally. It could even make for what is praised as a multicultural community; and indeed it was so for a long time. But then came the British Mandate and the Zionist incursion in the early twentieth century; conflict and sectarian divisions instituted by colonial design; the occupation of Palestinian lands that became the state of Israel in 1948; and in 1967 the occupation of east Jerusalem (and with it all the other occupations).

POWER CATS

Into this city of a motley population has now come a power with a single-minded goal. Since 1967, Israel and its Jerusalem municipality have implemented measures to Judaize the eastern part of the city. With West Jerusalem, in 1948, the Israelis got all the forcibly vacated Palestinian stone houses without paying for them. Now in east Jerusalem, the Judaizing plans are seen in new colonial suburbs built on confiscated land with Jewish contributions, and a house here or an apartment building there taken over by hook or by crook. These spaces of colonization are fenced in and well-protected, with large Israeli flags displayed, all designed to place mini-fortresses within and outside the Old City. Zionist organizations, or more usually their intermediaries, manage to concoct excuses for taking over a building or for wooing this person or that institution to sell property. This happened with the Greek Orthodox Patriarchy and a few Jerusalemite property owners—usually by trickery, when the Zionist system finds the weaker links.

Figure 9.3   Cat and Jet

It was natural to have various quarters exist in the Old City, and what happened between 1948 and 1967 was a historical gap in the continuity of a Jewish quarter. But it is another thing to expand the Jewish quarter at others' expense, to make it much larger than it was, and to use sheer force to destroy a Palestinian residential quarter to create a plaza in front of the Western Wall. Israel has taken over houses in the previous no-man's land, spread out into the French Hill and Silwan, enlarged the boundaries of the city by building huge colonies to increase the Jewish population, and separated Jerusalem from its natural West Bank extensions. It has also instituted policies that make it more difficult for non-Jewish Jerusalemites to live in their city and that stifle their existence, in an attempt to Judaize the city by force. It is a creeping many-pronged process that continues to be implemented with sacred sites and with place names (as I discuss in other chapters), as has already occurred with the Hebron mosque, now more than 60 percent controlled by

Jewish extremists, and as is planned for the Al-Aqsa Mosque and Dome of the Rock in Jerusalem.

In Silwan, just east of the Old City walls—or what some Zionist archaeologists like to call "the City of David" (although there is absolutely no evidence for that David, despite the many targeted excavations)—the plans are most insidious.[8] A richly funded corporation by the name of ELAD has been given free reign to implement the Zionist agenda, colonizing, taking over properties, finding excuses to evict Palestinians, and building for Jews in confiscated space—basically violating even Israeli antiquities laws that would prohibit such "development" in sensitive areas.[9] Archaeology is used or abused to support these nefarious activities, as when (funded by rightwing Zionist financiers from New York) a Zionist archaeologist declared the "discovery" of "King David's palace," despite objections by some Israeli archaeologists.[10] Find a structure or a pile of stones, provide no proof, and call it anything you like.

In such a situation, laden as it is with deceit, human relations are disrupted, turning a city that could have been a model of positive diversity into an odd cat's litter multiplied thousands of times. The Israeli system's control mechanism and its Judaizing designs have amplified the city's insularities and its fragmented identities. It is one mongrel in control, posturing as a pure breed, going through Machiavellian tricks to hem in or scatter a motley populace whose foremost concern becomes its immediate survival rather than the development of a larger communal interest. In such predatory conditions, raw power may continue to succeed for a while in breaking life-links among people and in diverting attention. Still, it does not seem possible that it could succeed in its aim of forcing an earth-bounded people, a *sha'ab*, out of existence.

10
Politics of Place Names

Why in the case of what was done to Palestine by Israel were there such frenetic initiatives to re-name ancient and modern places by the Zionist movement, in ways that could only be described as arrogantly inventive and ungrateful? This chapter analyzes the process of naming and related linguistic issues, and proposes new theories about how present place names relate to the ancient ones.

Normally, place names grow naturally, over time, as part of a culture. They are generated as responses by the continuous inhabitants of a region to the environment they live in and its distinctive features, as part of their lived experience. This process evolves naturally and does not have anything forced or sudden about it—except when a power, usually a colonizing or indoctrinating power, wants to assert its hegemony by altering the landscape and people's identification with it. Throughout history, there have been instances where geographical names were enforced—by the Romans in their empire, by the British and other colonial masters and geographical committees, by Soviet officials in the republics of the former USSR, by the fascists in Italy, and more recently by the Zionists in Israel and the other occupied parts of Palestine.

The "naming and unnaming" of Palestine by Israel, just as D. H. Lawrence also described it in fascist Italy, has a most unusual history.[1] This policy was undertaken by the Zionist movement for the purpose of Hebraizing the map of Palestine, before and after the creation of the State of Israel in 1948. While the process shares much with colonizing situations elsewhere, it is unlike any other in the extent of its disingenuous strategies, its misleading conceptions, its deceptive assumptions, and the insidiousness of its all-pervasive implementation on the ground.

Place-naming in Palestine and Israel takes on an unusual character in that while Zionist organizers were not natives of Palestine they assumed nativity for themselves in their claim system, at the same time denying native status to the indigenous inhabitants who originally coined the names or continued them, and from whom the Zionists often took place names in order to translate them. In this way, what would otherwise have been a clear case of colonial imposition is made to look like legitimate national recovery.

PLACE NAMES AS CENTRAL

If any single topic captures the essence of the conflict in Palestine and Israel it is this one. The paradigms and complexes at work in the region are encapsulated in this issue. They relate to power and entitlement, to assumptions in the Zionist claim system, to colonizing strategies and the response by the colonized, to the appropriation complex in its nefarious varieties, to the uses and abuses of history, traditions, and religions. It is extremely hard to fill the gaps, to find alternative perspectives, against the run of constructions that have accumulated over the past 2000 years or more, in the popular mind, in religious assumptions, and in the attitudes of scholarship. Place names in the "Holy Land" have been subjected more than other elements to a combination of developments that are difficult to trace: ancient and more recent natural naming by local people, forced actions by various powers in the past, oral transmission, transmission in religious texts, and finally impositions by naming committees.

If the issues relating to place names in Palestine and Israel could be disentangled and resolved this might hold out the possibility of advancing reconciliation and restitution of a measure of justice. Is it possible to find a compromise that would enable the redrawing of maps so as to restore a more accurate historical perspective?

WHICH NAMES ARE CLOSEST TO THE ORIGINAL?

In looking at a Western or Israeli map of Palestine or Israel, whether a historical or tourist map, one finds city names like Ashkelon and Akko/Acre. A map in Arabic, however, would have ʿAsqalān (عسقلان) and ʿAkka (عكا/عكّا) for these two old cities. It is clear there are significant differences in the vowels and consonants of such names, resulting not only from language differences or transcription (or mis-transcription) but also from divergent origins and perceptions. Which names are more genuine and ancient?

What complicates the problem here more than elsewhere are not just the linguistic intricacies but more immediately the contention, or pretence, by Zionist scholars and naming committees that they were restoring the "original" names. Ashkelon and Acco, both without the initial guttural ʿa (ʕin IPA) and other changes, are purported to be a return to the oldest and biblical names. In fact, names like "Ashkelon" and "Acco" have come about through a transcription tradition (which distorted many sounds) and were thus accepted in Jewish and Western usage. In other words, they are Israeli reinstatements of variants that are in effect fossils rather than originals, now placed on the map as tools for re-naming that aim to erase, scrape or chip away, and appropriate. Zionist claims assume that the Arabic forms are more recent and arose after the Arab/Muslim "conquest" in 638 CE, which changed or "distorted" place names, as if Arabic were a totally foreign language alien to its region.

Ironically, however, the same city names assumed to be more recent (that is, the ones used in Arabic, ʿAsqalān and ʿAkka) are much closer to the original names found in hieroglyphic that date back around 4000 years, as recorded in Egyptian sources, and a few hundred years later in cuneiform in the Tal el ʿAmarneh correspondence (ʿA[ʿI?]sqalānu or ʿAsqalān and ʿAkka). ʿAkka has not changed its name for more than 4000 years, while the Arabic ʿAsqalān is very close to the ancient name. They both represent a better preservation of the original than the biblical writings or Western renderings.

Figure 10.1   ʿAkka in hieroglyphic and Tal el ʿAmarneh cuneiform[2]

To explain the discrepancy in these and other names involves a number of linguistic matters concerning Arabic and Hebrew, including vowel shifts in Hebrew guessing (such as *ā—o*, *ʿa—a*, *a—e*) and consonant sounds (such as *q/k*, *b/v* and *p/f*), as well as issues relating to the transcription of the original sources and of the biblical and later renderings. In the case of ʿAsqalān/Ashkelon, the

Arabic form retains an initial guttural sound 'a, a q in the second syllable and ā in the last syllable, whereas the Hebrew and Western usage misses the initial guttural, has k in the middle, and ō in the last syllable.

Regardless of how such linguistic matters are settled, as I discuss them below, the most crucial factor to note is that the Arabic names are the continuous and natural forms as they evolved on the ground, as even Zionist scholars have to admit, indirectly, regardless of how much circumlocution they engage in (for example, by giving the impression that the sound ō is original or legitimate in the names). In inverse logic, a Zionist source cites "Acco, Canaanite 'Akā" without noting of course how exact the Arabic-Cana'anite correspondence is.[3] Little do they want to admit that varieties in Hebrew are largely the result of a transmission process through scholarly and religious traditions at a time when the language was practically dead or fossilized, or used only in scholarly and rabbinical practices—that in fact the Arabic variety, despite some natural changes, is a genuine one for the reason that Arabic preserved the original "Semitic" sound inventory, as I explain in the next section.

TRANSCRIPTION ERRORS

Yohanan Aharoni (one of the early authorities on Israeli geography) and others are forced to admit the errors in Hebrew transcription, even as they want to insist that biblical or other Hebrew sources of names are the genuine or original ones: "the biblical sources have undergone a long process of oral and written transcription ... some errors with regard to place names have crept in." At the same time, to give more credence to the Hebrew forms, Aharoni has to argue that transcription problems "exist mainly in the non-biblical sources, especially the Egyptian and Akkadian," although these are the only available and fairly reliable sources.[4] Yael Elitzur, a recent Israeli writer on toponymy (place naming), concedes the role of the "autochthonous inhabitants" in continuing the preservation of names, though who these undefined indigenous people are remains too sensitive for Elitzur to name them directly—viz. the Palestinians.[5]

Linguistically, both vowels o/ō and e/ē in Hebrew, according to Edward Lipinski, "do not belong to the common Semitic phonemes."[6] Rather, ā, ū, ī are the common proto-Semitic long vowels. That applies even more to consonants, especially gutturals. The importance of Arabic is confirmed by other standard authorities: "Arabic preserves the Proto-Semitic phonology almost perfectly."[7]

Arabic is not only the preserver of older languages and the best image of them: it is their natural and continuous descendent as well. One wonders, then, why there is this agenda to minimize and shrink Arabic as a major language and to limit it in terms of place names and its relationship to other languages to the kind of role assigned to it by Zionism and some Western scholars.

Even putting aside all linguistic arguments about Arabic and Hebrew, and all the ideological investments that attend toponymy, it is clear that current Western/Israeli transcription practices and conventions for ancient names are inaccurate as a reflection of actual epigraphic evidence. Erroneous habits are harder to break when a claim system that involves them is so ingrained and dependent on specific formulas.

THE ʿAQRŪN/EKRON INSCRIPTION AND TRANSCRIPTION

This was illustrated to me by an incident involving an inscription from the ancient city of ʿAqrūn/Ekron. I was discussing toponyms with a Palestinian archaeologist, trying to convince him how important it is to change his teaching maps because his students should know the original forms rather than only those given to them in Western and Israeli sources. He had invited me to the library of the Albright Institute in east Jerusalem where he was a "fellow." (I discuss the Albright's institutional structure in Chapter 8.) During the visit, he gave me a copy of an article about the Philistine city of "Ekron," whose remains date back to the Bronze Age, though the inscription comes from the seventh century BCE, at which time it was the largest olive oil processing center in the region. "But the name is not supposed to be Ekron," I told him after looking at the article. "Clearly, it should be ʿAqrūn, as the 'Phoenician' script clearly indicates, or to go Assyrian instead of Philistine its name is ʿAmqarūna, and it should have the initial guttural ʿa not e, q not k, and ū not o. It was identified because a Palestinian village close to it is called ʿAqr. In Western tradition it all started with early translations that simplified things or took on the tradition of how Hebrew was guessed. The ʿayn was elided by readers of Hebrew and of course by Western language speakers, and only some eastern Jews can pronounce this sound, and ū was guessed as an o. In addition, Hebrew often elides the distinction between ʿayn and aleph, since ʿayn and other difficult sounds become inaccessible outside the language context, whereas ʿayn is an all-important sound in Arabic as you know, which today in Arabic is still pronounced as the old guttural *'a* was. All the distortions in 'Ekron' are the result of transmission errors through Western sources, the condition of Hebrew before its revival, and how Western-based Jews read things."

Figure 10.2   'Aqrūn in a Philistine dedicatory inscription

Our argument was overheard by one of the authors of the article, director of the institute and co-excavator of "Ekron," Seymour Gitin, himself a biblical archaeologist, who approached to question my remarks. So I suggested: "Let's walk over to the poster of the inscription you dug up that hangs near the entrance of the institute and look at the name." Sure enough, both had to admit that the initial letter is unambiguously the guttural *'a* (ع; IPA /ʕ/) in "Phoenician" script followed by *q* (ق /q/) *r* (ر /r/) and *n* (ن /n/).[8]

MISLEADING TRANSCRIPTIONS

I am using Arabic letters in parenthesis because these signs represent the closest sounds to the original, since Arabic possesses the full inventory of the total "Semitic" language storehouse. It is one of the irritating and inaccurate conventions of scholarship, both Western and Israeli, to transcribe inscriptions in South Arabian (which, like modern Arabic, has 28 signs), Cana'anite/Phoenician, and Aramaic, using the 22-letter "square Hebrew" (square Aramaic really, as I explain later and in Chapters 1, 5, and 7). Unnecessarily and incompletely, Joan Copeland Biella in her dictionary of Old South Arabian decides on the following: "Entries in the dictionary are arranged by root, in the order of the Hebrew alphabet (with additions)."[9] Even a standard and generally reliable reference, *The World's Writing Systems*, arbitrarily decides to render the 30 alphabetic signs from Ugarit, almost completely identical to Arabic, in a chart that has "Ugaritic Scripts with Hebrew Equivalents." At the same time, the text tells us: "The wedge script records an inventory of sounds that is closer to that found in Classical Arabic (ca. 28 sounds) than to that found in Biblical Hebrew (ca. 22 sounds)."[10] What then is the purpose of giving an incomplete chart when a full and accurate chart is possible by using either Arabic (one of the five major world languages today) or the international phonetic transcription system?

This arbitrary and biased practice is also what Gitin et al. practice as they try to decipher the Philistine/"Phoenician" inscription from ʿAqrūn, introducing the notion of a "Hebreo-Philistine" script.[11] In another instance of fixation on Hebrew and the use of a Western linguistic tradition in application to regional place and personal names, a king mentioned in the inscription is called "Padi" (the consonants *p* and *f* have the same sign in Hebrew except for a dot mark introduced later in history). An obvious "Semitic" name would be Fadi (which means "one who sacrifices"). In this case, the name should be transcribed at least to posit both possibilities, as *F/Padi*, although *f* is more natural in this case (see later section on *f/p*).[12]

More strangely, indeed ludicrously, there is an attempt in the article to suggest that the inscription has some features of a script the authors call "Hebreo-Philistine," more definitely used (they say) in other Philistine inscriptions. As I pointed out in earlier chapters, this is a strategy that pervades the treatment of ancient languages in relation to Hebrew, for the languages are not identified as Canaʿanite, Ugaritic, Aramaic or Hebrew, but by the hyphenated "Hebrew-Aramaic" or "Hebrew-Canaanite" or now the much worse "Hebreo-Philistine" (taking over even the "enemy" script)— an attempt to appropriate the other languages, or to establish that Hebrew is more or less the same as them, or to elevate and expand it far beyond its actual size (as indicated in placing Hebrew first in the hyphenated compound), or to treat it as a very ancient script variety when in fact, as shown earlier, it is actually a takeover of a late script called square Aramaic.[13]

The practice is not simply that of appropriation, taking the language and culture of others at will; it also smacks of imperial pretension, as does the practice also of always writing "Jews and Arabs" or "Hebrew and Arabic," always in that order. It is uncanny how an innocent rabbinical script language used in the tradition has been exploited for all these extended uses. Ultimately, the objective is to implement the scholarly Zionist agenda of backdating its claims to the ancient Israelites and diluting the huge differences among the terms "Hebrew," "Israelite," and "Jew."

Other than famous names like ʿAsqalān and ʿAqrūn, there are thousands of place names in Palestine that have evolved over centuries and millennia—villages, towns, mountains, valleys, streams, and other geographic features. They had developed through a normal and gradual process—until the 1920s when the Zionist re-naming project began, formalized later in naming committees that prepared the way for a Hebrew map of Israel upon its establishment in 1948. After 1948 the names were officially employed in the State of Israel, and after the 1967 occupation of the West Bank, east Jerusalem, and Gaza, the process was imposed on the rest of Palestine. Of the Hebraized names only a few are ancient towns and cities, while a tiny percentage is of names associated with biblical narratives. As I show below, the great majority were fabricated by creating arbitrary biblical connections or by "translating" into Hebrew locally developed Arabic place names for topographic features that are descriptive and have no religious or historical association.

It is not only that this Zionist naming process is artificial. It also depends on fallacious linguistic and historical assumptions that are made to fit into a claim system intended to diminish Palestinian national rights. It even has little to do with the traditions of the minority of Jews who were in Palestine before European Jews and Zionist naming committees came on the scene.

EARLY NAMING PROJECTS

How did this unusual and complex problem come to develop over the centuries? Traditional Western usage over the past 1700 years or so had assumed either biblical or European referents for toponyms. To understand the evolution of the problem, it is necessary to trace how "scholarship" in relation to place names developed from the middle of the nineteenth century onward. This is historically important because Zionist practices in the twentieth and twenty-first centuries depend to a large extent on the exploitation of accumulated Western traditions about the "Holy Land," and on nineteenth-century sacred geography, even more than on Jewish tradition. As we have seen, in the mid nineteenth century, there grew up a Western fundamentalist wave of interest in Palestine, called Sacred Geography.[14] Reacting to scientific doubts raised about biblical accounts, it was thought that by going to Palestine sacred geographers might find literal verification for their faith in the "Land of the Bible" itself: the place is there, therefore the account is true, and thus their belief is confirmed. This type of thinking transformed earlier imaginings about the land from theoretical typologies into literal, physically oriented applications, not unallied to colonial ambitions. While that particular nineteenth-century doubt-belief crisis eventually resolved itself as a passing stage in Western thought, and although fundamentalism remains a phenomenon, it was a turning point with long-term consequences for the "Holy Land." Sacred geography laid the foundation and provided topographic models and various appropriative complexes that assisted, both politically and geographically, in the promotion of Zionist claims and the implementations that still rely on them. Place names were an essential part of this sacred geography.

Edward Robinson's *Biblical Researches in Palestine* (1841) is a formative work on this subject. Robinson and Eli Smith (his Arabic expert) are credited with inventing a method for finding towns and other locations of events mentioned in the Bible, something that was new in the exploration of Palestine and the region during the heyday of religious obsession. In the introduction to his book, Robinson explains his strategy of depending on "the ordinary tradition or preservation of ancient names among the native [Arab] population" and on a system of orthography not without parallel to that used for "writing the aboriginal names in North America and the South Sea Islands."[15] This method resulted in some reasonable conjectures but also many misguided identifications, sometimes hanging on far-fetched echoes. Robinson's argument assumed, first, that the Bible stories all actually occurred and, second, that the "original" biblical toponyms were Arabized after the Muslim conquest.

Later in the nineteenth century, Georg Kampftmeyer compiled and analyzed a list of 150 biblical names mentioned in earlier accounts by pseudo-scholars and travelers throughout the century.[16] Despite limitations and some unlikely identification, Kampftmeyer's study introduces an important linguistic factor. In explaining changes in the pronunciation of older names, he distinguishes between the "Arab tongue" (associated with the Muslim conquest in 638 CE) and the "Syrian tongue" (what people living in Palestine and the region spoke at the time, a colloquial language related to earlier dialects and ancient languages proximate to Arabic). This plausible explanation is generally attacked by Israeli scholars.[17] It is attacked because it tends to discredit the monolithic Zionist view that the "Arabs" all came from the Arabian Peninsula, populated the land, and adapted or changed its place names. Zionism dismisses the more natural explanation that the process was a gradual one and that the existing population in Palestine and Syria, Arabized over time but not "Arab" in the Zionist sense, had an equal if not more influential effect on how names evolved.

ISRAELI SCHOLARSHIP AND MYTHS OF CONNECTEDNESS

Israeli scholars dealing with this subject, despite their exhaustive scholarly practices, are interested mostly in fitting ancient place names into the Zionist claim system. While following in the tracks of Robinson and Kampftmeyer (on whom they need to rely as pioneers of biblical association), Israeli writers on toponyms have their own linguistic and historical assumptions based on Zionist prerogatives. These assumptions relate to the age of Hebrew, its relation to ancient languages such as Canaʿanite and Aramaic, as well as phonetic issues.

Yohanan Aharoni's *The Land of the Bible: A Historical Geography* is a typical early example of how Zionists deal with toponyms. For Aharoni, the place names are the ancient ones confirmed in the Bible, transmitted later in Aramaic, and then with the Muslim conquest in 638 CE they took on the "Arabic mouth." This fallacious premise leads to several linguistic jumps that contradict even his own list of toponyms that show ancient Egyptian or other regional variants are different from and more natural than the Hebrew. He says that the "k" was changed in Arabic to "kha" and "pe" appears in Arabic as "fa." Incredibly, he theorizes about a shift in Arabic pronunciation to justify "Ashkelon" as the original name: "At the beginning of a word it [the aleph] may shift to the stronger guttural *ayin* (Ashkelon—'Asqalan)."[18]

Shmuel Ahituv's *Canaanite Toponyms in Ancient Egyptian Documents*, based on his Ph.D. dissertation, is a curious book in that it has "Canaanite" in the title. Perhaps his assumption is that "Canaanite" is really Hebrew. While the agenda is obviously Zionist (he signed his introduction on "Jerusalem Day" to celebrate the occupation of east Jerusalem by Israel), all the evidence about place names he gives in fact points *away* from the Hebrew Bible as a source. Still, his toponymic listings and his index start with Hebrew as main headings. However, the transcribed forms from the Egyptian execration texts (about 4000 years old), el ʿAmarneh letters (about 3400 years old), Assyrian and other sources all show a substantial difference between the original names and the ones recorded in the Bible and later adopted in Israeli or Western usage, not to mention the closeness of the original names to the Arabic forms. For example, all these original "Canaanite" names are closest to current Arabic: ʿAkka (Western "Acre"; Israeli "Acco"), ʿAsqalana(u) (Israeli and Western "Ashkelon"), Ghazza (Hebrew ʿAzza; Western Gaza), Yāfa (Israeli "Yafo"; Western "Jaffa"), ʿAshdūd (Hebrew "Ashdod"), Majiddu (Hebrew and Western "Megiddo"), and ʿAriḥa (Hebrew "Yeriḥo"; Western "Jericho").

It is curious that Ahituv, like Elitzur after him, neglects to elaborate on Jerusalem in the ancient sources, a Canaʿanite/Jebusite city called Ur-salem, named as the place or foundation of the pagan god Salem. The irony should not be missed that "salem" in Jerusalem (Hebrew "Yerushalayim") is often mistranslated as "peace" and the city associated with the legendary story of David (City of Peace/City of David)—thus institutionalizing a process of both forgetting and appropriating the city's pagan and Canaʿanite ancestry.

Other Israeli writers attempt to maintain this illusion of continuity and naturalness in relation to the modern imposition of the Hebrew names. They want to consider the Arabic influence as a "distortion" and that the Hebrew names have now been "regained," contradicting the linguistic evidence and failing to give any credit to the Palestinian population that preserved the names: "many of the place-names were transmitted from ancient times, from one generation to another. This is true of Yerushalayim-Jerusalem or Akko-Acre."[19] It is left unspecified who these "generations" were, and why the original and present name ʿAkka is not mentioned. Yet, in a later article, the same authors, while repeating the standard mythologies and historical inventions about the Israelite Kingdom and the right of Jews to inherit it, cannot help marveling enviously at Palestinian villages in the occupied West Bank: "Instead, and ironically, the landscape reality of the present Arab village, with its densely-packed stone houses surrounded by olive groves and sparse pastures, better supports the Jewish myth for it evokes the Israelite settlements of old."[20]

Yael Elitzur's more recent *Ancient Place Names in the Holy Land*, like Ahituv's also based on a Ph.D. dissertation, is meticulous in its documentation. He acknowledges, as did nineteenth-century name seekers, the importance of the Arab "conquerors" in preserving place names, calling this inheritance a "miracle." However, his order of origin is "Hebrew, Aramaic, and Arabic." To make that sequence more convincing a bit of hyphenation is needed: "Hebrew-Aramaic" and "Hebrew-Canaanite."[21] Thus, as in other Zionist and some Western works, which elide much in this appropriation, Elitzur's chronology enshrines as coming first a script variety that came later and was less important in the larger picture of things.

On the issue of vowels, at some variance from ancient sources transcribed in his book that indicate an ā or ū for ʿA(ʿI) sqalūna/ʿAsqalān, Elitzur provides this convoluted and evasive explanation to try to lend authenticity to the end vowel in Ashkelon:

> In some cases, such as عسقلان = Ashkelon (which is frequently documented in sources earlier than the Arab conquest, always with /ō/), an explanation of the Arabic /ā/ may perhaps be that the name was known to the Arabs from Antiquity, being renowned as a southern metropolis and harbor; it therefore survived in the Arabic vocabulary with the ancient Semitic pronunciation of /ā/.

The "always" and before "the Arab conquest" contradict his recorded evidence and the earlier inadvertent transcriptions by Ahituv (which the latter could hardly have been expected to notice). In cases of the original guttural, the s, and the final vowel ā, Elitzur tries to argue for the Hebrew variants (initial *alif*, *š*, final ō) as being somehow original, though that contradicts actual transcriptions he himself provides (for example, he states that the "last vowel is /ō/ in all documentations," though earlier he cites the ancient instances of /a/ and /ā/).

Elitzur repeats the same kind of attempt at explanation for the /ō/ in the Hebrew change of ʿAkka to Acco. At first, he has to admit that the name of ʿAkka shows "perfect preservation of all elements," neglecting of course to mention that all these elements are in the present Arabic. Instead, he continues to try to show that somehow the final Hebrew /ō/ is parallel to the original final /a/ (in Egyptian lists) and /ū/ in el ʿAmarna, violating his evidence of consistency from the ancient Egyptian to the Greek forms. It is further noteworthy that the final Ugaritic, Phoenician, and Greek /ē/ is still reflected in the more colloquial Palestinian Arabic pronunciation of the city's name, in contrast to the more formal /a/. Insisting on the "Arabs" as invaders in the seventh century who changed pronunciation, rather than accounting for natural local transmission, he states: "Thus, one might conjecture that at least some speakers persisted in this pronunciation [the final /a/], from which the Arabs later inherited it."[22]

With a name like Dimašq (Damascus) and others to the north of Palestine, Elitzur and others have no trouble in maintaining (what for Zionists is unthreatening to their claims) that the name has been the same for many thousands of years and is documented as such in Akkadian, Assyrian, Aramaic, and Arabic. Why this rule would be contradicted by cities to the *south* in Palestine is not explained.

FALLACIES ABOUT ANCIENT LANGUAGES

To make their assumptions more convincing, Zionist and some Western scholars try to keep the Hebrew language closely affiliated with other ancient languages in the region, such as Aramaic, "Phoenician," and Cana'anite, while distancing it from Arabic. However, the contrary is closer to the truth. Arabic has the same sound system as Cana'anite, reflected in the 28-sign alphabets of both. Ugaritic also has the same sounds, except that the 30-sign alphabet has three signs for the aleph: *ā, ū, ē* (see Chapters 4 and 5). As the only live language in the region for many centuries, Arabic can be said to be the storehouse containing the inventories of the earlier languages. Hebrew, on the other hand, had been dead or read strictly as scholarly or religious writing, so that many of its features were fossilized and its pronunciation stipulative. Its revival as a spoken language in the twentieth century brought out some latent features and necessitated much guessing, borrowing, and improvisation to bring it into full use.

In guessing vowels in particular, Hebrew has diverged from close authenticity to the "Semitic" tongue as practiced in a live language like Arabic (as noted by Lipinski and Kaye above), and in many cases was influenced by its European environment (thus the difference between the more official Ashkenazi pronunciation and the Sephardic). It is theorized that some of these Hebrew sounds are in the northwest Semitic varieties, a somewhat incomplete theory. These are specific adaptations in guessing that influenced pronunciation, as in the vowel *o/ō* common in modern Hebrew (as in the way Israelis changed 'Akka to "Acco"), as well as the vowel *e/ē* (as in the way the Naqab Desert has been made into "Negev" by the Israelis), in this case adding another transmission difference from the Western use of "Negeb" by having *v* for *b*. (Hebrew signs for *v /b* and *f/p* are the same, except that dots were added later in the history of square Hebrew writing, after the introduction of diacritical marks in Syriac and Arabic).

FALLACIES OF GENERALIZATION

It is crucial to note that place names in Palestine and Israel have multiple ancestries. Thus, it is fallacious to generalize using a single argument about all the names. It is true, for example, that a process of adapting *foreign* names to the "Arab" tongue did occur clearly in the case of Greek, Roman, and Byzantine names (e.g., Neopolis becomes Nablus and Caesarea is Qāsariyye in Arabic). In addition, certain important cities were given appellations, Jerusalem being called Al-Quds (meaning "the holy") and Hebron Al-Khalil (meaning "the friend of Īl / El [God]").

However, in the case of indigenous ancient names thousands of years old, the pronounced and written forms in Arabic changed very little, if at all, from their original. Arabic is not only a native regional language that was close to the neighboring dialects and tongues; it also eventually became the live continuation and natural extension of the earlier languages as they were submerged. It cannot be viewed as a kind of disruption, a foreign language that became hegemonic, and "distorted" the original names, as Zionists want to see it. If the names evolved, the changes were not sudden but were organic adaptations, and were not forced as happened with re-naming by the Romans, the Fascists, or the Zionists. There was no need or motive for drastic phonetic or other changes in Arabic. Other city names in the region show the same tendency to be preserved now in Arabic almost exactly as they were known three or four or five thousand years ago, such as Dimašq (Damascus) and Ṣūr (Tyre). These places are all in parts of the region similarly affected by the "Arab"-Muslim influence after 638 CE.

Local Palestinian place names have had a long history of natural evolution, normal transmission, and continuity in the nature and environment that gave inspiration to them, as I show further in the following sections. On the other hand, the names as transmitted in the transcription-bound biblical tradition, or those later imposed by Israel, or those invented by committees to fit that tradition, illustrate the vagaries of linguistic disconnection, translation, and (mis)transliteration. Their forced application represents a calculated colonial erasure of native geography.

ALTERNATIVE VOICES

Two other works should be mentioned because they demonstrate this process of colonial erasure undertaken by the Zionist movement and the Israeli state. The first is a 1986 monograph by Thomas L. Thompson and F. C. Goncalvez entitled *Toponomie Palestinienne: Plaine de St Jean D'Acre et Corridor de Jerusalem*.[23] This study shows how the Zionist toponymy project, originally established as early as 1920 to "restore" Hebrew names or to create names of symbolic meaning, went much further than its original mandate. There was simply not enough tradition to go by, so it could only continue by picking out biblical or Jewish associations at random. It had to Hebraize Arabic names, or in other cases translate Arabic to Hebrew to give the location an ideologically consistent identity. For example, some locations were rendered from Arabic into the Hebrew phonetic system: Minet el-Muserifa became Horvat Mishrafot Yam and Khirbet el Musherifa was changed to Horvat Masref. Sometimes, in this artificial process, the committees forgot about certain genuine Jewish traditions, as in the case of the total canceling of the Arabic name Khirbet Hanuta, not recognizing that it probably rendered the Talmudic Khanotah. This forced exercise of re-naming often even went against biblical tradition, most notably in erasing the Arabic names Yalu and 'Imwās. Yalu became Ayallon, while 'Imwās, Western Emmaus, associated with the Christ story, was one of three villages, along with Beit Nuba, razed in 1967. The old stones from the villages were sold to Jewish contractors to lend local tradition and age to new buildings elsewhere, and the whole area was turned into the tragic Canada Park, made possible by millions from a Canadian donator. These are only three of the more than 450 villages in geographic Palestine that were destroyed or emptied of their Palestinian inhabitants by the Israelis in and after 1948.[24]

According to the Israeli writer Meron Benvenisti in *Sacred Landscape*, in order for a total map of the "Land of Israel" to be created, and since only a small number of place names could conceivably be linked to anything mentioned in the Bible, the renaming often became a forced exercise in making arbitrary connections, sometimes picking words at random from the Bible or translating to Hebrew the indigenous Arabic names and pretending they were Hebrew. One positive aspect of Benvenisti's work is that it recognizes the insidious nature of what the Zionists did to Arabic names, and what they did to the Palestinians: he documents Zionists interviewing and taking information from Palestinian villagers and Bedouins—to identify the original names, then adapting the names or translating them to Hebrew—the very people who were eventually dispossessed and their lands and villages taken from them by the Zionists.

While Benvenisti gives credit to Palestinian names and recognizes some of the injustices, he fails to extricate himself from two key Zionist linguistic and historical assumptions: "Had the Arabs not adhered closely to the ancient Hebrew-Aramaic names, the Zionists would not have been capable of reproducing a Hebrew map." Worse than the reiteration of "Hebrew-Aramaic," Benvenisti repeats almost verbatim one of Aharoni's linguistic inventions: "They [Arabs] after 638 CE had no difficulty finding Arabic forms for names such as Ashkelon—which they transformed into Asqalan."[25] There has been no response in Arab scholarship to this kind of linguistic fixation, nor is there an adequate Palestinian project or policy to counteract the Israeli naming program. In fact, there is nothing but literal repetition of lists.[26]

NATURALNESS LOST

Benvenisti describes with sensitivity the naturalness of Palestinian toponyms, as opposed to the artificial work of the Zionist naming committees. His work demonstrates the possibilities for a growth in consciousness and conscience, and he writes with a sense of sorrow and respect for what has been lost: "The wealth of Arabic toponymy is astounding in its beauty, its sensitivity to the landscape, its delicacy of observation and choice of images. Its metaphors have a poetic quality; its humor is sometimes refined, sometimes sarcastic."[27]

He also makes his own satirical allusions to the minutes of the Zionist committees, before and after 1948, showing how members argued about how best to invent names, or to arbitrarily turn them into Hebrew: "The settlement of Alon was called that because it is situated beside the Arab village of Sindiyanna, which means Oak (Alon): 'The name is ancient and one may assume that its source is Hebrew,' the committee stated." Often, the committee acted with crass arrogance, with unambiguous awareness of the fabrication it was pursuing. In the case of "Ramon Crater" in the Naqab/ Negeb, Benvenisti notes that an Israeli guidebook explains that the name "is derived from the Hebrew adjective 'ram' meaning 'elevated.'" The guidebook of course neglects to mention that the original name is actually the Arabic Wadi Rummān (*rummān* means "pomegranate"), as with many other geographical features in the area whose Arabic names have been modified to fit Hebrew phonology. In distorting Arabic names to make them sound Hebrew, the Israeli naming committee explains: "After all, it is likely that Hebrew names became garbled and acquired an alien form, and these are now being 'redeemed.'"[28]

A similar process of either Hebraizing the Arabic names or translating them applied to many villages and towns: ʿAin Kārem became ʿEyn Kerem (its Palestinian population has been totally replaced by a Jewish Israeli population), ʿAin el-ʿAllaq is now ʿEyn ʿAlleyet, and Suba is distorted as "Tzova" (a depopulated Palestinian village, with the colony of "Tzova" nearby). Whereas the process was made to look convincing in some cases, in most others it is meaningless—the only intention being to make the name sound Hebrew, so that through repetition and documentation it would be assumed to have previously or always had that name. This is clearest in the following cases, which combine translation of the first word and distortion of the second: Khirbet Ruseis (*khirbet* means "ruins"; *ruseis* means "pebbles" in Arabic) was changed to Horvat Rotsets, or Tel al Asmar (*asmar* means "dark" in Arabic) transformed to Tel Ashmar, Khirbat Ngass (*ngas* is "pear" in Arabic) to Horvat Agas.

LINGUISTIC PREMISES INVENTED

Whether it is in this totality of artifice of changing the map or in relation to the ancient names on the ground, or theories about ancient languages, there is a great deal of invention, guile, backdating, and fabricated justification. As a result, I question many linguistic premises in the study of ancient regional languages, whether in terms of phonetic rules or the relationship among languages. In addition, I am very skeptical of some of the standard encyclopedias and reference works, where knowledge has regressed to suit Zionist thinking (see Chapters 1, 5, and 7 for examples).

It is obvious that a "square Hebrew" exists, as a script, taken over from an Aramaic script. But there is no evidence that an "ancient" Hebrew script or language (and so called Paleo-Hebrew) existed—a "Hebrew" that is backdated, conveniently, to connect it to earlier biblical chronology. There is no "Paleo-Hebrew" or "ancient Hebrew," except if one falsifies things and appropriates "Canaanite" or later "Phoenician" or Aramaic. In fact, the distinct evidence is that square Hebrew is merely a script style that is known in Aramaic as square Aramaic. A scholar of Aramaic from the Aramaic-speaking village of Maʿalula in Syria spoke clearly of a "square Aramaic," which would have developed in the later periods of Aramaic—a fact that is now silenced. Yet some standard references have regressively (without scholarly questioning, or in some cases intentionally) shifted their scholarship to accommodate Zionist claims and linguistic assumptions that fit them. For example, any inscription found in the geographic area of Palestine is then assumed to be "ancient Hebrew" even when it is clearly identifiable as "Phoenician."[29]

In the case of cities I have discussed, ʿAkka and ʿAsqalan in particular, a reference work like *The Anchor Bible Dictionary* seems intent on hiding or avoiding certain facts in order to keep the names associated with Hebrew. By listing the city as "Acco" (adding "*Heb* ʿakkô" in parentheses) it suggests to readers that the name is originally Hebrew. There is no reference to the original Egyptian sources for the name, though we are later told: "According to Assyrian sources, the city (Akku) rebelled against Assyrian rule." The same dictionary transcribes ʿAsqalan as *ʾašqelôn*, without citing the exact original, but merely mentions that the "first recorded historical attestation of the name Ashkelon appeared in the Egyptian execration texts."[30] This is information and disinformation. A reader of all this would tend to be led to the conclusion that the Hebrew version is the original of these names.

TIME FOR RE-ASSESSMENT

I am appalled by the extent to which Arabic has been diminished in relation to other ancient languages and its importance in the region reduced in mainstream scholarship. A few scholars still make brave attempts to emphasize how far Arabic preserves the older languages, such as Ugaritic, Akkadian, and Canaʿanite/Phoenician. I am skeptical too of the transcription conventions still pervasive in scholarly use, which are based on the past tradition of learning Greek, Latin, and Hebrew as necessary for a Western education. Frequently, an incomplete phonetic equivalence is adopted while neglecting to use the advantages of Arabic, or at least the international phonetic system, to reflect the full inventory of sounds and so posit all possibilities.

I have explained (above and in Chapters 1, 4, 5, and 7) the problems with the transcription system for ancient languages, such as using the 22-sign square Hebrew to transcribe "Phoenician" or South Arabian and, worse, to transcribe Ugaritic. In matters of phonology, even when an *f* sound could be suggested, scholars who are already so predisposed assume a *p* and therefore don't draw potential conclusions. The almost exact similarity of the Ugaritic alphabet and its vocabulary to Arabic is transparent to anyone who has some acquaintance with Arabic (see Chapter 4), yet most scholars (out of habit or convention) neglect to use that facility and instead mention inexact similarities to Hebrew in glosses or in discussion. Generally excellent works on Ugarit and the relevance of its mythology to monotheistic religions would still have benefited from a knowledge of Arabic in understanding the meaning of certain Ugaritic words and concepts.[31]

F/PISGAH

One instance that could help to change thinking on the subject is the famous "Pisgah," assumed to be the name of the mountain peak from which Moses viewed the Promised Land he never had the chance to set foot in, according to the biblical account. In William Bradford's *Of Plymouth Plantation* (1620), which tells the story of the early Puritan pilgrims in New England, Bradford wants so much to climb to a Pisgah from which to better view the promised land of America. This "mountain" looms large in the religious mind and in the typology of conquest.

But is "Pisgah" a mountain, as assumed and as indicated in its meaning in Hebrew? Is it to be pronounced as "Pisgah"? Is *p* the correct sound? In some biblical dictionary entries and commentaries on "Pisgah," there is mention of the fact that "Pisgah" is used with the definite article, which suggests it cannot be a proper name. *The Anchor Bible Dictionary* alludes to Jerome's curious rendering of the word:

> Most interesting is Jerome's translation of "Fasge" (Pisgah) by the Lat *abscisum*, meaning "steep" or "broken off." This corresponds to the LXX's translation of Hebrew *pisgā* with Gk *laxeuō*. Thus, LaSor (*ISBE* 3: 873) notes that the name Pisgah, which derives from Heb *pāsag* ("split," "cut off"), means "cleft." It is suggested that Pisgah's projection from the plateau had this appearance when viewed from the E.[32]

What if, instead, as suggested by the definite article and the other evidence cited, the word is not the name of a mountain at all but a geographical feature? Why is Jerome using an f rather than a p? Has the word become fossilized incorrectly as "Pisgah" in both sound and sense? Equally suggestive is that Jerome's rendering, possibly the word itself, or at least the language or feature's name associated with the Moses account, could relate to the noun *faskha*, from the root *fasakh*, which in Arabic means "to break off or separate," thus suggesting a slit or break in the rock or elevated land forming a cliff.[33]

Jerome either reflected how he heard or guessed the sound being made. There is also the evidence that both the Samaritan Pentateuch and the Greek Septuagint (several centuries before Jerome) include an initial *f* in words and names. In contrast the medieval Masoretic system adopts an initial *p*, which was the pedagogical basis for synagogue reading and cannot therefore be a basis for accurate pronunciation or exclusion of an initial *f*. The Samaritan and Septuagint readings, which use the initial *f* for *felistim*, for example, are sufficient evidence that one cannot exclude (in fact, one should prefer) an initial *f* in contrast to *p*.[34] All this has other implications for the nature of the languages used in those ancient times and the theories developed about them.

SEARCHING FOR INCLUSIVENESS

I have raised questions about how Israeli state power has re-written names and changed historical perceptions. My belief is that people need to have genuine meaning in the names they use. Names should not be tools of control or reminders of oppression. And when they are generated by the use of purely mythic associations unrelated to people's lives, they cause distortions in the human imagination that stifle healthy development and exaggerate obsessions. What could possibly justify such false alterations? What should be done in such cases, especially when witnesses to the distortions are still alive and present? Why these impositions? Even today the artificial changes continue to be enforced. A highway sign about 10 km before Tel Aviv showing the exit to 'Annaba (عنابا), which was accidentally written correctly in Arabic, has had an alternative plastered on the old sign changing the name to 'Annava (written in small Arabic script as عنافا, always placed below Hebrew, with an unnatural three dots for the *v*!).[35] Should one accept fabrications that cover up realities? Or could there be "negotiation" of a naming scheme that all sides could share, find meanings they can live with, within their language and also their conscience?

Palestinians could possibly accept Ur-salim (or Yabous) as a suitable name for Jerusalem, while also retaining Al-Quds out of respect for tradition, if they were not made to feel that "Yerušalayim" is politically enforced and is part of a Zionist claim. Meanwhile, Jews may wish to continue using Yerušalayim, while recognizing it is only their transcription tradition. It would be factually real and historically faithful to continue to call Gaza Ghazza (rather than 'Aza, as it has been transformed in Hebrew), to adopt the name ʿAsqalān rather than Ashkelon, and ʿAkka instead of Acco. I would prefer "Ekron" to be called what it was: ʿAqrūn, even if the guttural is not pronounced and the spelling simplified for easy Western usage (for example, as *Aqrun*). And there is less harm in calling the desert in the south of the country not the Negev (Western Negeb) but what people in the region have called it for thousands of years: the Naqab.

There is a compelling need to change—which now means to reverse—the naming and language enforcement policies used by Zionist committees, ministries, and municipalities. One side invents and exploits while the other side tries to resist what is being forced and sees it as a neo-colonial framework for disempowerment and dispossession. Israel and Zionism are free to name as they like, but should not be allowed to get away with fabricating names or normalizing their distortions or erasing the past. The long and organic process of naming over the millennia is too rich and too dear to be expunged from maps, or manipulated and disfigured on replacement maps. What an excellent achievement it would be if regional maps in all languages could be redrawn to reflect the variety of cultural traditions in Palestine and a modicum of historical accuracy.

11
Epilogue:
Retrieving the Ancient Subaltern

The people of Palestine are ancient. Their ancientness is not a fabricated one. It is not assumed. It is real. They do not need to constantly assert it or to reassure themselves they are an ancient people or insist on how ancient they are. But Palestine's wholeness was shattered in 1948, and its direct links to that wholeness and its relatedness to the region have been disrupted. In this situation, how possible is it to maintain a naturalness that has been subject to such an attack? How can the lived past be recovered when its presence is now only infrequently recorded, silently, in what people say and do? How does one search for what is left of the indigenous Palestinian culture in an environment contaminated by the savagery of the present?

This is not my last chapter. It is the beginning of another book.

UNRECOGNIZED CONNECTIONS

A graduate student once approached me after a lecture I gave in Toronto with the following question: What sources are there for studying the connections between present Palestinian culture and ancient cultures in the region? I gave her a list of possible sources but pointed out that the subject is almost untouched, indeed almost untouchable. That is the problem: there is very little available documentation, and what is available is sketchy, fragmented, and often unscholarly. Most of all, the prevailing scholarly attitudes seem to be obstructive. Ancient Palestinian roots have been buried over the centuries by a combination of elision, rewriting, neglect, and now by brutal dispossession and occupation. On the one hand, people have continued to live and to mix in the region over millennia; on the other hand, other voices—not those of the people—have presented what was written as allegory or literary narrative as if it were history, thus sidelining important facts and contexts, and magnifying distorting perspectives. The people themselves have been variously disempowered, their heritage and culture appropriated, becoming forgetful of aspects of their history, and preoccupied with more recent identities.

The question of connections is important for reasons related to both public and scholarly perceptions in the West, in Israel, and among the Palestinians themselves. In the West and Israel, the dominant view of Palestine involves chronology convenient to chroniclers of an overarching framework, mostly intended to emphasize biblical associations and Jewish presence, based on legendary religious narratives and other transmitted traditional assumptions, often fallacious. There are stories that have been assumed to be historical and some facts about conquests and empires. As I suggest in Chapter 2, note 32 and the passage from Sozomen in Chapter 3, there are suggestions in old texts that negate common assumptions about the ethnic or religious composition in Palestine for those periods. Monotheistic sequencing remains one of the most damaging assumptions about the history of Palestine and its people. Without regard to earlier presences or people's existence, it sequences periods according to mainstream religions (Judaism, followed by Christianity, then Islam) and major imperial events such as occupations and conquests. While imaginative minds throughout history may have crafted religious discourses as explanatory tools to understand the world and humanity, now such tools are used methodically, particularly in regard to East Mediterranean discourse, to distort, or to construct presences out of past absences.

Palestinians generally comply by associating their presence with either the Christian or Muslim conquests, thus accepting the dominant discourse and participating unknowingly in abbreviating their own cultural history. On the other hand, the Israelis construct their identity and history on the basis of misleading ties to ancient idealized entities like "Hebrews" and "Israelites," and use other biblical justifications. By sheer force of relying on a religious book as an excuse (a book primarily crafted out of much earlier cultural antecedents), these notions have a serious impact on common perceptions in diverse areas—from perspectives about history, politics, and religion to questions of identity and continuity. Countering such dominant interests and hegemonies with available alternative information would have wide-ranging effects on both Palestinian self-understandings and understandings by and about others.

New strategies are needed to create a framework that could free discourse, and just as importantly a reflective willingness and the academic capability to write the actual history of the land and its people. In particular, establishing concrete links to the past outside the dominant paradigm would go a long way toward altering the view of human development in Palestine. Yet the task, which may appear to be straightforward, calls for a seismic shift in attitudes and a letting go of the comforting but inaccurate repetition of stories about the development and history of the region. Most of all, it has to be done by the Palestinians and other people in the region themselves, for the most part—and that has its requirements and complications.

INVISIBILITIES

Palestinian native life as it has been observed by outsiders can be summarized in one word: invisibility (or, from the other side, blindness). However, the symptoms of invisibility today are different from what they were in the nineteenth century and early twentieth century.

A common way to dehumanize is to ignore the agency of those whose land is desired: the "land of milk and honey" is lauded yet the people who have worked that land over centuries have no value, are disposable (see Chapter 1). In its application to the native people, the intersection of religious and colonial thinking finds strategies for denying their existence and de-legitimizing their rights, expressed in double acts of demonizing or making invisible: the natives must be either made into savages or not seen at all, except perhaps as hidden background or anthropological curiosities.

A major difficulty for sacred topographers resulted from how to interpret or explain the presence of the inhabitants of Palestine (villagers, townspeople, and Bedouins), especially since they visibly carried the only reminders of the ancient past. In their single-minded mission, sacred topographers could not possibly identify with these people as continuous occupants of the land; they observed, used, and denied them at the same time. They imagined Palestinian customs, lifestyle, clothing, and habitat as reminders of "biblical" characters and biblical life, de-contextualized from current realities. While useful as fossilized remains or as opportunities for visual evidence of biblical scenes, Palestinian villagers were invisible as present human beings, becoming almost phantoms of some esoteric, unexplainable existence.[1] Nineteenth-century travelers, who illustrated the people and the land with biblical eyes, refused to see the actual people they encountered as real—a peculiar precursor perhaps to the Zionist notion of a "land without [seen] people."

While earlier travelers used Palestinians and their landscape for mere illustration, what can be surmised today about ancient life is generally appropriated by Zionism, and so culturally Palestinians become an absence, more literally invisible. Still, whether through villagers or Bedouins, aspects of what constitutes the Palestinian population have remained the only reflection and reminder of the way things were in the past. There is no other reference.

Today, Zionist writers still suffer the same difficulty as the sacred geographers. They use Palestinian scenes and Palestinian life for illustration, yet must keep the people unmentioned. As I point out in Chapter 7 (and note 10 there), there are many book covers by Israeli and Western Zionist writers that include pictures of farmers or shepherds, or typical Palestinian villages and scenes. The trend is duplicated in tourist postcards, where biblical stories are suggested in the pictures used of Palestinian scenes (such as a postcard showing a present shepherd and his sheep under the title "Shepherd's Field"). In some texts, the Bedouins may be mentioned (this is acceptable in the Zionist agenda since "Arabs" are to be seen as nomadic), but Palestinian farmers and villagers are largely ignored.

One extended example of this invisibility of Palestinians is a book that claims to give an account of "daily life in biblical times." Its cover, like others of its type, shows somewhat bare hills in Palestine with a flock of sheep (that, unmentionably, are shepherded by a Palestinian). All the details given of lifestyle and diet, and such like, are of course theoretically derived from the Bible. In places, this book wants to lend contemporary relevance to the old ways of doing things, such as churning milk in goatskin or using a clay container or eating certain wild plants. Particular vessels, the author ventures to write, are "still used in some present-day societies," and some plants like wild dandelion are "still picked by the locals for salads."[2] One wonders if this ambiguity is intended to make some readers think that Israeli Jews are the "locals," or if it is a colonial erasure of the Palestinian population that "still" does such things.

This form of silent appropriation is not unlike an expensively produced folio *The Holy Land: A Unique Perspective*, which contains impressive pictures: aerial shots acquired from NASA and landscape and habitat photographs of Palestinian villages and towns. The text, however, is silent about the actual, living Palestinians, concentrating instead on all sorts of biblical quotations, related or unrelated. Below one photograph of a hill terrace, the text makes a claim for the Israelite "invention" of terrace agriculture—a claim that disagrees with all known information about terraces. A

Palestinian farmer working the terrace in the photograph is erased from the text.[3] Here certain humans are erased from the land to make room for others to displace them and claim their history and heritage, not unlike a palimpsest where the land and the people are the original writings on an old parchment scratched out to incise a different text. Another, more scholarly Zionist work is obliged to supply documentation about the development of terrace agriculture much earlier than the existence of any possible "Israelites," yet still goes on to make the same argument and give the Israelites credit for inventing terracing.[4]

It is rare to find an investigative history of Palestine that is a people's history. Thomas L. Thompson attempts to provide that in *The Mythic Past*. His Chapters 5–9 make an impressive sweep of Palestine's history, starting significantly with the "Genesis" in 1,400,000–6000 BCE (in opposition to the title of the Bible's creation myth) and ending with a note about "our ignorance" and the biases of historical invention by biblical scholars ("Fiction is the clear creation of the bearers of tradition"). Despite the changes and historic events that affected the population, Thompson postulates a significant degree of human continuity regardless of turns in official belief in one religion or the other.[5]

TOPOMANIA AND ETHNOGRAPHY

Ethnographic observations over the past two centuries confirm this continuity of the Palestinian population, whether the intentions of the observers were "biblical," Zionist-oriented, ill-intentioned or well-intentioned. Yet, the present situation has been transformed whereby such issues are much less in the foreground.

These earlier ethnographic observations of Palestinian life, as well as some recent DNA studies, tend to support the idea that the Palestinians as a whole, especially the villagers, represent ancient indigenous populations dating back many thousands of years, and that the same people have gone through first pagan and then various monotheistic or other affiliations. A study by a group of Israeli and U.S. scientists (carried out in the aftermath of the Oslo peace process) concluded that Palestinian Arabs have close genetic similarity to Jews, findings which agree with historical records indicating that "Moslem Arabs in this country [Palestine and Israel] descended from local inhabitants, mainly Christians and Jews, who had converted after the Islamic conquest in the seventh century AD."[6]

While they have the potential to reveal unexpected human commonalities, DNA studies in particular must be undertaken with more careful sampling criteria in the future, and efforts made to avoid all kinds of historical preconceptions that could prejudice the results. It is not possible, for example, to start such a study by assuming that the Palestinians are descendents of the "Philistines," or that present Jews are related to ancient "Israelites," or that the Jews being studied are descendents of past Jews! Further, the study mentioned above seems to have been encouraged in its conclusion by the existence of a "peace process." Sampling, as far as I know, has not been done to compare present populations in Palestine and Israel with the DNA from bones or other remains in the region from specific periods (a most crucial comparison). For results to be more definitive, the present villages or populations and the ancient samples would have to be meticulously chosen after extensive research.

As I have indicated, the subject of continuity has not been adequately studied in the Palestinian context or from the Palestinian point of view, and the approaches taken by outsiders are not always balanced. With renewed Western interest in Palestine, the nineteenth century produced thousands of travel and "anthropological" accounts by clergy and lay people (see Chapter 1 and Chapter 3). Some of these writers, whether famous or obscure, advocated crusading campaigns and expressed racist sentiments. But most of the topographers were simply obsessed with finding any scrap of evidence, literal or invented, for the "veracity" of the scriptures. Finding no real evidence, they imagined the land and plants, farmers and shepherds of Palestine as oriental fossils from a biblical past. The people were mere conduits for their illustrative topomania. With careful accounting for cultural and religious bias, however, it is possible to use this material as a partial, albeit weak, source.

Inadvertently, even some of the most biased nineteenth-century writers gave credence to the connection of present Palestinians with the most ancient populations. A work somewhat more insidious than the average sacred geography text is the book *Palestine Peasantry* by Elizabeth Anne Finn, missionary wife of the British consul in Jerusalem during the nineteenth century (discussed in Chapter 1). Finn's millennial zeal inspired her weird association of the Palestinians with ancient pre-biblical inhabitants. Her sympathies for Jewish women, with the intention of converting them, did not extend to non-Jewish women in Palestine, except pictorially perhaps. (The frontispiece of Finn's *Home in the Holy Land* is shown as Figure 11.2.)[7] In 1924 Finn's daughter published her mother's *Palestine*

Figure 11.1 Nizam ʿAshour plowing around an olive tree on a terrace, Al-Jīb, Palestine, 2009

Peasantry, and adds her own opinion in an introduction to the effect that "the people in question" (meaning the great majority, Palestine's "Arab" Muslims) are really more pagan than Muslim, and so "most probably of Canaanite origin." The villagers retain many old unbiblical customs, she says, preparing the way for her political argument that they do not deserve self-determination.

According to the mother, the customs and habits of Palestinian farmers are mostly inherited from the biblically condemned Canaʿanites, Jebusites, and Philistines. These Palestinian "fellaheen" are only "nominal Moslems" since their practices "violate Mosaic strictures." It does not matter if the strictures are themselves

Figure 11.2   Bethlehem peasant traveling to Jerusalem to sell grapes (1877)

ridiculous. "Thou shalt not plow with an ox and an ass together" is one rule Mrs. Finn says the farmers violate, although Palestinian farmers usually use mules or donkeys for this purpose. It does not really matter if she exaggerates (they "cook lambs only a few days old"), or gives examples that may equally apply to Europe (they consult "diviners and astrologers"), or invents others (they eat snails and hyena, and sons "beat their mothers"—hardly likely in view of the sacredness of the mother in Palestinian society). However, she also puzzlingly concedes that some of their customs "are derived from those of the Israelites." Even as she provides such biased observations, Finn is in a way confirming the antiquity of the Palestinian villagers.[8]

This conflation of images of Palestinians with ancient peoples (or even contemporaneous others, such as the "Indians" or others fated to colonial condemnation) is common among other travelers during the nineteenth century. One oddity, though more typical than an exception, is William Francis Lynch, who wrote a narrative of an expedition to "Lake Asphaltites or Dead Sea." He proudly reports that he received official permission from the highest U.S. authorities and that he wrote an "official report" in 1849, before publishing the account to a "liberal and enlightened community" in 1852. (His original report is reproduced by the University of Michigan's "Makers of America" series, and has been translated to Hebrew.)

Lynch is a curious combination of military thinking, fake refinement, religious preconditioning, and quasi-scientific purpose. He proudly informs readers in the introduction that he has commanded a supply ship "formerly called the 'Crusader.'" His mission—as he declares it after the surrender of Vera Cruz in 1847, leaving him with "nothing to perform" anymore—is to explore the Dead Sea: "the extent, configuration, and depression of which ... are as much desiderata to science as its miraculous formation, its mysterious existence, and wondrous traditions respecting it, are of thrilling interest to the Christian." So he bids farewell to his "native land," all prepared with boats and supplies, to launch a trip, which of course does not come to much because there are no ruins of Sodom and Gomorrah. Probably his only real discovery is that birds don't immediately die when they fly over the waters of the Dead Sea (as had been reported by some of the early hoax accounts such as John Mandeville's). Instead, his exploration often takes the form of colonialist geographical description, the type usually intended to prepare the way for future conquest. The fundamental conflation of the religious and colonial minds surfaces in his observations about the local people. He cannot stop blending stereotypes by associating the people with "Indians," with "African blacks," or with the South Sea Islanders, adding to those all the ingrained Old Testament based genealogical biases that predetermine his observations. Upon sighting some of the villagers from Mazra'a close to the Dead Sea, he concludes that they are "much darker, and their hair more wiry and disposed to curl than any Arabs we have seen. Their features as well as their complexion are more of the African type, and they are short and spare built, with low receding foreheads, and the expression of countenance is half sinister and half idiotic. ... They all, men and women, seem to bear impressed upon their features, the curse of their incestuous origin." (By "incestuous," one guesses, he means that all are descended from the sexual intercourse between Lot and his daughters.)

Exemplifying how colonials seek to divide and conquer, Lynch patronizes the Bedouin tribes in Karak, Jordan, because they are mostly Christians, enticing them against their neighbors. In turn, the leaders of the Christian Arabs seem to want to exploit him for aid as a rich foreigner and give him petitions to take back home. Simultaneously, he is constantly suspicious of other local people. He classifies Arabs into two camps: the useful and the "bad Arabs." His preconceptions determine how he thinks and acts. His outward courage rages on an undercurrent of mistrust and fear, which recall Henry Maundrell, an often-quoted traveler, whose "fear" of Bedouins amounts to paranoia. Lynch is constantly "preparing for hostility," thinking of "Indian warfare," against people who have little value in his eyes. His guns are always at the ready to shoot apparently unoffending tribesmen, even when there is nothing hostile in their behavior (as he describes it) to warrant such drastic precautions. Lynch's narrative and its incidents give an eerie forecast of complicated and massive events to come, whether in how "sacred geography" has been realized in state creation in the region or in how colonial powers have behaved and still behave in terms of policy and military action.[9]

U.S. biblical orientalism took other forms that are consistent with its peculiar Protestant ethic, its sense of exceptionalism, and its appropriation of the idea of the U.S. as another Promised Land. Whether the travel was real or vicarious did not make much difference to how the Holy Land was interpreted. In the later nineteenth century and early twentieth century, several models of Palestine and Holy Land parks were built throughout the U.S., where the public was treated to various "you-are-there experiences of Bible times." One famous attraction was called "Palestine through the Stereoscope," which contained 200 photos of Palestinian scenes with commentary. Burke O. Long analyzes this commentary as a double or multiple invented vision, in which Palestinians are used as tools in an "orientalizing gaze" that suggests how much of their way of life duplicates that of two or three thousand years ago. At the same time, the present-day people and land are cast as degraded and ruined copies of an idealized biblical past that is compared in its values to the superior and progressive American present, which then requires action to exercise power and domination. For one photo, entitled "A barley harvest near Bethlehem," the text informs the viewer that this scene takes them back to Old Testament days. However, the ten figures in the photo (obviously a single family of men, women, and children) are presented by the commentary as showing a Palestine that is oppressed and stratified between poor and rich. An old man standing is assumed to be the "master" watching the others slaving at work (in fact, he was most likely the grandfather in the family, resting). While parallels are drawn to biblical characters, the present people are described as inferior and shoddy in comparison to characters like Ruth and Boaz who must have been better dressed and lived in a time of quiet, prosperity, and freedom, which the text identifies with the U.S. or the prospect of a Judeo-Christianized future. Such attitudes (a mixture of ethnography, geography, biblical literalism, and ideology) were replicated in texts, maps, and the establishment of institutes to serve the enterprise: "Biblical scholars continue to play a role in the old story. If not a model, then a photograph. If not a photo, then a map. If not a map, then a painting. If not these, then assemblages of Holy Land knowledge shaped for political relevance. All desire to convey a touch of the real, while all enable a fantasy of a real-imagined place of surrogate travel."[10]

One positive anthropological study was undertaken by Hilma Granqvist, a doctoral student from Finland during the period 1925–31.[11] She started out intending to study women in the Old Testament, but ended up doing intensive field work in Artas, a village close to Bethlehem—the kind of work that made her supervisor disqualify her. She concentrated on marriage customs and relied in her findings on observations and interviews with local women, "excavating" this one village in an anthropological sense, as opposed to making comparisons. Granqvist's methods are the kind worth repeating regarding various topics in villages and towns across the region, with modifications, although the point of such work should be cultural rather than biblical or Islamic in its assumptions.

In contrast to Western orientalism, the history of interaction between Zionists and the native Palestinians is changeable from a cultural perspective. Some early Zionists did not shy away from seeing the Palestinians as rooted in the land from prehistoric times. For Yitzhak Ben-Zvi, who became the second president of Israel, the Palestinian Arabs are really the descendents of the ancient Israelites (an opinion suggested by travelers, including Mark Twain, who says "Arabs" are the only remaining real trace, if there is any, of "Israelites"). Of course, Ben-Zvi mixed up the "Canaanites" with the "Israelites," thinking the latter evolved from the first (now rejuvenated in some theories, as I explain in Chapter 1 and note 41). His research led him to the view, as reported by Uri Avnery, that the population of the country had not really changed from the earliest times: "The Canaanites mixed with the Israelites, became Jews and Hellenists, and when the Byzantine Empire, which then ruled this country, adopted Christianity, they too became Christians. After the Muslim conquest, they gradually became Arabs. In other words, the same village was Canaanite, became Israelite, passed through all the stages and in the end, became Arab." But when the Israeli-Palestinian conflict gathered momentum, adds Avnery, this theory was forgotten.[12]

Early "pioneer" Zionists tried to establish roots and to find proof of connections between ancient Judaism and the exotic East, which led to a peculiar mixture of orientalist thinking, romanticizing, biblical referencing, and colonial attitudes. One object of attraction was the "Arab," who, as reflected in early Zionist literary works, was used as a model of courage and "manhood" to be emulated. While some writers can be seen to be "mimicking" the local Palestinians, seeing them as "inspiring" cultural symbols, in other instances, inversely, the "Arab" is viewed as primitive and inferior. Until the 1930s, many Zionist theorists saw the Palestinian farmers or "fellahin" as descendents of Judean peasantry, as Jews who converted to Islam to avoid taxation and were still "primitive" enough to be easily assimilated.[13]

It is a strange thing that any "affinity" early Zionists felt toward the local Palestinians, for utilitarian cultural reasons, has now disappeared overall and been replaced by antagonism or dismissal. Zionist ideology and its relation to the people and land adapt variously with time. In the 1940s and 1950s, a movement of Young Hebrews gained strength, its members known as "Canaanites" because they distanced themselves from Jewish religious heritage and "exilic history" and instead identified with a cultural past and wanted to root themselves by reviving it in the local landscape.[14] This renegade "Canaanite" movement looked for unity among "Hebrews," and though still essentially Zionist it could not be accepted by mainstream Zionism because it advocated "not ... an anachronistic Jewish religious exclusivism ... but a secular entity that will ... assimilate all other non-Arab minorities ... into a new Hebrew confederation."[15]

More recently, post-Zionism arrived as a deconstructive movement, though it appears to have weakened. Now the Israeli system, as expressed in its media and its policies, and in most Israeli scholarship, has fallen generally within the parameters outlined by the overall Zionist claim system and its assumptions. As implied in a study of Israeli archaeology, Palestinians are to be restricted to the more recent periods that follow the arrival of Islam (anything farther back than that is viewed with ridicule, anxiety or fear), whereas the Israelis have control of the more ancient periods. In place of the earlier adaptive and necessary use of the local inhabitants, Zionism has moved in the main onto different strategies, now that its earlier aims have been largely achieved. The Israelis have appropriated a semblance of nativity and have relegated the Palestinians to cultural invisibility or active demonization within the Zionist system, in general drawing parameters for the study of the "Arabs."[16]

For the Palestinian past to be rediscovered on fresh grounds will require that all previous findings and records be integrated, or reinterpreted, as well as new anthropological and archaeological studies initiated that are uninfluenced by religious or ideological biases, assumptions, and agendas. While the study of nomadic Bedouins could complete the total picture, it should be done only as supplementary to the altogether different task of studying village and farming life and its popular heritage. The history of Palestinians and the record of Palestinian life need to be seen as consecutive and cumulative in terms of preservation of heritage and influences from the various periods of its continuous existence.

PALESTINIAN ETHNOGRAPHY

Tawfik Canaan was one of the first Palestinians to study the country's folklore and customs, under the auspices of British institutions. He produced several essays, both short and extended, most of which were published in the *Journal of the Palestine Oriental Society*, including "Haunted Springs and Water Demons in Palestine" (1921), "Mohammedan Saints and Sanctuaries in Palestine" (1924; continued 1927), "Plant-lore in Palestinian Superstition" (1928), and "Modern Palestinian Beliefs and Practices Relating to God" (1934). One of his arguments is that the Palestinian village population holds beliefs and practices that predate current religious affiliations. He begins his continuation of "Mohammedan Saints" with this important statement:

On the whole, the conceptions of the people of Palestine have been surprisingly little changed, considering the extraordinary vicissitudes to which this land has been subject. Invasions, conquests and occupation by new races have modified their beliefs by giving them a different colour, but they were unable to extirpate them entirely. Even the great revolutions produced by the three monotheistic religions, whose cradle lay in or near Palestine, were not able to suppress all primitive beliefs.[17]

He laments that, even within the compass of a few years, it has become much more difficult to collect folkloric information, hence the urgency of the task. Despite reservations one may have about Canaan's Western-inspired scholarly habits and terminology (such as using "Mohammedan"), it is clear his essays contain solid scholarship and valuable details of customs and beliefs. Some of these customs have already been lost, and so his recording of them should be collated and organized.

Since Tawfik Canaan, the work of Palestinians on this subject has been not only sparse but also of not wholly satisfactory quality. This is clearly due in part to the constricted environment and fragmented circumstances within which they work. Whether recent or not so recent, the brochures and booklets that describe present Palestinian heritage such as popular arts, landscape, proverbs, and sayings are generally poorly produced and have limited circulation. A work such as Nimr Sarhan's *al-mabāni el kana'anyya fi falastīn* [*Cana'anite Buildings in Palestine*] (1989) is unable to deliver on its promising title in any significant way. A volume in English entitled *Folk Heritage of Palestine* (1994), edited by Sharif Kanaana, is badly printed and has mostly meager content. Its most useful essay, by Abdul-Latif Barghouthi, "Palestinian Folk Heritage: Roots and Characteristics," makes an attempt to link ancient and modern Palestine, but uses somewhat outdated scholarship and is inconsistent in the quality of its approach to ancient history and its sources. In fact, ancient history remains a major source of confusions and self-colonizing misconceptions in Palestinian self-understanding and in the understanding of Palestine's total cultural heritage.

There are a few good monographs on embroidery. However, as I discuss in Chapter 8, tourism information in print and on the internet is in general ill-prepared and poorly presented. It also makes no attempt to present in any realistic or interesting manner the daily life of the people and the aspects of their heritage that are likely to be of interest to visitors.

Recently, an "artist-cum-anthropologist" recorded some remnants of sacred trees associated with *walis* (holy men) and the barely surviving practice of human burial in caves in areas south of Jerusalem (a custom that definitely contradicts current religious traditions). His study also notes evidence of how the veneer of a Christian calendar and of Muslim practices (often conflated, with Muslims adopting Christian symbolism and vice versa) are overlaid on Cana'anite and other ancient symbols, rituals, seasonal practices, and customs.[18]

OLD GODS LIVE ON

Despite all the distractions of survival in an old place troubled by eternal, zealous conflict, in pockets there are still remnants of ancient customs and popular beliefs, old signs, the little fragments that are left.

The use of ancient terms among Palestinians and other people in the region is unconscious and simple. On the steps to Damascus Gate in east Jerusalem one day, I watched an elderly Palestinian woman wearing an embroidered traditional dress, sitting cross-legged on the stone pavement, with baskets of fruit in front of her that she had brought from a village. She had carried her load across checkpoints, or avoided them, to make the little she would get to support herself or her family. To advertise her tiny pears, she called out, "Pears, Pears, Ba'al ["bʕl"] Pears." The people passing by knew what she meant: the pears are small because they are not mass-produced in orchards that are irrigated and fertilized. Most people today prefer to buy plump and perfect looking fruits, even though they do not have as much taste. Ba'al fruits and vegetables are those grown on moisture left from the rains: they may be imperfect and blemished, small in size, but their flavor is concentrated and special. I bought a kilo from her because these pears, left to grow naturally on their own, are the most aromatic and satisfying. In a kind of second exchange, I asked: "What does it mean that your pears are ba'al?" She explained what she meant, but was obviously unable to articulate fully an ancient memory that the meaning originates from a pagan god and his attributes.

I was satisfied. For her, as for other people in the region, this word and many such expressions have retained thousands-of-years-old associations they are unaware of—associations that are not fossilized remnants but rather surviving and functional folk traditions, subaltern meanings from past inventories conveying a host of values that merit being rediscovered.

Figure 11.3   Village women selling vegetables and fruits inside Damascus Gate, east Jerusalem, Palestine (2009)

But there are ironies in how these distant memories are preserved, and how they relate to more recent identifications. This was vividly illustrated to me during a summer visit to a Palestinian village west of Ramallah called Kfr Niʿmeh (*kfr* is an ancient word for "village" common in names across the region). August and September are months of agricultural plenty: including grapes, figs, and other fresh fruits and vegetables. We sat on a roof that overlooks the distant Mediterranean to the west, sipping tea, eating grapes and figs. An old farmer came to greet us. After a while, he remarked: "How good the fruits and vegetables used to taste when they were grown *baʿal*." Yes, I agreed, I always look for *baʿal* vegetables and fruits, so rare and difficult to find these days, if not impossible. His usage struck me nevertheless and I wanted to know more, so I asked: "Why is this word used to describe agricultural produce that is not irrigated or fertilized?" He didn't answer, nor could any of the others present. I tried to explain, somewhat proudly, that it is a term inherited from the ancient gods worshipped in our region thousands of years ago, in particular in reference to natural soil moisture credited to the rains generated by Baʿal, the Canaʿanite god of thunder. The old man looked at me; perhaps he did not get my drift or the enthusiastic tone of my explanation. Instead he responded indignantly: "We have nothing to do with those Cana'anites. They were pagans and idol worshippers condemned by Allah in the Qur'an."

A last illustration of inadvertent Palestinian use of an ancient past—of which people seem unaware and, therefore, with which they are unable to identify fully—came to me by accident as I was traveling from the "Allenby" Bridge to Jerusalem. I was sitting in the backseat with a man and his wife. The man was working his prayer beads—made up of 33 pieces, which repeated three times complete the 99 names of Allah. Suddenly, he exclaimed aloud, "*Ya Latīf*" (literally meaning "Oh, beneficent one" or "Oh, kind and pleasant one"). In my ignorance, having been away in the West for a long time, I assumed one usage of this expression to which I had been exposed in popular exchange, something like "May God protect us from this" or "Oh, what a terrible situation." Since there was nothing to warrant such an expression of concern, I turned to him and asked, "What do you mean by *Ya Latīf*?" His answer was simple: "I am calling out one of the names of Allah."

Immediately my mind turned to a translation of myths from Ugarit (see Chapter 4), the city in northwest Syria now called Ras Shamra that dates to 3200–3800 years ago, where the same name is given as one of the qualities of the chief god Īl (El).

And it is not only Īl and Ba'al that people have preserved without completely knowing of their inherited meanings, present still in words and expressions (for instance in the name of the city of Baalbek in Lebanon). There is the god Mōt (meaning "death"), who in the Ugaritic stories kills Ba'al, the god of fertility, who is later resurrected with the help of the goddess 'Anat, another "virgin" goddess. In popular usage, when the weather is unbearably hot, we say it is *ḥar mōt*, meaning "the heat [is] deadly."

Other ancient pagan gods are still present in the names of many cities, such as in Jerusalem (*ur-salem*, associated with the pagan god *salem*, son of 'Ashtar, a "virgin" goddess, who is immaculately impregnated by the chief god Īl / El) and in Bethlehem/Beit-Laḥem ("house of the [Cana'anite] god *laḥm*). As I show with place names (Chapter 10), it is a trait of the region as a whole that villages, towns, cities, and topographic elements have a long history with little change in their names over the past four or five thousand years.

POPULAR ARTS, CUSTOMS, FARMING PRACTICES

Aspects of heritage such as dress, popular customs, ceremonies and farming practices, superstitions, and common habits could be particularly significant in the search for ancient parallels. Old habits and customs are harder to trace back than language usage. People in villages near Hebron, Jerusalem, and Ramallah, or in villages like Birzeit or in the Galilee, have everyday cautions relating to simple things that we normally would not think of today. For example, after taking a hot bath, one is told it is necessary to wash one's feet in cold water before leaving the bathroom, or to drink cold water before leaving the house. Most Palestinians would remember their mothers or grandmothers always asking them to drink before leaving the warm house, especially in colder weather. One would acclimatize oneself in this way and avoid getting sick by going outside abruptly and having one's "chest" exposed to the elements, to diminish the chance of getting sick from what we call *lafḥet hawa* ("a blast of the wind").

The biblical suggestions can be worked in reverse: instead of finding biblical parallels in present-day life, it is possible to explain the Bible using what is still left of local customs and material culture. I suggested in Chapter 10 how "Pisgah" (or rather *Faskha*) can be better understood in reference to Arabic. A curious thing happened in the Naqab (the desert in southern Palestine that is called Negeb/Negev in Western and Israeli usage) when one of the Arab schools organized a Bedouin tent exhibition. Labels were put up showing parts of the tent and items inside, such as a skin for churning milk and a cloth for keeping bread fresh, written in Arabic with Hebrew transcription. Visiting rabbis were amazed to see the words illustrated live and said they could now better understand some of the meanings and uses in the Hebrew Bible.

There are in practice many rituals and amulets used to safeguard one's children and oneself against "the evil eye," or to acquire protection with the blue eye (of Horus?). People still engage in popular medicine and have "prescriptions" they use, or are prepared by specialists in herbal medicine, outside of what is available from modern doctors in the way of chemical pharmaceutical products. And in places, traditional marriage and funeral customs are still practiced and could be examined with an eye to finding the less recent aspects of rituals that are not prescribed by present religions or are imitations of Western marriage celebrations.

How old are such habits and customs? Which ones are relatively more recent and which very ancient? Are they one thousand, two thousand, three thousand years old, or even older? How (and where) does one find corroboration for them in available ancient texts or inscriptions, dating back as far as possible, in various parts of the region?

Figure 11.4   The Palestinian village of Deir Samet, Hebron region

Farming practices are important clues to the connectedness of people to ancient times, and it is still possible to record old farming terminology, methods, and the rituals associated with seasons and harvests: when the agricultural "calendar" starts and how it is related to ancient patterns; how people anticipate the rain, how they feel the weather, how they prepare the soil, when and where they plant, how they celebrate, what they call various tools and tasks, and how they relate to the land. Modern (and Israeli) farming has overwhelmed Palestinian agriculture and very little of it is left (let alone the fact that most of the refugees now removed from their land were farmers). As a result, it is necessary to supplement what has remained by observing farming practices in distant parts of Syria or Lebanon. Farming terminology may be a very fruitful area for gleaning similarities, even if only a few terms are located that relate to ancient times. Such a task requires a group of researchers who among them have the requisite knowledge and skills to detect a parallel or close parallel when it occurs. Because the old practices are fast disappearing and difficult to date, the fixed features of the agricultural landscape are also significant, such as hill terraces, which warrant systematic study. Though some aspects may have been documented here or there, what is necessary is to connect them more definitively to the past and have them presented in their totality.

Such connection to ancient times has already been attempted with Palestinian embroidery. There are striking similarities between women's traditional dresses (especially of Jericho and Bethlehem today) and what the ancients from this region are shown to be wearing, say in ancient Egyptian wall paintings or other sources.[19] A multiplicity of knowledge practices and access to various historical sources and periods would be needed to begin to retrieve what has yet to be recorded, and to have all the findings concentrated in one place. Changes and influences naturally occurred over the millennia, important to note as one traces the continuities and reaches as far back as possible to the most distant past.

Some of the customs and traditions, rare, difficult to identify, and surely changed to some extent, have already been shown to be remnants of ancient cultural habits covered up, or purposely washed away, or modified by subsequent religious, political, and cultural developments. In other words, there is already evidence of continuities, though recent historical events in particular over the last 60 years have accelerated the process whereby these old links and customs are being lost. As the evidence (either direct or by comparative methods) is retrieved systematically, it becomes possible to make a strong case for more extensive continuities that would reflect positively on Palestinian consciousness and generate alternative historical perceptions. Given the importance of this region symbolically for people throughout the globe, and despite how ravaged it remains by misconceptions and colonial actions, it should now be possible to mobilize the human intellectual resources and will needed to evolve a new understanding and a resultant new consciousness of spiritual values.

WHAT IS LEFT FOR THE FUTURE

Uncovering hidden histories and countering hegemonic narratives are challenging but not impossible tasks. Even when it is difficult and painstaking to establish connections between past and present, there will be significance in exploring gaps and inconsistencies, and much to gain from comparative study. The comparative method could be rewarding, by linking existing scholarship on ancient regional customs and habits to present parallels in Palestine, Jordan, Syria, and Lebanon. Ethnographic observations, including "field" observations and old descriptions in travel accounts or earlier ethnographic research over the past centuries, could also be used to supplement new findings.

It is essential to start by listing and annotating all books, articles, and archives related to Palestinian and regional heritage, as well as existing scholarship and documentation from all sources, in all languages. An inventory of ancient regional customs, popular medicine, farming practices, religious beliefs, superstitions, and language expressions should also be charted out from any possible ancient sources in the region. The aim would be to see how some of these could be connected to present customs, daily habits, superstitions, ceremonies, farming terms, place names, popular medicine, sayings, and vernacular language.

These are essential steps for retrieving Palestinian and regional subaltern culture. The intention would be to uncover the hidden and to give what is due, without any agenda—not to idealize or create an alternative mythic history. It would be a laborious and far-reaching project, with the results not at all certain at the outset, and certainly a major challenge in terms of funding and time investments. Additionally, science can be brought to bear by conducting *new* DNA studies in Palestine and the region, under balanced criteria unaffected by historical preconceptions. A potentially fruitful approach involves comparing Lebanese and Syrian customs with Palestinian customs and habits, using ethnographic observations about the region (particularly about Bedouins and farmers). These in turn would be compared to scholarly findings and texts relating to ancient customs and long-standing traditions. Once scattered or undirected sources and resources begin to be canvassed, it may be possible to proceed to establish the subject of cultural continuity as an important field of study in this region.

It is doubtless that such an exhaustive anthropological inventory of past and present will yield significant results. Initial areas of connection can be charted out and framed in the context of continuity so that the inventory search would have clearer targets and could supply not only the data but also some of the strategies for future study—and not too far in the future since the remnants of a human heritage are constantly being destroyed and fast disappearing, making them increasingly more difficult to recover.

SUBALTERN RECOGNITION

If I seem to have focused much on the ancient peoples in our region, or their gods, their remains, and their connections to us, it is because I believe it is crucial to retrieve what has been left behind both for its value in the present and for its potential meaning in the future, as much as for recovering the meaning of the past, which needs to be reframed. It is not that I think all Palestinians, Lebanese, Syrians, Jordanians, and Iraqis today are descendents of the Cana'anites, Philistines, Arameans, Assyrians, Babylonians, Moabites, or other ancient peoples whatever they may have called themselves or are called by others—though most surely are. It is not certain at all—in fact except in isolated areas it is doubtful—that these ancient peoples thought of themselves as having a kind of identity in the way we think of identity today. Their city states or empires often competed with each other, and some of these people seem to have liked to move about and establish new ventures. I imagine their identity may have been strengthened in places to which they migrated or where they put down new roots, even in periods much later than has been thought, overwritten since by newer identities.[20] Among others, the Cana'anites had an extended presence in the region over millennia and a great impact throughout the Mediterranean, establishing settlements and expanding knowledge in places surrounding the basin of this sea and its islands from as far back as 3500 years ago or even earlier. Their impact can be seen in locations as wide apart on the coasts of that sea as the Iberian Peninsula, North Africa, Malta, Sicily, Crete, Croatia, and probably still further afield as far as Ireland and Britain. They invented and spread the alphabet that most languages use today.

In both West and East, recognition of the region's contributions is inadequate, in some cases wholly absent, mostly because giving its ancient peoples proper credit would contradict the negative treatment most of them have had grafted onto them, in uncreative creations, in religious narratives, and in the construct of Western civilization. However, incorporating these ancient peoples, known by different names, into regional identity and self-understanding is now essential in order to overcome many present self-colonizing notions. Within existing conceptualizations, it would remain difficult for some to revise their thinking and to consider the Palestinians or other modern or ancient peoples not in terms of how they have been dehumanized for others' self-interested purposes but instead as tenacious inhabitants of the land and as carriers of knowledge. To open minds and effect this revision in thinking would involve no less than a challenge to the authority of the myths that currently prevent people from escaping blindness and beginning to see more clearly.

So I see in these ancients something I also see in all other peoples who have since been devalued or demonized by racist or imperialistic systems—symbols of what was important but is inadequately felt, what has been elided or covered up by a homogenized history that needs to resurface. And more than being improperly recognized or constantly marginalized, their accomplishments are appropriated when useful or convenient, while their roots are simultaneously denied. To me, the Cana'anites and other ancient people of our region stand for what has been forgotten, submerged and subaltern, and what is closer to primal inclusiveness and diversity. I imagine they stand for more benign values that are worth retrieving in humanity. Their existence and their fate are representative of the oppressed and dispossessed. In this sense, whether literally or figuratively, they are the ancestral Palestinians.

One wonders at the multitude of other revelations that could come to light but that lie buried in the daily language and customs of people in this old and deep region. For nothing primal can be completely edited out of existence. Like the Etruscans in D. H. Lawrence's poem "Cypresses," the ancients still appear in *our* dark cypresses. We live under their trees; we harvest their olives, their figs, and their grapes. Our farmers still plough their hill terraces. We still wait for the rain that Ba'al, Rider on the Clouds, brings, and a man and a woman refer to each other as *ba'lati* and *ba'li*. We still use their place names. Near some villages the vegetation is unusually prolific in old sacred locales where superstition prevents the cutting of trees.

The culture of the region may have become more layered, the people more mixed, religious beliefs more exclusive, self-colonizing identities more fractured, appropriations more distracting, but the lives of the people who have always inhabited the place still retain their deep historical roots. They show in small gestures, in farming practices, in fetishes and old remedies, in sayings and words, in the faces and eyes of a people who have lived here and mixed here since times primordial. Neither the heat of dogma nor the fog of history can erase or wash away these ancients. Their writings and their spirits are still alive in the myths and gods that the religions of today have taken from them. Their signs and letters are present in this very text.

Notes

CHAPTER 1

1. Genesis 9: 20–7, 19: 31–7, among other instances of genealogical exclusion or preparatory cursing.
2. Michael Prior, in *The Bible and Colonialism: A Moral Critique* (Sheffield: Sheffield Academic Press, 1997), shows how Old Testament notions were used to build frameworks of rights and exclusions. Robert Allen Warrior, a Native American academic, "read[s] the Exodus stories with Canaanite eyes," and Takatso A. Mofokeng notes how in apartheid South Africa the Bible was used as "an ideological instrument of colonization, oppression and exploitation" (105, 43).
3. See Chapter 7 for part of a speech made by William Thomson at the first public meeting of the Palestine Exploration Fund in 1865.
4. John Davis, *Landscape of Belief: Encountering the Holy Land in Nineteenth-Century American Art and Culture* (Princeton: Princeton University Press, 1996). Perry Miller's classic *Errand into the Wilderness* (Cambridge: Belknap, 1956) is an early work on this theme.
5. William Bradford's *Of Plymouth Plantation* (1620), an account of Puritan landing, readily available in anthologies of U.S. literature, is essentially the foundation of the U.S. national myth. (See Chapter 10 on "Pisgah" as a "mountain.")
6. John Winthrop's sermon "A Model of Christian Charity" (1630) is another founding document which explains why charity (rather, philanthropy, in this context) is in the self-interest of the wealthy and why various "Canaanites" are excluded from his "city upon a hill." Winthrop is of course misusing Christ's Sermon on the Mount which begins with "How blessed are the poor ... Blessed are the gentle": "You are light for the world. A city built on a hill-top cannot be hidden" (Matthew 5: 3–14).
7. Harriet Beecher Stowe, *Uncle Tom's Cabin*, Chapters 7 and 12.
8. Burke O. Long, *Imagining the Holy Land: Maps, Models, and Fantasy Travels* (Bloomington: Indiana University Press, 2003), 1–6; an excellent study of U.S. model parks, travel, biblical scholarship, and its institutions. Chapter 8 discusses some of these U.S. institutions in Jerusalem.
9. Readers will be familiar with more recent films that are sympathetic to American natives, such as *The Mission* and *Dances with Wolves*. Jack G. Shaheen's *Reel Bad Arabs: How Hollywood Vilifies a People* (New York: Olive Branch Press, 2001) documents the bias against "Arabs." However, the bias in Hollywood films runs deeper, affecting the whole region and its ancient history, as I point out in notes 22 and 23.
10. George Sandys, *A Relation of a Journey Begun An Dom 1610, Containing a Description of the Turkish Empire, of Egypt, of the Holy Land* (London: W. Barrett, 1615), 218; G. Frederick Owen, *Abraham to Allenby* (Grand Rapids: Wm. B. Eerdmans, 1939); Barbara Tuchman's popular Zionist interpretation of

British involvement in *Bible and Sword: England and Palestine from the Bronze Age to Balfour* (New York: Ballantine, 1984 [1956]); D. V. Lucas, *Canaan and Canada* (Toronto: William Briggs, 1904).

11. Basem L. Ra'ad, "Primal Scenes of Globalization: Legacies of Canaan and Etruria," *PMLA* 116.1 (2001), 90. See also Silvia Federici, ed., *Enduring Western Civilization: The Construction of the Concept of Western Civilization and Its "Others"* (Westport: Praeger, 1995).

12. For the comments by Walter Burkert, see his *The Orientalizing Revolution: Near Eastern Influence on Greek Culture in the Early Archaic Period*, 1984, trans. from the German by Margaret E. Pinder and Walter Burkert (Cambridge: Harvard University Press, 1992), 1, 4–5. Burkert notes, ironically it seems, that the word *canon* derives from Akkadian (38). Dictionaries, however, give the source as Greek. In Arabic, the word is *qanūn*, meaning "law."

13. An example of such contradiction is William Foxwell Albright, a biblical archaeologist, who praises "superior" Roman paganism while justifying the extermination of Cana'anites and "Indians" because they were pagan (for more, see Chapter 5 and note 3 there and Chapter 8, "Academic Colonization"). On monotheism, see Chapter 2, and on parallels to the Greek pantheon, Chapter 2, note 21.

14. *The Travels of Sir John Mandeville*, translated with an introduction by C. W. R. D. Woseley (London: Penguin, 2005 [1983]), 43–5. The translator takes liberties by identifying Mandeville's scrambled place names, and is lenient with Mandeville's inventiveness and vicious statements about Bedouins and Islam, saying that his outlook is "fair, sensible, and detailed" (27)! George Sandys, though considered a secular traveler and a humanist, expresses similar sentiments in his preface "To the Prince" that introduces *Relation of a Journey*. Many later travellers, especially during the nineteenth century, also assume Palestine is theirs to own by right. One does not need to explain much how Zionism has translated this sentiment.

15. X. J. Kennedy and Dana Gioia, *An Introduction to Poetry*, ninth edition (New York: Longman, 1998), 8; Eric J. Leed, *The Mind of the Traveler: From Gilgamesh to Global Tourism* (New York: Basic Books, 1991), 28; Marshall McLuhan, *Understanding Media: The Extensions of Man* (New York: McGraw-Hill, 1964), 87. On the alphabet see Chapter 5.

16. Notes 18 and 21, and especially the latter, explain my use of scare quotes. Among books on the "Canaanites" are Niels Peter Lemche, *The Canaanites and Their Land* (Sheffield: Sheffield Academic Press, 1991) and Jonathan Tubb's *The Canaanites* (London: British Museum, 1998) and his *Bible Lands* (New York: Knopf, 1991). One problem with scholarship such as Tubb's is that it directly or indirectly appropriates all real cultural heritage of the region under what is called "Bible Lands." To books on the Cana'anites add all those on "Phoenicians." See Mark S. Smith's reservations about the terms "Canaan" and "Canaanite" in *The Origins of Biblical Monotheism: Israel's Polytheistic Background and the Ugaritic Texts* (Oxford: Oxford University Press, 2001), 14–18.

17. Thomas L. Thompson, *The Mythic Past: Biblical Archaeology and the Myth of Israel* (New York: Basic Books, 1999), 126.

18. "Interrogati rustici nostril quid sint, punice respondents chanani: If you ask our peasants who they are they will answer in Punic, 'Canaanites'" (Augustine, *Ep. Ad Romanos inchoate exposition* 13 Migne, *Patrologia Latina*, XXXV,

p. 2096; quoted in Lemche, *The Canaanites and Their Land*, 56–7). For more see note 21.

19. An impressive volume *The Phoenicians*, ed. Sabatino Moscati (New York: Rizzoli, 1999; originally published as *iFenici* [Milan: Bompiani, 1988]) maps out and illustrates the influence of Cana'anite culture across the Mediterranean.

20. This maybe says something about Matthew, placed as the first gospel though not the earliest.

21. I use scare quotes for "Arab" because of the confusion in its meaning, and especially its misuse to obscure the distinction between nomadic or desert Arabs and Arabized people in the region. I place "Phoenicians" in quotation marks because it seems to have been the name given by the Greeks to coastal Cana'anites, but mostly because I want to remind readers that the two terms are equivalent rather than to allow "Phoenician" to be used as a kind of euphemism to avoid "Cana'anite." Greek *phoiniké* also become what the Romans called their enemies the Carthaginians, *Poenicus*, thus the derogatory sense of "punic" in English. One scholar, Glenn E. Markoe in *Phoenicians* (Berkeley: University of California Press, 2000), states that the term is "a Greek invention" (10). However, another, Charles R. Krahmalkov, is of the opinion that "Phoenician" is a term which the people "called both themselves and their language and which is the origin of the Greek [word]," at the same time that it was "the dialect of city state of Tyre and Sidon, adopted by all Phoenicians as the Standard literary language," *Phoenician-Punic Dictionary* (Leuven: Uitgeverij Peeters, 2000), 10–11. Krahmalkov still refers to "the region of Canaan" and to the Augustine reference (see note 18). Regardless of who coined the term "Phoenician," and even if "*Pon(n)īm*" referred to the particular dialect of the two cities and a "language," it does not exclude the wider Cana'anite identification. Whether the term was Greek (more likely) or local, it may have become more common or extended during the time the region was Hellenized. In the Gospels, "Phoenicia" seems limited to an area in the north of Palestine and just north of it. For more, see Chapter 5 (and note 1) and Chapter 6 (and note 10).

22. I avoid using "denigration" (instead of "vilification") because of its offensive etymology. A mainstream attack on multilingual education using "Babel" is made by Arthur M. Schlesinger, Jr. *The Disuniting of America* (New York: Norton, 1992), 18. The term "whores of Babylon" is quoted in Giles B. Gunn's *The Interpretation of Otherness: Literature, Religion, and the American Imagination* (New York: Oxford University Press, 1979), 99. This notion of "whores of Babylon" may well have inspired the film *Eyes Wide Shut*, and another well-crafted film, *Magnolia*, seems to preach biblical values as against Egyptian corruption (the frogs, as in Exodus, rain down at the end and a placard with a biblical quotation is flashed subliminally). Spielberg's *Prince of Egypt* is an example of how stereotypical notions about other peoples are popularized in films for children, while the more recent film *300* is transparently anti-Persian (Iranian). Other built-in prejudices in Hollywood movies are discussed in my article "Subliminal Filmic Reflections of Ancient Eastern Mediterranean Civilizations," *Quarterly Review of Film and Video* 22.4 (2005), 371–7.

23. One rare exception I discuss in the article cited above is Jim Jarmusch's independent film *Dead Man* (1995), which contains several scenes that allude to "Philistines" with the intention of deconstructing the frontier mentality. In one scene, Bible-reading pioneers quarrel over who should be the one to abuse

and sodomize the protagonist, William Blake, each claiming him to be his "Philistine."

24. George Sandys, *Relation of a Journey*, 151; Henry Maundrell's 1703 *A Journey from Aleppo to Jerusalem in 1697* (Beirut: Khayats, 1963 [reprint]), 111, 146; Edward Henry Palmer, *The Desert of the Exodus: Journeys on Foot in the Wilderness of the Forty Years Wandering* (Cambridge: Deighton, Bell, 1871), 297–9; and W. F. Lynch, *Narrative of the United States' Expedition to the River Jordan and the Dead Sea* (Philadelphia: Blanchard and Lea, 1852), 221, 223–4, 231, 242. The idea of "incestuous origin" Lynch applies to people near the Dead Sea comes from the story of Lot's daughters who beget children from their father in Genesis. For more on these travelers, see Chapter 3 and Chapter 11.

25. Thomas Fuller, *A Pisgah-Sight of Palestine* (London: M. F. for John Williams at ye Crowne in St. Paules Churchyard, 1650), 5.

26. Jonathan Haynes, *The Humanist as Traveler: George Sandys's "Relation of a Journey Begun An. Dom. 1610"* (Rutherford: Fairleigh Dickinson University Press, 1986), 15, 18.

27. Sandys, *Relation of a Journey*, 150–1, 218.

28. D. H. Lawrence, *Etruscan Places* (London: Folio Society, 1972 [1932]), 32. Though the Romans borrowed from Etruscan arts, material culture and religion, and converted the Etruscan script (originally from Cana'anite) into Latin, their tropes portray Etruscans as decadent.

29. "Sacred Geography," *Quarterly Review* XLIV (March 1854), 353–84.

30. John MacGregor, *The Rob Roy on the Jordan* (London: Murray, 1870).

31. Elizabeth Anne Finn, *Palestinian Peasantry: Notes on Their Clans, Warfare, Religion, and Laws* (London: Marshall, 1923), 5–6, 70–6, 86, 89–94, 69.

32. Lucas, *Canaan and Canada*, 21, 33, 42, 55–6.

33. Apart from reprints by Zionist publishers (as in a series called "America-Holy Land Studies"), one collection expressly intended to quote and promote anti-Arab sentiments is *Famous Travellers to the Holy Land* (London: Prion, 1989), compiled by Linda Osband.

34. Such a tack is taken by Joan Peters in *From Time Immemorial* (New York: Harper & Row, 1985), to which David Hirst responds adequately in the third edition of *The Gun and the Olive Branch* (London: Faber & Faber, 2003).

35. The Zionist claim system's assumption that "Arabs" in Palestine or Israel should go to one of the many Arab countries is too common to need documentation. A propagandistic book by Ramon Bennett, *Philistine: The Great Deception* (Jerusalem: Jerusalem Arm of Salvation, 1995), says that peace should not be made with the Palestinians because they are deceptive like the ancient Philistines. In a speech, Israeli ex-prime minister Yitzhak Shamir referred to the Palestinians as "Canaanites," as did Yitzhak Ben-Zvi, the second president of Israel (see Chapter 11). The "Arab" connection to "Ishmael" comes from the biblical story about how Abraham, at the urging of Sarah, throws his eldest son and Hagar into the desert—a story quite different from the high appraisal given to Isma'īl/Ishmael in the Qur'an.

36. Ilan Pappe, *The Ethnic Cleansing of Palestine* (Oxford: Oneworld Publications, 2006); Walid Khalidi, *All That Remains: The Palestinian Villages Occupied and Depopulated by Israel in 1948* (Washington: Institute for Palestine Studies, 1992).

37. Graham Philip, *Palestine Exploration Quarterly* 130 (1998): 172–3.

38. T. E. Levy, ed., *The Archaeology of Society in the Holy Land* (London: Leicester University Press, 1995).There are innumerable uses of "Holy Land" in book titles, among them: Yehoshua Ben-Arieh's *The Rediscovery of the Holy Land in the Nineteenth Century* (Jerusalem: The Magnes Press/The Hebrew University and Israel Exploration Society, second edition, 1983; first edition, 1979); Joel Elitzur's *Ancient Place-Names in the Holy Land: Preservation and History* (Jerusalem/Winona Lake, Indiana: The Hebrew University Magnes Press and Eisenbrauns, 2004); a clearly Zionist collection of papers from a conference held in Johannesburg during apartheid: Moshe Sharon, ed., *The Holy Land in History and Thought* (Leiden: E. J. Brill, 1988); and Bryan F. Le Beau and Menachem Mor, eds., *Pilgrims & Travelers to the Holy Land* (Omaha: Creighton University Press, 1996). A bibliographic search will produce many more such works.

39. Keith W. Whitelam's *The Invention of Ancient Israel: The Silencing of Palestinian History* (London: Routledge, 1996) studies some aspects of this industry.

40. One such descendant is Eilat Mazar, who came to the conclusion that a place uncovered in Silwan outside Jerusalem is David's Palace, for which even other Israeli archaeologists say there is no evidence (see Chapter 9). In the case of the Kuntilet 'Ajrud find, Johannes C. de Moor notes, in *The Rise of Yahwism: The Roots of Israelite Monotheism*, second edition (Leuven: Leuven University Press, 1997), 11, how J. H. Tigay and others attempt to "remove the name of Asherah from the inscriptions." Stretching happens with other finds like the *dwd* stone. On why the *dwd* stone could be fake or has been tampered with, see Niels Peter Lemche, "'House of David': The Tel Dan Inscription(s)," in *Jerusalem in Ancient History and Tradition*, ed. Thomas L. Thompson (London: T & T Clark, 2003), 46–67. For a discussion of Israeli archaeology, see Nadia Abu El-Haj's *Facts on the Ground: Archaeological Practice and Territorial Self-Fashioning in Israeli Society* (Chicago: University of Chicago Press, 2001).

41. Israel Finkelstein, *Archaeological Discoveries and Biblical Research* (Seattle: University of Washington Press, 1990), 37–84, and Amihai Mazar, *Archaeology of the Land of the Bible 10,000–586 B.C.E.* (New York: Doubleday, 1990), 328–38; Israel Finkelstein and Neil Asher Silberman, *The Bible Unearthed: Archaeology's New Vision of Ancient Israel and the Origin of Its Sacred Texts* (New York: Free Press, 2001); for comments, see Mark Zvi Brettler's "The New Biblical Historiography," in *Israel's Past in Present Research: Essays on Ancient Israelite Historiography*, ed. V. Philips Long (Winona Lake, Indiana: Eisenbrauns, 1999), 43–50. Jonathan Tubb's *The Canaanites* also subscribes to the theory that "Israelites" are later "Canaanites." This theory is not detected as dangerous by scholars keen to debunk biblical historicity: Nur Masalha in his otherwise excellent chapter on biblical un-historicity in *The Bible and Zionism* (London: Zed Books, 2007), 253–4, seems to praise Finkelstein and others for the Israelites-are-Canaanites theory, praise I have also heard from some Palestinian archaeologists. But such a theory in effect appropriates Cana'anite culture as it supplies a replacement for old stories of conquest and other foundations of Zionist claims which have been shown to lack historicity.

42. There are exceptions. One in particular is a historian from Syria, Firas es Sawwah, who offers some original perspectives and keeps apace with Western scholarship.

43. Thomas L. Thompson, in email correspondence, May 28, 2009. I was earlier alerted to this fact by a Syrian Aramaic expert in Ma'lulah, one of the few

places where Aramaic is still spoken, when he talked of square Aramaic as a late script development. When I asked an expert at the École Biblique in Jerusalem (whose name I withhold because I have not asked him, and he is unlikely to agree) he concurred with the above assessment that "square Hebrew" is an act of appropriation of square Aramaic by present Jews.

44. On transcription, to highlight one of the examples I provide in other chapters, even as it acknowledges the exact similarity of Ugaritic to Arabic, Peter T. Daniels and William Bright's *The World's Writing Systems* (New York: Oxford University Press, 1996), 92, uses square Hebrew to transcribe inscriptions. The article on "Aramaic" in *The Anchor Bible Dictionary* (New York: Doubleday, 1992) is pretty clear in explaining how "square Hebrew" developed later from Aramaic script, so is the *Ecyclopaedia Judaica* (1971 edition). However, the *Anchor* article on "Hebrew Scripts," as well as the generally excellent source *The World's Writing Systems* (89), still insist on a "Paleo-Hebrew" and even an "ancient Hebrew," though both mention that the latter derived from "Phoenician"; in fact, it *is* "Phoenician" (or rather later Cana'anite), and there is no reason to consider it an "ancient Hebrew." See remarks on the "Gezer Calendar" in Chapter 5 and note 9 there and Chapter 7 (note 16).

45. Seymour Gitin, Trude Dothan, and Joseph Naveh, "A Royal Dedicatory Inscription from Ekron," *Israel Exploration Fund Journal* 47 (1997): 1–15. While the authors argue that this inscription is not completely "Hebreo-Philistine" they still speak of such a script for the Philistines (13–14). For additional discussion, see Chapters 5, 7, and 10.

46. Only a couple of the examples I give of such names have been mentioned in scholarship. It is useful to note Burkert's *The Orientalizing Revolution*, especially page 153. Recognizing "Canaanite" and Egyptian influences is a major aim of Martin Bernal's *Black Athena: The Afroasiatic Roots of Classical Civilization. Vol. I: The Fabrication of Ancient Greece, 1785–1985* (New Brunswick: Rutgers University Press, 1987), although unfortunately the book has become embroiled in racial and classicist controversies that are specific to U.S. and Western scholarship. Bernal holds contradictory attitudes toward Israel (is it a colonial state or an affirmation of Jewish strength?), and his interest in "Canaanite/Phoenician" influence involves a mild form of appropriation, as he wants to connect Jews to "Canaanites" in a manner similar to older scholars like M. C. Astour and Cyrus Gordon, and a renegade movement within Zionism whose followers call themselves "Canaanites" (for more on this movement, see Chapter 11).

CHAPTER 2

1. Much of the atheistic criticism popular today, such as Michel Onfray's *Atheist Manifesto: The Case Against Christianity, Judaism, and Islam*, trans. Jeremy Leggatt (New York: Arcade Publishing, 2007; original French edition, 2005), seems misguided in that it launches polemics against the doctrines and practices of Christianity and Islam, and to a lesser extent Judaism—as if this could disprove the existence of God—rather than probing the origin of these religions. Karen Armstrong provides a perspective on the God idea in *A History of God: From Abraham to the Present: The 4000-year Quest for God* (London: Vintage, 1999 [1993]). Armstrong, however, often falls into repeating old myths, as when, in *The Bible: The Biography* (London: Atlantic Books, 2008), she talks

of "the Hebrew words that God had spoken on Sinai" (211) or that "Yahweh had ousted El in the divine assembly" by the eighth century (16) when the much later Dead Sea Scrolls tell us otherwise.

2. See my article "Updike's New Versions of Myth in America," *Modern Fiction Studies* 37 (1991), 25–33. My reference here to some U.S. writers comes from a belief that the initial brutal effects of colonizing the American continent and its landscape brought reminders of primal processes that eventually led to creative perceptions in some of these writers who were later attempting to make sense of their environment and history.

3. There is a trend to exaggerate the influence of Babylonian and Egyptian mythology on "Canaan," and so to underestimate Cana'anite specificity; as for example in Karen Armstrong's *A History of God* (17), and Tom Harpur's *The Pagan Christ: Recovering the Lost Light* (Toronto: Thomas Allen, 2004), which is discussed later in this chapter.

4. It has been suggested that Moses adopted Yaw/Yahweh from the Midianites (noted by Armstrong, *A History of God*, 30). However, that stays within the biblical narrative, though a Bedouin origin is not unlikely! A good summary on the god Il / El (90–3), but a less satisfactory one on Yahweh (105–12), and other regional gods and heroes is provided in David Leeming's *Jealous Gods, Chosen People: The Mythology of the Middle East* (Oxford: Oxford University Press, 2004). Monotheism that predates later biblical narratives had been attempted in the region, not only in Egypt but later in Mesopotamia. One of these episodes is uncovered more in Erik Hornun's *Akhenaten and the Religion of Light*, trans. David Lorton (Ithaca: Cornell University Press, 1999; original German edition 1995).

5. George Smith, *The Chaldean Account of Genesis, Containing the Description of the Creation, the Fall of Man, the Deluge, the Tower of Babel, the Times of the Patriarchs, and Nimrod; Babylonian Fables, and Legends of the Gods; from the Cuneiform Inscriptions* (London: Sampson Low, Marston, Searle, and Rivington, 1876).

6. Quite puzzling is a much later fragment preserved by Eusebius from Philo of Byblos, who reports the myth that [the Greek father god] Kronos, "whom the Phoenicians call El," sacrificed his son Ieoud, "the Only"; *Philo of Byblos: The Phoenician History* (Washington, D.C.: Catholic Biblical Association of America, 1981), 63.

7. James Bennett Pritchard, *Ancient Near Eastern Texts Relating to the Old Testament*, third edition (Princeton: Princeton University Press, 1969); a useful general introduction to antecedents is John B. Gabel et al., *The Bible as Literature: An Introduction*, fifth edition (New York and Oxford: Oxford University Press, 2006).

8. In *Egypt, Canaan, and Israel in Ancient Times* (Princeton: Princeton University Press, 1992), 422, Egyptologist Donald B. Redford points out the ironies in Cana'anite folklore memories being copied and appropriated in Greek and Hebrew stories, the Sojourn and Exodus. See the discussion in Gabel et al., *The Bible as Literature*, and the entry "Exodus," in *The Oxford Companion to the Bible*, ed. Bruce M. Metzger and Michael D. Coogan (New York: Oxford University Press, 1993).

9. Angel Manuel Rodriguez, "Ancient Near Eastern Parallels to the Bible and the Question of Revelation and Inspiration," *Journal of the Adventist Theological Society* 12 (2001): 43–64, 62, 64; italics in the original.

10. T. C. Mitchell, *The Bible in the British Museum: Interpreting the Evidence* (London: British Museum, 1988), 24, 69.

11. E. C. B. MacLaurin, "A Comparison of Two Aspects of Ugaritic and Christian Theology," *Oriental Studies: Presented to Benedikt S. J. Isserlin*, eds. R. Y. Ebied and M. J. L. Young (Leiden: E. J. Brill, 1980), 76.

12. R. Alter and F. Kermode, eds., *The Literary Guide to the Bible* (Cambridge: Harvard University Press, 1987), 1; Northrop Frye, *The Great Code: The Bible and Literature* (New York: Harcourt Brace Jovanovich, 1982), xviii, xxii.

13. David Hume, "Natural History of Religion," in *Four Dissertations* (Bristol: Thoemmes Press, 1995), 61–2, 1, 3, 48.

14. Noted by Johannes C. de Moor in *The Rise of Yahwism: The Roots of Israelite Monotheism*, second edition (Leuven: Leuven University Press, 1997), 11. For a description of this discovery, see Zeev Meshel, "Kuntilet ʿAjrud: A Religious Centre from the Time of the Judaean Monarchy on the Border of Sinai" (Jerusalem: The Israel Museum, 1978 [Cat. No. 175; items reportedly transferred to Egypt after the peace treaty?]).

15. Judith M. Hadley, *The Cult of Asherah in Ancient Israel and Judah: Evidence for a Hebrew Goddess* (Cambridge: Cambridge University Press, 2000), 209.

16. That confusion was assisted by Masoretic substitution of "Adonai" for Yahweh in several instances in the manuscript ("Adon" = Lord; also the name of a separate god).

17. Jonathan Kirsch, *God Against the Gods: The History of the War between Monotheism and Polytheism* (New York: Viking Compass, 2004), 21. Kirsch shares with Karen Armstrong the habit of romanticizing and embellishing biblical accounts as if they were historical while also briefly indicating here and there that they are mythic or lack historical support.

18. Other suggestions of polytheism come from the reference to "sons of God [El]" in Genesis 6: 2 and Exodus 6: 2–3. Yet, despite the presence of "Council of Il (El)" in the Hebrew, the Stone Edition of *The Tanach* still insists on this translation of Psalm 82: "God stands in the Divine assembly, in the midst of judges shall He judge" (New York: Mesorah Publications, 1996). The New Revised Standard Version (1989) has: "God has taken his place in the divine council: in the midst of the gods he holds judgment."

19. Julie A. Duncan, "The Book of Deuteronomy," article in *Encyclopedia of the Dead Sea Scrolls*, 2 Vols., eds. Lawrence Schiffman and James C. VanderKam (Oxford: Oxford University Press, 2000). See the notes in some scholarly Bible versions and *The Complete Parallel Bible* (New York: Oxford University Press, 1993).

20. *The HarperCollins Bible Commentary*, rev. edition (San Francisco: Harper-SanFrancisco, 2000), 212, has the following comment on Deuteronomy 32: 8–9: "Israel's story begins with the nation's election at the time of the origin of all peoples (vv. 8–9). When parceling out the peoples of the earth to their gods, God kept Israel as a personal inheritance." For more analysis of this Deuteronomy passage, examine current translations and commentaries as well as *The Complete Parallel Bible*.

21. Philo of Byblos equates the Greek god Kronos with Il / El (Creator in the Canaʿanite pantheon) and Zeus with Baʿal, both thunder and rain gods (*Philo of Byblos: The Phoenician History*, 55, 63); noted in B. C. Dietrich, *The Origins of Greek Religion* (Berlin: de Gruyter, 1973), 44–65. Other scholars discuss such influences, among them: Walter Burkert, *The Orientalizing Revolution:*

Near Eastern Influence on Greek Culture in the Early Archaic Period, 1984, trans. Margaret E. Pinder and Walter Burkert (Cambridge: Harvard University Press, 1992); Martin Bernal, *Black Athena: The Afroasiatic Roots of Classical Civilization. Vol. I: The Fabrication of Ancient Greece, 1785–1985* (New Brunswick: Rutgers University Press, 1987); and Robert Turcan, *The Cults of the Roman Empire*, trans. Antonia Nevill (Oxford: Blackwell, 1996; original French edition 1992). For the equation of Baʿal and Zeus in the fragments remaining of Philo's work, see *Philo of Byblos: The Phoenician History*, 41.

22. Al Fayrūz ʿAbādi, *al qamūs al muḥīṭ* (Beirut: Al-Resalah, 1986).

23. Matthew (1: 1–17) connects Jesus to the main line of Old Testament genealogy, while Luke has a somewhat different genealogy and takes Jesus back further to Adam (Luke 3: 23–37).

24. "Some scholars have proposed that the book [Job] was originally written in Aramaic or Arabic," *The HarperCollins Bible Commentary*, 369. Jerome more definitively states in the preface to his translation of Daniel (392 CE): "For we must bear in mind that Daniel and Ezra, the former especially, were written in Hebrew letters, but in the Chaldee language, as was one section of Jeremiah; and further, that Job has much affinity with Arabic," quoted in Ronald H. Worth, Jr., *Bible Translations: A History Through Source Documents* (Jefferson, N.C.: McFarland, 1992), 22.

25. F. Nietzsche, *Beyond Good and Evil*, Chapter 3: The Religious Mood, Section 52.

26. Freya Stark, *The Journey's Echo: Selections from Freya Stark* (London: John Murray, 1963), 5.

27. Christopher Hitchens, another popular atheist, lists many other instances of mythological virgin births from Perseus and Krishna to Genghis Khan, in *God Is Not Great: How Religion Poisons Everything* (Toronto: McClelland & Stewart, 2007), 23.

28. Harpur, *The Pagan Christ*, 27, 77–8, 39–40; Harpur does not note that "Iusa" is the same name used for Jesus in Arabic (ʿIssa), which is close to "Jesus" anyway if one takes out the Greek ending and allows for the Germanic "J." See the discussion by D. M. Murdock (Acharya S), *Christ in Egypt: The Horus-Jesus Connection* (n.p.: Stellar House Publishing, 2009), 322–4.

29. Thomas L. Thompson, *The Messiah Myth: The Near Eastern Roots of Jesus and David* (London: Jonathan Cape, 2006).

30. MacLaurin, "A Comparison of Two Aspects of Ugaritic and Christian Theology," 72–82.

31. J. M. Robertson, *Pagan Christs*, second edition (London: Watts & Co., 1911 [1903]); discussion of Christ predates even these books, including such early works as David Friedrich Strauss's 1835 *Das Leben Jesu* on the gospels as messianic construction and *The World's Sixteen Crucified Christs* by Kersey Graves, first published in 1875.

32. See Mark 15: 34 and Matthew 27: 46 for this sentence: "Eli [Elahi], Eli, lama sabachthani?" traditionally translated as "My God, My God, why have you forsaken me?" (Other interpretations are possible!) One wonders if the gospels in this case reflect the worship of Il / El and that Jesus is expressing a popular, not strictly mainstream Jewish, belief system that still gave allegiance to the Supreme God Il (El), or a generic god at least, rather than only to the national god of the Israelites, Yahweh. While Matthew's genealogy tries to trace Jesus, fallaciously through his non-father Joseph, to David and Abraham, Luke, as

mentioned above, has a different genealogy. The gospel of John, however, provides additional clues that Jesus is not to be associated with the Israelites or their god. John 1: 43–7 relates a tit for tat between Jesus and Nathanael. Nathanael, thinking Jesus cannot hear, asks the satiric question "Can anything good come out of Nazareth?" to which Jesus retorts, in apparent irony (v. 47): "Here is truly an Israelite in whom there is no deceit." The point is not just whether Jesus is responding in kind by typifying Israelites as deceptive. Rather, more importantly, the comeback clearly implies that Jesus does not consider himself to be an Israelite. Curiously, the NRSV and NJB agree on basically the same sense of what Nathanael and Jesus say, but both NAB and REB translations (*Complete Parallel Bible*) appear to *reverse* the meaning of what Jesus says in a way that does not make sense in that context! (REB: "Here is an Israelite worthy of the name; there is nothing false in him"; NAB: "Here is a true Israelite. There is no duplicity in him.") John 8 is also useful in examining how Jesus addresses Jews. Such texts (to which one could add Sozomen's observations from the fifth century; see Chapter 3) also carry implications related to the religious and ethnic composition of the population in those periods, which should be studied along with other sources.

CHAPTER 3

1. Pertinent to what I say here are books by Thomas L. Thompson: *The Mythic Past: Biblical Archaeology and the Myth of Israel* (New York: Basic Books, 1999) (also published as *The Bible in History: How Writers Create a Past* [London: Jonathan Cape, 1999]) and *The Messiah Myth: The Near Eastern Roots of Jesus and David* (London: Jonathan Cape, 2006). Regarding Jesus, there is a long tradition of seeing him as an accumulation of traits from previous mythologies, discussed under "Pagan Christs" in Chapter 2. Some standard sources suggest support for what I say here about pagan ancestry, such as several entries in *The Oxford Companion to the Bible*, eds. Bruce M. Metzger and Michael D. Coogan (New York: Oxford University Press, 1993) and a valuable guide by John B. Gabel, Charles B. Wheeler, and Anthony D. York, *The Bible as Literature: An Introduction*, fifth edition (New York: Oxford University Press, 2006).

2. Hawthorne's short story "The May-pole of Merry Mount" (1835) and Achebe's *Things Fall Apart* (1959), Chapter 22, both agree on this point about the puritanical demonization of Ba'al.

3. Bertolt Brecht, *Baal* (1918–20), trans. Peter Tegel, in *Collected Plays* (London: Methuen, 1970; New York: Pantheon, 1971), Vol. I, 1–58. Golding's novel was published in 1954.

4. See Constantine's letter quoted in Hunt's book (see note 7, below). It can be argued that using the sites for Christian purposes was made easy or convenient because of connections to earlier myths. For example, the Milk Grotto adjacent to the Nativity site was associated with a fertility god, Adonis, who dies and is resurrected and for whom (Jerome reports) the pagan women of Bethlehem used to weep. On the other hand, priestly arguments reverse this thinking by saying that the Romans suppressed the places where Christian events occurred by placing pagan temples there.

5. See Chapter 2, note 21, concerning eastern Mediterranean influences on Greek and Roman mythology and the fragments from a lost work by Philo

of Byblos, which leave little doubt about the direct links between Greek and earlier Cana'anite/Phoenician mythology.

6. Twain's 1869 *Innocents Abroad; or The New Pilgrim's Progress*, Chapter 53; Edward Robinson, *Biblical Researches in Palestine, Mount Sinai and Arabia Petræa* (London: John Murray, 1841), II: 80.

7. E. D. Hunt, *Holy Pilgrimage in the Late Roman Empire AD 312–460* (Oxford: Clarendon Press, 1982), 102, 136.

8. Sozomen, *Historia Ecclesiastica* Book II, Chapters 4–5, who continues to describe the measure taken by Constantine to punish practice of former rites; discussed in Elizabeth Key Fowden, "Sharing Holy Places," *Common Knowledge* 8.1 (2002), 124–46, 127. Sozomen's statement also indirectly enlightens the issue of the ethnic and religious composition of Palestine, and questions monolithic assumptions about the population in this or any other period. See Chapter 2, note 32, for the potential implications of John 1: 47.

9. For such additional stories about Abraham, see Sayyid Mahmūd el Qumni, *an-nabi ibrahīm wa et tarīkh al majhūl* [*Prophet Abraham and the Unknown History*] (Cairo: Madbūli es Saghīr, 1996).

10. Ernest L. Martin, *The Temples That Jerusalem Forgot* (Portland: Associates for Scriptural Knowledge, 2000).

11. An imaginative rendering is Kanan Makiya's *The Rock: A Tale of Seventh-Century Jerusalem* (New York: Vintage, 2002). Identifying both "temples" with the Muslim site (obscuring the distinctions among the three) is carelessly, if not intentionally, done in the media, as in an article by Tom Mueller, "Herod," *National Geographic* (December 2008). A reader of Mueller would think that all Palestinians are nomadic Bedouins.

12. John Strange, "Herod and Jerusalem: The Hellenization of an Oriental City," *Jerusalem in Ancient History and Tradition* (London: T & T Clark, 2003; 97–113), 112.

13. Noteworthy is Kamal Salibi's theory that the events of ancient Israel occurred in the Arabian Peninsula, as he demonstrates through the repetition of place names.

14. A typical example is Rivka Gonen's *Contested Holiness: Jewish, Muslim, and Christian Perspectives on the Temple Mount* (Jersey City, N. J.: KTAV Publishing House, 2003).

15. The Islamic Museum in Topcapi (the Ottoman sultan's government center in Istanbul) displays all sorts of incredible items: Prophet Muhammad's sandals and hair from his beard, King David's sword and Jacob's turban, surprisingly un-aged. Unexpectedly, the museum also displays a gold sheet ripped off from the Ka'ba, presumably brought there after the Ottoman armies occupied Mecca.

16. Hilton Obenzinger, *American Palestine: Melville, Twain, and the Holy Land Mania* (Princeton: Princeton University Press, 1999), 7.

17. "Sacred Geography," *Quarterly Review* XLIV (March 1854): 353–84, 378.

18. Meron Benvenisti, *Sacred Landscape: The Buried History of the Holy Land since 1948* (Berkeley: University of California Press, 2000), 273–9. See also Chapter 10 on Benvenisti.

19. The old photo, about 1880, shows Beit Jala in the background.

20. For an instance of Rachel's Tomb being described as a "Turkish structure," see Henry Maundrell's 1703 account, *A Journey from Aleppo to Jerusalem in 1697* (Beirut: Khayats, 1963), 117. In an unlikely concession, Nadia Abu El-Haj, *Facts on the Ground: Archaeological Practice and Territorial Self-Fashioning*

in Israeli Society (Chicago: University of Chicago Press, 2001), 281, appears to accept some historicity for Joseph's Tomb: "It [the attack on it] needs to be understood in relation to a colonial-national history in which modern political rights have been substantiated in and expanded through the material signs of historic presence." Additionally, El-Haj does not seem to see the lack of connection between what is ancient "Israelite" and what is Jewish tradition, or the traps that result from traditions that have been kept by Islam. Who started a certain tradition and when seems now very difficult to answer.

21. "Netanyahu to present Obama with Twain's Holy Land memoir," *Haaretz*, May 19, 2009; available at: http://www.haaretz.com/hasen/spages/1086234.html. Twain's *Innocents Abroad*, however, debunks sacred geography and satirizes biblical narratives, but because of its complex narrative ironies, isolated passages can be exploited to demonstrate views contrary to what Twain intends.

22. Both excellent books, they still fall into the easy conclusion that such travelers vilify Palestine's landscape: Nur Masalha, *The Bible and Zionism* (London: Zed Books, 2007), 44, and Raja Shehadeh, *Palestinian Walks: Forays into a Vanishing Landscape* (New York: Scribner, 2007), xiv, xv, 10.

23. Melville's first novel *Typee* drew sharp attacks from missionaries and fundamentalists, and its first edition was published in the U.S. only after the offending passages were excised. For Melville's views about missions in Palestine and Syria during his 1856–7 visit, see his *Journals* (Evanston and Chicago: Northwestern University Press and the Newberry Library, 1989), 91–94, where he ridicules their aims and actions.

24. Melville, *Journals*, 94.

25. Herman Melville, *Clarel: A Poem and Pilgrimage in the Holy Land*, 1876 (New York: Hendricks House, 1960), II.xvi.106.

26. Twain, *Innocents Abroad*, Chapter 45.

27. Twain, *Innocents Abroad*, Chapter 46.

28. This process is explained in my articles "The Death Plot in Melville's *Clarel*," *ESQ* 27 (1981), 14–27, and "Ancient Lands," *Companion to Herman Melville*, ed. Wyn Kelley (London: Blackwell, 2006), 129–45.

29. Melville, *Clarel* II.xi.83–94; *Journals*, 89 and note on 574. Strangely, the editors of this edition of the *Journals* decide to use "terrific" instead of Melville's final "ghastly." This rendition could mislead readers since "terrific" is now often used colloquially to mean something like "wonderful," a sense not available in Melville's time! Melville tried several words to describe the theology: "diabolical," "terrible," and "terrific," but (as an editorial note is forced to explain) all were consecutively "cancelled" and finally replaced by "ghastly." On the pyramids and "the idea of Jehovah born here," see *Journals* 75–8.

30. See http://www.tourism.gov.il/tourism/default/homepage.aspx. See also the discussion in Chapter 1, under the section "National Myths."

CHAPTER 4

1. To her credit, Elaine Pagels mentions the Egyptian peasant as a discoverer many times in her *The Gnostic Gospels* (New York: Random House, 1979).

2. Simon B. Parker, ed., *Ugaritic Narrative Poetry* (Atlanta: Scholars Press, 1997), 157.

3. On the *f/p* sound and transcription, see my discussion in Chapter 10 and note 34.

4. For a fuller discussion, see E. C. B. MacLaurin, "A Comparison of Two Aspects of Ugaritic and Christian Theology," *Oriental Studies: Presented to Benedikt S. J. Isserlin*, eds. R. Y. Ebied and M. J. L. Young (Leiden: Brill, 1980), 72–82.

5. *The Cuneiform Alphabetic Texts: from Ugarit, Ras Ibn Hani and Other Places* (KTU), ed. Manfried Dietrich, et al., second enlarged edition (Münster: Ugarit-Verlag, 1995), 4.

6. See discussion and note 21 in Chapter 2.

7. As I document in Chapter 2, note 24, Jerome and some commentators suggest that the Book of Job (Ayyūb), acclaimed as one of the most profound and poetic books of the Old Testament, is Arabic in origin.

8. Frank Moore Cross, *Canaanite Myth and Hebrew Epic: Essays in the History of Ancient Israel* (Cambridge: Harvard University Press, 1973), vii.

9. "Ugaritic," in *The Oxford Companion to the Bible*, eds. Bruce M. Metzger and Michael D. Coogan (New York: Oxford University Press, 1993).

10. William L. Moran, "The Hebrew Language in its Northwest Semitic Background," in G. Ernest Wright, ed., *The Bible and the Ancient Near East* (Garden City: Doubleday, 1961), 58; Robert Alter, *The Art of Biblical Narrative* (London: George Allen and Unwin, 1981), 13; similarly, Jonas C. Greenfield, "The Hebrew Bible and Canaanite Literature," in R. Alter and F. Kermode, eds., *The Literary Guide to the Bible* (Cambridge: Harvard University Press, 1987), 546; Foster R. McCurley, *Ancient Myths and Biblical Faith: Scriptural Transformations* (Philadelphia: Fortress Press, 1983), cover and viii–ix.

11. Wilfred G. E. Watson and Nicholas Wyatt, eds., *Handbook of Ugaritic Studies* (Leiden: Brill, 1999), 5, 82, 89, 614.

12. Peter T. Daniels and William Bright, *The World's Writing Systems* (New York: Oxford University Press, 1996), 92.

13. In addition to *The World's Writing Systems*, see as an example Niels Peter Lemche's excellent critical essay "'House of David': The Tel Dan Inscription(s)," in Thomas L. Thompson, ed., *Jerusalem in Ancient History and Tradition* (London: T & T Clark, 2003), 46–67, which nevertheless transcribes the obvious "Phoenician" in square Hebrew.

14. On why *f* is at least a strong possibility rather than *p*, see discussion in Chapter 10 and note 34 there.

15. J. C. L. Gibson, ed., *Canaanite Myths and Legends*, second edition (Edinburgh: T & T Clark, 1978); N. Wyatt, *Religious Texts from Ugarit: The Words of Ilimilku and His Colleagues* (Sheffield: Sheffield Academic Press, 1998); Wyatt, despite his good translation effort, discounts Arabic in his introduction and has the usual habit of mentioning "Hebrew and Arabic" and "Hebrew, Aramaic" thus disregarding rules of importance.

16. Mark S. Smith, *The Origins of Biblical Monotheism: Israel's Polytheistic Background and the Ugaritic Texts* (Oxford: Oxford University Press, 2001), 12.

17. Smith, *The Origins of Biblical Monotheism*, 43.

18. Manfried Dietrich, "Aspects of the Babylonian Impact on Ugaritic Literature and Religion," in N. Wyatt, et al., *Ugarit, Religion and Culture* (Münster: Ugarit-Verlag, 1996), 37. See also the discussion about Ugaritic and Arabic above, and Manfried Dietrich and Oswald Loretz, "The Ugaritic Script," in Watson and Wyatt, eds., *Handbook of Ugaritic Studies*, 81–90. Another discussion is Alan S. Kaye's, "Does Ugaritic Go with Arabic in Semitic Genealogical Sub-classification?" *Folia Orientalia* 28 (1991): 115–28.

CHAPTER 5

1. See remarks in Chapter 1 (and notes 18 and 21) and Chapter 6 (and note 10 there) for more on the terms "Phoenician" and "Cana'anite."
2. Marshall McLuhan, *Understanding Media: The Extensions of Man* (New York: McGraw-Hill, 1964), 87.
3. The adjective "true" is used by Steven Roger Fischer, *A History of Language* (London: Reaktion, 1999), 97, 108.
4. Quoted in Keith Whitelam's *The Invention of Ancient Israel: The Silencing of Palestinian History* (London: Routledge, 1996), 83–4.
5. Graeme Barker and Tom Rasmussen, *The Etruscans* (Oxford: Blackwell, 1998), 96–7.
6. Martin Bernal, *Black Athena: The Afroasiatic Roots of Classical Civilization. Vol. I: The Fabrication of Ancient Greece, 1785–1985* (New Brunswick: Rutgers University Press, 1987), 413.
7. Peter T. Daniels and William Bright, *The World's Writing Systems* (New York: Oxford University Press, 1996), 88.
8. Leonard Shlain, *The Goddess Versus the Alphabet: The Conflict Between Word and Image* (New York: Viking, 1998), 68–71.
9. Robert K. Logan, *The Fifth Language: Learning a Living in the Computer Age* (Toronto: Stoddard, 1995), 144; Marc Zvi Brettler's *The Creation of History in Ancient Israel* (London: Routledge, 1995), 143; Thomas L. Thompson's *The Messiah Myth: The Near Eastern Roots of Jesus and David* (London: Jonathan Cape, 2006); H. W. F. Saggs, *Civilization Before Greece and Rome* (New Haven: Yale University Press, 1989), 83. The "Gezer" calendar is so transparently unlike square Hebrew, and so close to Moabite and "Phoenician" signs of that period, it is incredible how anyone can claim it as Hebrew.
10. Saggs, *Civilization Before Greece and Rome*, 83–4.
11. Michael D. Coogan, ed., *The Oxford History of the Biblical World* (New York: Oxford University Press, 1998), 58.
12. See the discussion of Aramaic and Hebrew in Chapters 1, 7, and 10.
13. Jorge Luis Borges, "The Library of Babel," in *Labyrinths: Selected Stories and Other Writings* (New York: New Directions, 1964); Michel Foucault, *Language, Counter-Memory, Practice: Selected Essays and Interviews* (Oxford: Basil Blackwell, 1977), 29–31, 51, 60, 66–7.
14. David Tracy, "Writing," in Mark C. Taylor, ed., *Critical Terms for Religious Studies* (Chicago: University of Chicago Press, 1998), 392.
15. The translation is taken from N. Wyatt, *Religious Texts from Ugarit: The Words of Ilimilku and His Colleagues* (Sheffield: Sheffield Academic Press, 1998), 78, and the transcription from J. C. L. Gibson, ed., *Canaanite Myths and Legends*, second edition (Edinburgh: T & T Clark, 1978), 49. I suggest that the third-to-last line could be rendered, "I show thunderbolts that the sky cannot contain."
16. Manfried Dietrich, "Aspects of the Babylonian Impact on Ugaritic Literature and Religion," in N. Wyatt, et al., *Ugarit, Religion and Culture* (Münster: Ugarit-Verlag, 1996), 42.

CHAPTER 6

1. Sharon Herbert has given this lecture about her research on second-century BCE seals in various places. See http://www.archaeological.org/webinfo.

php?page=10224&lid=145, among other sites. For a marvelous recording of the extent of Canaʿanite / "Phoenician" civilization across the Mediterranean, see Sabatino Moscati, ed., *The Phoenicians* (New York: Rizzoli, 1999), originally published as *iFenici* (Milan: Bompiani, 1988).

2. Trude and Moshe Dothan, *People of the Sea: The Search for the Philistines* (New York: Scribner, 1992); Seymour Gitin, Trude Dothan, and Joseph Naveh, "A Royal Dedicatory Inscription from Ekron," *Israel Exploration Fund Journal* 47 (1997), 1–15. Jonathan N. Tubb's *Canaanites* (London: British Museum Press, 1998) and the work of Israeli archaeologist Israel Finkelstein, among others, suggest the theory about "Israelites" being "Canaanites." Among mid-twentieth-century Israeli intelligentsia, there developed a now largely defunct "Canaanite" movement.

3. Eric M. Meyers, "Israel and Its Neighbors Then and Now: Revisionist History and the Quest for History in the Middle East Today"; available at: http://www.bibleinterp.com/articles/emeyers.shtml

4. This misunderstanding does not need documentation as it is so common in the West and of course in Zionist scholarship. A work like Barbara Tuchman's classic Zionist interpretation of British history in relation to Palestine, *Bible and Sword: England and Palestine from the Bronze Age to Balfour* (New York: Ballantine, 1984 [1956]), is replete with this typical confusion between present Jews and ancient people: the Hebrews and "the modern survivors of the Old Testament" have been gathered from "exile" in the "restoration of Israel" with the partial (she insists it is partial) help of British biblically affected thinking along the same lines.

5. For an Israeli example see my discussion of author Abraham B. Yeshoshua's confused use of "Israelite," "Jew," and "Israeli" in "Editing in a Time of Dispossession," *Profession 2009* (Modern Language Association), 150–1. I suggest that even critics of the Zionist system don't make the distinction: for example, both Nur Masalha, in a good chapter about the un-historicity of the Bible in *The Bible and Zionism* (London: Zed Books, 2007), and Nadia Abu El-Haj in her competent analysis of the role of archaeology in Israeli society in *Facts on the Ground: Archaeological Practice and Territorial Self-Fashioning in Israeli Society* (Chicago: University of Chicago Press, 2001), fail to notice that "Jewish" and "Israelite" are altogether two different things. In his keen criticism of traditional biblical history, Masalha goes so far as to praise theorists like Israel Finkelstein for the appropriate notion that "Israelites" emerged peacefully from "Canaanites." Shlomo Sand, who demolishes Zionist mythology about a "Jewish people" and their "exile" and "return" (see below), does not seem to make the distinction clear between Judaism and the biblical tradition about "Israelites."

6. For more, see the discussion of DNA and other studies in Chapter 11. On issues related to population, see the works I mention in Chapter 1, and specifically Thomas L. Thompson in his *The Mythic Past* and an article "Biblical Archaeology and the Politics of Nation Building," *Bible and Interpretation* (August 21, 2009) (available at http://www.bibleinterp.com/opeds), an expanded version of which appears in *Holy Land Studies* 9.2 (2009). On David, see Thompson's *The Messiah Myth: The Near Eastern Roots of Jesus and David* (London: Jonathan Cape, 2006) and its references to other studies about the un-historicity of a King David, and also Marc Zvi Brettler, *The Creation of History in Ancient Israel* (London: Routledge, 1995), 143. On the myth of Exodus, see Chapter 7 (note 11).

7. Arthur Koestler, *The Thirteenth Tribe* (New York: Random House, 1976); Paul Wexler, *The Non-Jewish Origins of Sephardic Jews* (New York: SUNY, 1966). Shlomo Sand's book *The Invention of the Jewish People*, trans. Yael Lotan (London: Verso, 2009) was published in Hebrew as *mattai ve'ekh humtza ha'am hayehudi?* [*When and How the Jewish People Was Invented*] (Tel Aviv: Resling, 2008). The main section on Berbers is on pages 199–210; on Hasmonean forced conversion and later centuries, pages 154–81; on the Palestinian fellahin being "the people of the land," the descendents of the most ancient populations, pages 182–9. A review of the Hebrew edition by Israel Bartal "Inventing an Invention" criticizes Sand's historical method but does not challenge his facts (available at: http://www.haaretz.com/hasen/spages/999386.html). Another review, by Raymond Deane in *The Electronic Intifada* (October 22, 2009), notes Sand's fears of academic censure since he admits having "waited until he was a full professor" before publishing the book. For more on this topic see Uri Avnery's "On Jewish History: The Lion and the Gazelle," available at: http://www.counterpunch.org/avnery04212008.html

8. Nikos Kokkinos, *The Herodian Dynasty: Origins, Role in Society and Eclipse* (Sheffield: Sheffield Academic Press, 1998), 28.

9. A report about a DNA study conducted by Dr. Pierre Zalloua, Assistant Professor of Medicine at the AUB Faculty of Medicine, is entitled "Are We Phoenicians After All?" *AUBulletin Today* 6.6 (May 2005). Noteworthy here is the National Geographic genographic project.

10. Whether "Phoenician" is a Greek term or a local one that became more widespread is not as material here as the way it is being employed (see Chapter 1, notes 18–21, and Chapter 5 and note 1 there). A competent discussion of "Phoenicianism" is Asher Kaufman's *Reviving Phoenicia: The Search for Identity in Lebanon* (London: I. B. Tauris, 2004). There was a strong literary movement in mid-twentieth-century Lebanon and Syria that went back to ancient regional cultures, and in terms of politics the idea of regional unity is represented in such parties as the Syrian Nationalist Party.

11. A source on aspects of national identity is the double issue I edited of the *Palestine-Israel Journal* 8.4/9.1 (2002), particularly Yoav Peled's "Inter-Jewish Challenges to Israeli Identity" and Issam Nassar's "Reflections on the Writing of the History of Palestinian Identity."

12. See the discussion, mostly interviewing Israeli archaeologists, in Nadia Abu El-Haj, *Facts on the Ground*, 249–58. On "national consciousness," see Rashid Khalidi, *Palestinian Identity: The Construction of Modern National Consciousness* (New York: Columbia University Press, 1997).

13. Amin Maalouf, *On Identity* (London: Harvell Press, 2000; original French edition, 1996), 17, 81–9, 129.

14. R. Radhakrishnan, "Postcoloniality and the Boundaries of Identity," in Linda Martin Alcoff and Eduardo Mendieta, eds., *Identities: Race, Class, Gender, and Nationality* (Oxford: Blackwell, 2003), 318. A well-known discussion of nationalist constructions is Benedict Anderson's *Imagined Communities* (London: Verso, 1991).

CHAPTER 7

1. Ranajit Guha, "Dominance without Hegemony and Its Historiography," *Subaltern Studies VI* (1989), 210.

2. PEF archives, London PEF/1865/2/8, "Report of the Proceedings at a Public Meeting," June 22, 1865 (emphasis is in the original).

3. The website of the Israeli Ministry of Tourism offers ample illustration. Among the many books that perpetuate such assumptions about Israeli "national dishes" is Tami Lehman-Wilzig and Miriam Blum's *The Melting Pot: A Quick and Easy Blend of Israeli Cuisine* (Herzlia, Israel: Palphot, n.d.), 10. A critical essay on the subject is Yael Raviv's "National Identity on a Plate," *Palestine-Israel Journal* 8.4/9.1 (2002), 164–72, which cites promotional Israeli government publications distributed by embassies.

4. Ziva Amir, *Arabesque: Decorative Needlework from the Holy Land* (n.p.: Massada Press, 1977; New York: Van Nostrand Reinhold, 1977).

5. "Clothing," *The World Book Encyclopedia* (2005 edition and previous editions). This encyclopedia has been translated into Arabic, but the Saudi publishers merely changed "Israel" to "Palestine." The U.S. publisher informed me that the illustration has now been dropped "for cause" from the 2009 edition (personal correspondence, July 9, 2009), and the editors will be reviewing new information. While dropping the illustration is positive, it may be appropriate to retain an illustration and correct the identification.

6. Check Maha Saca's own website: www.palestinianheritagecenter.com. There is striking resemblance between the present Jericho dress and clothing worn by "Semitic" women in an ancient Egyptian wall painting (see the reproduction in Philip K. Hitti, *History of Syria, including Lebanon and Palestine* [London: Macmillan, 1951]). The similarities to ancient dress are noted in a competent Wikipedia article "Palestinian Costumes," which also has a bibliography including Shelagh Weir's *Palestinian Costume* (London: British Museum, 1989) and Leila el Khalidi's *The Art of Palestinian Embroidery* (London: Saqi, 1999).

7. Ilan Pappe, *The Ethnic Cleansing of Palestine* (Oxford: Oneworld Publications, 2006) and Walid Khalidi, *All That Remains: The Palestinian Villages Occupied and Depopulated by Israel in 1948* (Washington, D.C.: Institute for Palestine Studies, 1992).

8. On 'Ein Houd, see Susan Slyomovics, *The Object of Memory: Arab and Jew Narrate the Palestinian Village* (Philadelphia: University of Pennsylvania Press, 1998).

9. *The Jerusalem Post Magazine* (October 2, 1998), 27.

10. Chapter 11 gives more examples of invisibility. On "biblical" plants, see David Darom's *Beautiful Plants of the Bible: From the Hyssop to the Mighty Cedar Trees* (Herzlia: Palphot, n.d.), 24, 7. In Oded Borowski's *Daily Life in Biblical Times* (Atlanta: Society of Biblical Literature, 2003), despite the cover photo and descriptions of native foods, any reference to Palestinians is absent (66, 71). The photos in *The Holy Land: A Unique Perspective* (Oxford: Lion, 1993) are unacknowledged for their sources; instead the book overwhelms the reader with biblical quotations and credit-taking. The cover photo of Yoel Elitzur's *Ancient Place Names in the Holy Land: Preservation and History* (Jerusalem: The Hebrew University Magnes Press and Winona Lake, Indiana: Eisenbrauns, 2004) is a typical Palestinian olive grove scene.

11. One historical perspective is provided by the Egyptologist Donald B. Redford, who points out the ironies in Cana'anite folklore memories being preserved in Greek and Hebrew stories (Sojourn and Exodus), which were "appropriated from the earlier cultures they were copying" (*Egypt, Canaan, and Israel in Ancient Times* [Princeton: Princeton University Press, 1992], 422). A good

summary is given in the entry "Exodus," *The Oxford Companion to the Bible,*
eds. Bruce M. Metzger and Michael D. Coogan (New York: Oxford University
Press, 1993). Among the skeptics are Israeli archaeologists like Ze'ev Herzog,
who caused uproar by stating that decades of archaeology contradict biblical
stories; see "The Bible: No Actual Findings," *Ha'aretz,* weekend magazine,
(October 29, 1999), 36–8, and Haim Watzman, "Archaeology vs. the Bible,"
Chronicle of Higher Education (January 21, 2000), A19–20.

12. Some fairly random examples of such titles: Anson F. Rainey and R. Steven
Notley, *The Sacred Bridge: Carta's Atlas of the Biblical World* (Jerusalem:
Carta, 2006); Michael D. Coogan, ed., *The Oxford History of the Biblical
World* (New York: Oxford University Press, 1998); Alan Millard, *Treasures
from Bible Times* (Tring: Lion Publishing, 1985); and T. C. Mitchell, *The Bible
in the British Museum: Interpreting the Evidence* (London: British Museum,
1988). Incidentally, no real "evidence" is exhibited anywhere in the British
Museum about "ancient Israel," except for a posted text reportedly written by
Jonathan Tubb, who also wrote *Bible Lands* (New York: Knopf, 1991). Many
other biblical "atlases" fit into this category. For further discussion see Chapter
1. The U.S. occupation of Iraq has led Israeli reporters to incorporate that
country—according to Yigal Schleifer ("Where Judaism Began," *The Jerusalem
Report,* June 16, 2003, 38–43), Iraq is where "patriarch Abraham" started out,
the place of the Diaspora and the Babylonian Talmud, where a "large Jewish
community" lived for 2500 years and left lots of remains.

13. For more documentation, see the appropriate sections of Chapter 1 and Chapter
10.

14. Leonard Shlain, *The Goddess Versus the Alphabet: The Conflict between
Word and Image* (New York: Viking, 1998), 68–71; Seymour Gitin, Trude
Dothan, and Joseph Naveh, "A Royal Dedicatory Inscription from Ekron,"
Israel Exploration Fund Journal 47 (1997), 13–14. For additional discussion,
see Chapter 1 and Chapter 10.

15. *The Holy Land: A Unique Perspective,* 153.

16. Oded Borowski, *Agriculture in Iron Age Israel* (Winona Lake, Indiana:
Eisenbrauns, 1987), 15–17. Borowski follows with a long section on the
"Gezer" calendar, claiming it to be Israelite and written in Hebrew, though it
could only have been written in "Phoenician" (with some features of Moabite
writing). On the "Gezer Calendar" as "Phoenician," see Chapter 5 and note 9
there. In particular, H. W. F. Saggs, *Civilization Before Greece and Rome* (New
Haven: Yale University Press, 1989), states that the calendar is "Phoenician"
(83).

17. Mark Twain, *Innocents Abroad, or The New Pilgrim's Progress* (1869), Chapter
46.

18. More on Sataf is given by Pappe, *The Ethnic Cleansing of Palestine,* 232–35,
who details the fate of many other villages. Also, check "Sataf" on the internet.

19. This reverse complex reminds me that several people have since claimed as their
own effort the Arab Community Centre of Toronto I founded and directed in
the 1970s, as well as a conference, "Landscape Perspectives on Palestine," held
in October 1998 at Birzeit University, that I initiated and developed.

20. Robert J. C. Young, *White Mythologies: Writing History and the West,* second
edition (London: Routledge, 2004), 35.

CHAPTER 8

1. "Yāfa" and "Jaffa" are in fact the same. The problem is that in early transcriptions the Germanic "J" (= Y) was used, so the letter started to be pronounced as a "J" in languages such as English. The same applies to other place names and to personal names like Jesus or Joseph. "Joseph" is sometimes used as a male name by Arab Christians, with the intention of distinguishing it from the more obviously Arabic original "Yūsef." Similarly, a Palestinian company uses "Jericho" in Arabic script as the brand name on its water bottles. See Chapter 1 and Chapter 10 for more examples of how transcription errors lead to such name transformations.

2. See my discussion in "Subliminal Filmic Reflections of Ancient Eastern Mediterranean Civilizations," *Quarterly Review of Film and Video* 22.4 (2005), 371–7.

3. Elsewhere, especially in Chapter 6, I provide more detailed answers to Zionist claims: Jews of today have nothing except tradition to relate them to ancient Jews, or Hebrews, or Israelites; in fact, these three terms are unrelated. Ancient Judaism did not have this sense of ethnicity attached to it, and most present Jews are the result of various historical conversions rather than any connection to ancient Jews in the region, or to Israelites. In contrast, many indigenous Palestinians and other people in the region would have been pagan in old times, were converted to one religion or another later, but essentially a large portion of the population remained on the land throughout the ages. I don't limit this statement to Palestine but include the whole region as well, since there is no reason to find much distinction among people in the region except now through the colonially imposed boundaries, nor was (or is) there reason for them not to move from one part of the region to another.

4. Chapter 3 on the invention of sacred places provides more instances of the Zionist exploitation of local traditions. Chapter 2 points out some differences among the three monotheisms in terms of connections to earlier polytheistic gods and beliefs.

5. Frantz Fanon, *The Wretched of the Earth*, (Harmondsworth, England: Penguin, 1967 [1961]), 119, 123, 125. At one conference I attended, in a paper presented by American Bible Society members the authors prided themselves on making sure the names used in translating the Bible to Senegalese did not remind the converts how close the biblical and qur'anic names are (that, for example, "Joseph" is really "Yūsef" in both texts). This strategy adopted in parts of Africa reminds me of similar Zionist designs and media campaigns. Fanon explains how colonialism "pulls every string shamelessly" to sow divisions and turn Africans against Arabs, Christian converts against Muslims, and blame Arabs for the slave trade to get black people to hate them (*The Wretched of the Earth*, 129).

6. Interestingly, the Palestine Exploration Fund changed its objective to a neutral one in 1978, removing the reference to "biblical illustrations," but it then recanted and reinserted "biblical aspects" in a 1996 re-revision.

7. Chapter 2 shows how the NJB better reflects aspects of the original text.

8. Such views fit nicely into the paradigm of Western civilization I describe in Chapter 1; Albright's 1957 *From Stone Age to Christianity* is quoted extensively in Keith W. Whitelam's study of the biblical industry, *The Invention of Ancient*

Israel: The Silencing of Palestinian History (London: Routledge, 1996), to demonstrate Albright's racist privileging of Roman and biblical values.

9. Seymour Gitin, personal communication, Albright Institute (June 4, 2000); see also another scholar of similar persuasion, William G. Dever, "What Remains of the House That Albright Built?" *Celebrating and Examining W. F. Albright*, special issue of *Biblical Archaeologist*, 56.1 (1993), 25–35. Burke O. Long provides an astute overview of Albright's scholarly motives in *Imagining the Holy Land: Maps, Models, and Fantasy Travels* (Bloomington: Indiana University Press, 2003), 131–46.

10. See http://www.visit-palestine.com/Jerusalem.htm

11. Department of Antiquities and Cultural Heritage (Ramallah: Ministry of Tourism, Palestinian National Authority, 2005).

12. Frantz Fanon, *Black Skin, White Masks* (New York: Grove Press, 1967 [1952]), 8–9.

13. Ngugi wa Thiong'o, *Decolonizing the Mind: The Politics of Language in African Literature* (Portsmouth: Heinemann Educational Books; London: James Curry, 1986).

14. Paulo Freire, *Pedagogy of the Oppressed* (New York: Herder and Herder, 1972).

CHAPTER 9

1. The word "cat" and its varieties in Western languages probably derive from North African and Asiatic roots, which in Arabic is *qiṭṭa* (feminine) and *qiṭ* (masculine).

2. T. S. Eliot, *Old Possum's Book of Practical Cats* (London: Faber, 1939).

3. Robert Darnton, *The Great Cat Massacre, and Other Episodes in French Cultural History* (New York: Basic Books, 1984), 74–105.

4. Darnton, *The Great Cat Massacre*, 95, 78, 96.

5. Quoted in Darnton, *The Great Cat Massacre*, 103.

6. See, for example, a study by Meir Margalit, *Discrimination in the Heart of the Holy City* (Jerusalem: International Peace and Cooperation Center, 2006), which details the discriminatory policies of the Israeli-controlled municipality. Margalit minces no words in saying that all state authorities do their part "to keep East Jerusalem down" through preferential treatment of Jewish areas, "deprivation" of Palestinian areas, and other racist actions (11, 177, 180).

7. The Palestine Museum is where my father worked until 1948. I should mention that I enter the country and city of my birth technically as a "visitor" on a foreign passport, and have to rent somewhere to live, though my family has properties in what is now West Jerusalem. In 1948 my immediate family and my grandparents were forced to leave, and were never allowed to return or to regain their properties or their contents. Israel enacted an Absentee Property "law" in 1950 to allow the government to take over any house or land whose owner (Palestinian owner that is) was not present in the country. Most Palestinians were already refugees in other countries and were prevented from returning after 1948, so that law was de facto confiscation. Such a "law" of course contradicts international law and UN resolutions, not to mention the standards Jews and Zionist organizations have used to claim assets and properties in Europe. As with houses and lands owned by hundreds of thousands of Palestinians, my family's properties were not sold to the Israelis, and so their current occupants are there without permission or legal right. In the areas occupied in 1967, the

Israelis have built many colonies on public or confiscated lands and have evicted residents in order to take over their properties, particularly in east Jerusalem, using various pretexts.

8. The Absentee Property Law and "security" reasons have also been applied to internal refugees, i.e. Palestinian Israelis who are still not allowed to go back to their original villages within pre-1948 areas.

9. Some Israeli archaeologists and activists have protested against the exploitation of Silwan through an organization for alternative archaeology (see www.alt-arch.org). There is inadequate support for belated and poorly funded local protests. These Israeli archaeologists are also campaigning against the disregard of ethical standards in building plans and the manipulation of information about the site.

10. Steven Erlander, "King David's Palace Is Found, Archaeologist Says," *New York Times* (August 5, 2006). It is unbelievable that totally unfounded conclusions about a discovery can be given the appearance of history and be prominently advertised as such without any proof. The whole City of David "finding" is a concoction.

CHAPTER 10

1. Lawrence uses the phrase to comment on fascist policies in his 1932 travel book *Etruscan Places* (London: The Folio Society, 1972), 44.

2. After E. A. Wallis Budge, *An Egyptian Hieroglyphic Dictionary* (London: John Murray, 1920).

3. Shmuel Ahituv's *Canaanite Toponyms in Ancient Egyptian Documents* (Jerusalem: Magnes Press, 1984), 48. Ahituv gives these ancient names more or less accurately as I describe them, probably as a matter of course for his Ph.D. dissertation, but still insists on the main listings as "Acco" and "Ashkelon," though this obviously contradicts the original Egyptian sources of "Canaanite" names he alludes to. Yoel Elitzur's more recent *Ancient Place Names in the Holy Land: Preservation and History* (Jerusalem: The Hebrew University Magnes Press and Winona Lake, Indiana: Eisenbrauns, 2004) at least lists ʿAkka and ʿAsqalān in the main headings, though in documentation sometimes strangely lists Jewish sources before ancient Egyptian ones. However, the general thrust of his interpretation is not that much less circumventive than Ahituv's, as I illustrate later in the section on Israeli scholarship.

4. Yohanan Aharoni, *The Land of the Bible: A Historical Geography*, trans. from the Hebrew by A. F. Rainey (Philadelphia: Westminster Press, 1967), 104, 100.

5. Elitzur, *Ancient Place Names in the Holy Land*, 2.

6. Edward Lipinski, *Semitic Languages: Outline of Comparative Grammar* (Leuven: Peeters, 1997), 107.

7. Alan S. Kaye, "Arabic," in *The World's Major Languages* (New York: Oxford University Press, 1986), 665.

8. Seymour Gitin, Trude Dothan, and Joseph Naveh, "A Royal Dedicatory Inscription from Ekron," *Israel Exploration Fund Journal* 47 (1997), 1–15, which attempts also to interpret Philistine script as "Hebreo-Philistine" (13–14)! A book by Zakaria Muhammad, *nakhlet et tay': kašf lughz el filasṭīniyyīn* [*Nakhlet Tay': Uncovering the Riddle of the Philistines*] (Ramallah: Dar esh Shurouq, 2005), provides a theory about the origin of the Philistines, challenging the interpretation of Gitin and others as motivated by ideological and biblical

biases intended to erase the historical depth of Palestinians. Muhammad gives a new rendering of names and dates, theorizing that it is not a goddess mentioned in the inscription but an adjective that contains a clue pointing not to Hellenistic origin but rather to the Philistines as an ancient "Semitic" people who migrated from the Arabian Peninsula, Najd in particular, where remnants of them are still left (the "tay'" tribe). The word "filisti" is a compound of "filis" (the main god) and the name of this tribe. But Muhammad falls into one trap of Arabic literalism, for while Gitin's rendering is defective, Muhammad gives Gitin's "Padi" as "Badi" (confusing *p* and *b* is common in Arabic pronunciation), and asserts: "The second name (Badi) is common among Arab tribes until today" (44). As I explain later, what is transcribed as *p* is more likely an *f*, thus "Fadi" ("one who sacrifices"), a more natural common personal name then and now in the whole region.

9. Joan Copeland Biella, *Dictionary of Old South Arabic: Sabaean Dialect* (Chicago: Scholars, 1982), ix. Even scholars who generally debunk Zionist interpretations adopt this convention, as does Niels Peter Lemche by transcribing Phoenician in square Hebrew in "'House of David': The Tel Dan Inscription(s)," in Thomas L. Thompson, ed., *Jerusalem in Ancient History and Tradition* (London: T & T Clark, 2003), 97–113.

10. Peter T. Daniels and William Bright, *The World's Writing Systems* (New York: Oxford University Press, 1996), 92. See also the discussion in Chapters 1, 5, and 7.

11. Gitin, et al., "A Royal Dedicatory Inscription from Ekron," 9–14.

12. This is not to be confused with the p/b difference, and the difficulty some Arabic speakers have in making the *p* sound. Some Arab scholars transfer Western-transcribed *p* in ancient languages to *b*. Thus, in one case what is transcribed as Ugaritic *itpn* is thought to be "*itbn*" in an Arabic source, rather than a more useful *itfn* (Khaza'al el Mājidi, *al āliha al kan 'aniyya* [*Cana'anite Gods*], Amman: Dar Azmina, 1999), 49. Chapter 4 gives more examples of how an *f* makes more sense in Ugaritic.

13. See note 29.

14. See sections on sacred geography in Chapters 1 and 3.

15. Edward Robinson, *Biblical Researches in Palestine, Mt. Sinai, and Arabia Petraea, a Journal of Travels in 1838, by E. Robinson and E. Smith, undertaken in Reference to Biblical Geography* (Boston: Crocker and Brewster, 1841), viii–x.

16. Georg Kampftmeyer, "Alte Namen im Heutigen Palästina und Syrien," *Zeitschrift des Deutschen Palästina-Vereins* 15 (1892): 1–116; 16 (1893): 1–71.

17. One example of such attack is in Elitzur, *Ancient Place Names in the Holy Land*, 4–8.

18. These glaring constructions are found on pages 108 and 110 of Aharoni's book.

19. Saul B. Cohen and Nurit Kliot, "Israel's Place-Names as Reflection of Continuity and Change in Nation-Building," *Journal of the American Name Society* 29.3 (1981), 227–48 (232–3).

20. Saul B. Cohen and Nurit Kliot, "Place-Names in Israel's Ideological Struggle over the Administered Territories," *Annals of the Association of American Geographers* 82.4 (1992), 653–80, (656).

21. Elitzur, *Ancient Place Names in the Holy Land*, 2, 11, 44; the myth about this sequencing of Hebrew-Aramaic-Arabic is so ingrained that even a commentary that pretends to be analyzing the "power" system, in this case Neil Asher

Silberman's "Power, Politics and the Past: The Social Construction of Antiquity in the Holy Land," in Thomas E. Levy, ed., *The Archaeology of Society in the Holy Land* (London: Leicester University Press, 1995), 13–14, uses that sequence and further gives credence to the work of the Zionist naming committees by saying that the Hebrew names were "linguistically and historically approved by the British Mandatory Government."

22. Elitzur, *Ancient Place Names in the Holy Land*, 44, 121–3, 163–7, 198–9; cf. Ahituv, *Canaanite Toponyms in Ancient Egyptian Documents*, 48, 60–71.

23. Louvain La Neuve: Institut Orientaliste, Universite Catholique de Louvain, 1988.

24. Walid Khalidi, *All That Remains: The Palestinian Villages Occupied and Depopulated by Israel in 1948* (Washington: Institute for Palestine Studies, 1992); Ilan Pappe, *The Ethnic Cleansing of Palestine* (Oxford: Oneworld Publications, 2006).

25. Meron Benvenisti, *Sacred Landscape: The Buried History of the Holy Land Since 1948* (Berkeley: University of California Press, 2000), 46, 47. Despite his excellent scholarship, in commenting on forced naming by Israel, following Benvenisti's assumptions, Rashid Khalidi by-passes original pre-biblical sources of some place names by saying that Palestinian toponyms are "ironically" based on "earlier Hebrew, Aramaic, Greek, Latin, or French Crusader names"; see Rashid Khalidi, *Palestinian Identity: The Construction of Modern National Consciousness* (New York: Columbia University Press, 1997), 14–15, 214.

26. One recent comprehensive list is composed by Shukri 'Arraf to record the names in Arabic, English transcription, and the name assigned in Hebrew *almawā qe' aj jughrāfiyya fi filasṭīn: al asma' el 'arabiyya wa at tasmiyāt el 'ibriyya*, *Geographic Sites in Palestine: Arabic Names and Hebrew Denominations* [English title as provided in the text] (Beirut: Institute of Palestine Studies, 2004).

27. Benvenisti, *Sacred Landscape*, 49.

28. Quoted in Benvenisti, *Sacred Landscape*, 35, 19.

29. See discussion and documentation in Chapter 1, "Politics of Ancient Languages," and notes 43–5, in Chapter 5, and also Chapter 7, notes 14 and 16.

30. *The Anchor Bible Dictionary*, 6 Vols., eds. David Noel Freedman, et al. (New York: Doubleday, 1992).

31. For example, the glossary in J. C. L. Gibson's *Canaanite Myths and Legends*, second edition (Edinburgh: T & T Clark, 1978), N. Wyatt's *Religious Texts from Ugarit: The Words of Ilimilku and His Colleagues* (Sheffield: Sheffield Academic Press, 1998), and Mark S. Smith's *The Origins of Biblical Monotheism: Israel's Polytheistic Background and the Ugaritic Texts* (New York: Oxford University Press, 2001) (the last an important work of scholarship, despite its typos) would have all arrived at different translations by using Arabic. They are discussed in Chapter 4.

32. *Anchor Bible Dictionary*, Vol. V, 374.

33. Kamal Salibi, who has a theory about a Western Arabian location for the biblical land of Israel based on the repetition of place names there, mentions in *The Historicity of Biblical Israel: Studies in 1 & 2 Samuel* (London: NABU Publications, 1998), 222, that *pisgah* is "a feminine noun formation from the verb *pasagh* (cf. Arabic *fasaqa*) meaning 'passing between'" and so is not a mountain summit.

34. It seems ill-justified to exclude *f* partly on the basis of an exclusive initial *p* used in medieval Masoretic, copied in synagogue readings, as a norm for how to pronounce the sound or to generalize to all "northwest Semitic" languages. As a general phonetic rule, if a language has one voiceless labial, it is more likely to be an *f*. At least one should posit both possibilities. There is no justification for transcribing all northwest "Semitic" languages using *p* to the exclusion of *f*.

35. A recent Israeli Knesset "law" (of July 6, 2009), and a decision by the Israeli Minister of Transport to use only transliterations of Hebrew forms on road signs, even for Arab Palestinian towns and cities, are intended to wipe out what is left of the original names.

CHAPTER 11

1. Some of the research for this chapter was assisted by a small grant from the Palestinian American Research Center. For other studies of related phenomena, see Issam Nassar's *Photographing Jerusalem: The Image of the City in Nineteenth-Century Photography* (Boulder, Colorado: East European Monographs, 1997) and Burke O. Long's description of vicarious creations of "Palestine" in the U.S., *Imagining the Holy Land: Maps, Models, and Fantasy Travels* (Bloomington: Indiana University Press, 2003).

2. Oded Borowski, *Daily Life in Biblical Times* (Atlanta: Society of Biblical Literature, 2003), 66, 71.

3. *The Holy Land: A Unique Perspective* (Oxford: Lion, 1993), 153. Thomas L. Thompson's *The Mythic Past: Biblical Archaeology and the Myth of Israel* (New York: Basic Books, 1999), 118, mentions that terracing was developed in the region more than 5000 years ago, and Ugaritic epics, dating to between 3200 and 3500 years ago, refer to terraces as a feature of the landscape. See the section "Terraces" in Chapter 7 for more and Figure 7.3 for the terrace photo.

4. Oded Borowski, *Agriculture in Iron Age Israel* (Winona Lake, Indiana: Eisenbrauns, 1987), 15–17.

5. Thompson, *The Mythic Past*, also published as *The Bible in History: How Writers Create a Past* (London: Jonathan Cape, 1999), 206. These chapters in particular deserve careful reading.

6. Almut Nebel, et al., "High-Resolution Y chromosome haplotypes of Israeli and Palestinian Arabs reveal geographic substructure and substantial overlap with haplotypes of Jews," *Human Genetics* 107 (2000), 637. Research by the same group found Jews to be more closely related to populations in the northern Fertile Crescent: Almut Nebel, et al., "The Y Chromosome Pool of Jews as Part of the Genetic Landscape of the Middle East," *American Journal of Human Genetics* 69 (2001), 1095–1112. Another genetic study by Antonio Arnaiz-Villena, et al., "The Origin of Palestinians and their Genetic Relatedness with Other Mediterranean Populations," *Human Immunology* 62 (2001), 889–900, caused a furore after its publication, and the journal took the unusual step of asking subscribers and libraries to disregard or preferably tear out the article. Some libraries have kept the publication under lock and key for fear of destruction by ideologically motivated readers.

7. Elizabeth Anne Finn, *Home in the Holy Land* (London: John Nisbet, 1877).

8. Elizabeth Anne Finn, *Palestinian Peasantry: Notes on Their Clans, Warfare, Religion, and Laws* (London: Marshall, 1923), 5–6, 70–6, 86, 89–94, 69.

9. W. F. Lynch, *Narrative of the United States' Expedition to the River Jordan and the Dead Sea* (Philadelphia: Blanchard and Lea, 1852), 28–9, 221, 223–4, 134–6, 231, 242.

10. Long, *Imagining the Holy Land*, 102–28, 208; Long comments in detail on the American School of Oriental Research, renamed the Albright Institute (129–46), which I discuss in Chapter 8. Another perspective on U.S. scholarship is given in Bruce Kuklick's *Puritans in Babylon: The Ancient Near East and American Intellectual Life, 1880–1930* (Princeton: Princeton University Press, 1996, 7): "The paradox in the evolution of Near Eastern studies was the manner in which the pursuit of Bible truth might undermine the truth of the Bible."

11. Kirsti Suolinna, "Hilma Granqvist: A Scholar of the Westermarck School in its Decline," *Acta Sociologica* 43 (2000), 317–23. The photographic collection and written reports documented by Catholic monks since 1894 in *Revue Biblique* are another potential source for later nineteenth century and early twentieth-century Palestinian life.

12. Uri Avnery, "Whose Acre?" (available at: http://www.counterpunch.org/avnery08182009.html). It is curious, however, why Avnery decides to use the crusader word "Acre" for the city's name. His intention is probably to avoid both Arabic 'Akka and Hebrew Acco, as a compromise in troubled times. Yet, 'Akka is the name preserved from the most ancient times, as explained in Chapter 10.

13. Yaron Peleg, *Orientalism and the Hebrew Imagination* (Ithaca: Cornell University Press, 2005), 9, 76, 139; Shlomo Sand, *The Invention of the Jewish People*, trans. Yael Lotan (London: Verso, 2009), 182–9.

14. Peleg, *Orientalism and the Hebrew Imagination*, 132–5; for my discussion of this movement, see "Primal Scenes of Globalization: Legacies of Canaan and Etruria," *PMLA* 116.1 (2001), 96.

15. James S. Diamond, *Homeland or Holy Land?: The Canaanite Critique of Israel* (Bloomington: Indiana University Press, 1986), 3; also Yaacov Shavit, *The New Hebrew Nation: A Study of Heresy and Fantasy* (London: Frank Cass, 1987), and my article "The Cana'anite Factor: (Un)Defining Religious Identities in Palestine and Israel," *Palestine-Israel Journal* 8.4/9.1 (April 2002), 108–20, published in Hebrew in *Qeshet ha Hadasha* 4 (2003), 106–14.

16. See Nadia Abu El-Haj's interviews with Israeli archaeologists and other citations, in *Facts on the Ground: Archaeological Practice and Territorial Self-Fashioning in Israeli Society* (Chicago: University of Chicago Press, 2001), 249–58.

17. Tawfik Canaan, "Mohammedan Saints and Sanctuaries in Palestine," *The Journal of the Palestine Oriental Society* VII (1927), 1–88.

18. Ali Qleibo, *Surviving the Wall: The Formation of Palestinian Cultural Identity from the Crimean War to the Wall* (Jerusalem: privately printed, 2009).

19. Chapter 7 (and note 6) discusses Palestinian embroidery and cites works on this art.

20. New findings should enable revision of previous theories and biases about ancient people such as the Philistines. Chapter 1 and notes 16–21 comment on the origin and uses of "Cana'anite" and cite Augustine's allusion to people identifying themselves as Cana'anites as late as the fourth century CE.

References

Note: The following list does not include the various interviews, minor newspaper articles, films, and language dictionaries mentioned in the text or notes. A few famous works of literature are cited without specific publication details, since they are available in different editions. Specialized reference works are cited here but not the specific entries from them discussed in the text or notes.

'Abādi, al Fayrūz. *al qamūs muḥīṭ* [early fifteenth-century Arabic dictionary]. Beirut: Al-Resalah, 1986.

Abu El-Haj, Nadia. *Facts on the Ground: Archaeological Practice and Territorial Self-Fashioning in Israeli Society*. Chicago: University of Chicago Press, 2001.

Achebe, Chinua. *Things Fall Apart*. 1959.

Aharoni, Yohanan. *The Land of the Bible: A Historical Geography*. Trans. from the Hebrew by A. F. Rainey. Philadelphia: Westminster Press, 1967.

Ahituv, Shmuel. *Canaanite Toponyms in Ancient Egyptian Documents*. Jerusalem: Magnes Press, 1984.

Albright, William Foxwell. *From Stone Age to Christianity: Monotheism and the Historical Process*. New York: Doubleday, 1957.

Alter, Robert. *The Art of Biblical Narrative*. London: George Allen and Unwin, 1981.

Alter, Robert, and Frank Kermode, eds. *The Literary Guide to the Bible*. Cambridge: Harvard University Press, 1987.

Amir, Ziva. *Arabesque: Decorative Needlework from the Holy Land*. n.p.: Massada Press; New York: Van Nostrand Reinhold, 1977.

The Anchor Bible Dictionary. New York: Doubleday, 1992.

Anderson, Benedict. *Imagined Communities*. London: Verso, 1991.

Ankori, Gannit. *Palestinian Art*. London: Reaktion, 2006.

"Are We Phoenicians After All?" *AUBulletin Today* 6.6 (May 2005).

Armstrong, Karen. *The Bible: The Biography*. London: Atlantic Books, 2008.

—— *A History of God: From Abraham to the Present: The 4000-year Quest for God* [1993]. London: Vintage, 1999.

Arnaiz-Villena, Antonio, et al. "The Origin of Palestinians and their Genetic Relatedness with Other Mediterranean Populations." *Human Immunology* 62 (2001): 889–900.

'Arraf, Shukri. *Geographic Sites in Palestine: Arabic Names and Hebrew Denominations*. Beirut: Institute of Palestine Studies, 2004.

Avnery, Uri. "On Jewish History: The Lion and the Gazelle." http://www.counterpunch.org/avnery04212008.html

—— "Whose Acre?" http://www.counterpunch.org/avnery08182009.html

Barker, Graeme, and Tom Rasmussen. *The Etruscans*. Oxford: Blackwell, 1998.

Bartlett, William Henry. *Walks About the City and Environs of Jerusalem*. London: George Virtue, 1844.

—— *Forty Days in the Desert on the Tracks of the Israelites*. London: Arthur Hall, Virtue, 1845.

Bennett, Ramon. *Philistine: The Great Deception*. Jerusalem: Jerusalem Arm of Salvation, 1995.

Benvenisti, Meron. *Sacred Landscape: The Buried History of the Holy Land Since 1948*. Berkeley: University of California Press, 2000.

Ben-Arieh, Yehoshua. *The Rediscovery of the Holy Land in the Nineteenth Century*, 2nd ed. Jerusalem: The Magnes Press/The Hebrew University; Israel Exploration Society, 1983.

Ben-Yehuda, Nachman. *The Masada Myth Collective Memory and Myth-Making in Israel*. Madison: University of Wisconsin Press, 1995.

—— *Sacrificing Truth: Archaeology and the Myth of Masada*. Amherst: Humanity Books, 2002.

Bernal, Martin. *Black Athena: The Afroasiatic Roots of Classical Civilization. Vol. I: The Fabrication of Ancient Greece, 1785–1985*. New Brunswick: Rutgers University Press, 1987.

Biella, Joan Copeland. *Dictionary of Old South Arabic: Sabaean Dialect*. Chicago: Scholars, 1982.

Blake, William. "The Marriage of Heaven and Hell." 1794.

—— "The Tyger." 1792.

Borges, Jorge Luis. "The Library of Babel." *Labyrinths: Selected Stories and Other Writings*. New York: New Directions, 1964. 51–8.

Borowski, Oded. *Agriculture in Iron Age Israel*. Winona Lake, Indiana: Eisenbrauns, 1987.

—— *Daily Life in Biblical Times*. Atlanta: Society of Biblical Literature, 2003.

Bradford, William. *Of Plymouth Plantation: 1620–1647*. New York: McGraw-Hill, 1981.

Brecht, Bertolt. *Baal* [1918–20]. Trans. Peter Tegel. *Collected Plays*. Ed. Ralph Manheim and John Willett. Vol. I. London: Methuen, 1971 [New York: Pantheon, 1971]. 1–58.

Brettler, Mark Zvi. *The Creation of History in Ancient Israel*. London: Routledge, 1995.

—— "The New Biblical Historiography." Long, ed. *Israel's Past in Present Research*. 43–50.

Budge, E. A. Wallis. *An Egyptian Hieroglyphic Dictionary*. London: John Murray, 1920.

Burkert, Walter. *The Orientalizing Revolution: Near Eastern Influence on Greek Culture in the Early Archaic Period* [1984]. Trans. from the German by Margaret E. Pinder and Walter Burkert. Cambridge: Harvard University Press, 1992.

Canaan, Tawfik. "Mohammedan Saints and Sanctuaries in Palestine." *The Journal of the Palestine Oriental Society* VII (1927): 1–88.

"Clothing." *The World Book Encyclopedia*. 2005 ed.

Coetzee, J. M. *Waiting for the Barbarians*. 1980.

Cohen, Saul B., and Nurit Kliot. "Israel's Place-Names as Reflection of Continuity and Change in Nation-Building." *Journal of the American Name Society* 29.3 (1981): 227–48.

—— "Place-Names in Israel's Ideological Struggle over the Administered Territories." *Annals of the Association of American Geographers* 82.4 (1992): 653–80.

The Complete Parallel Bible. New York: Oxford University Press, 1993.

Conrad, Joseph. *Heart of Darkness*. 1899.

Coogan, Michael D., ed. *The Oxford History of the Biblical World*. New York: Oxford University Press, 1998.

Cooper, James Fenimore. *The Last of the Mohicans*. 1826.

Cross, Frank Moore. *Canaanite Myth and Hebrew Epic: Essays in the History of Ancient Israel*. Cambridge: Harvard University Press, 1973.

Cummings, E. E. "anyone lived in a pretty how town." 1940.

Daniels, Peter T., and William Bright. *The World's Writing Systems*. New York: Oxford University Press, 1996.

Darnton, Robert. *The Great Cat Massacre, and Other Episodes in French Cultural History*. New York: Basic Books, 1984.

Darom, David. *Beautiful Plants of the Bible: From the Hyssop to the Mighty Cedar Trees*. Herzlia: Palphot, n.d.

Davies, Philip R. *In Search of "Ancient Israel"*. Sheffield: Sheffield Academic Press, 1995 [1992].

Davis, John. *Landscape of Belief: Encountering the Holy Land in Nineteenth-Century American Art and Culture*. Princeton: Princeton University Press, 1996.

de Moor, Johannes C. *The Rise of Yahwism: The Roots of Israelite Monotheism*, 2nd ed. Leuven: Leuven University Press, 1997.

Dever, William G. "What Remains of the House That Albright Built?" *Celebrating and Examining W. F. Albright*, special issue of *Biblical Archaeologist* 56.1 (1993): 25–35.

Diamond, James S. *Homeland or Holy Land?: The Canaanite Critique of Israel*. Bloomington: Indiana University Press, 1986.

Dietrich, B. C. *The Origins of Greek Religion*. Berlin: de Gruyter, 1973.

Dietrich, Manfried. "Aspects of the Babylonian Impact on Ugaritic Literature and Religion." *Ugarit, Religion and Culture*. Ed. N. Wyatt, et al. Münster: Ugarit-Verlag, 1996. 33–47.

Dietrich, Manfried, and Oswald Loretz, "The Ugaritic Script." Watson and Wyatt, eds. *Handbook of Ugaritic Studies*. 81–90.

Dietrich, Manfried, et al., eds. *The Cuneiform Alphabetic Texts: from Ugarit, Ras Ibn Hani and Other Places* (KTU), 2nd enlarged ed. Münster: Ugarit-Verlag, 1995.

Dothan, Trude and Moshe. *People of the Sea: The Search for the Philistines*. New York: Scribner, 1992.

Duncan, Julie A. "The Book of Deuteronomy." *Encyclopedia of the Dead Sea Scrolls*, 2 Vols. Ed. Lawrence Schiffman and James C. VanderKam. Oxford: Oxford University Press, 2000.

Eliot, George. *Daniel Deronda*. 1876.

Eliot, T. S. *Old Possum's Book of Practical Cats*. London: Faber, 1939.

—— "The Waste Land." 1922.

Elitzur, Joel. *Ancient Place Names in the Holy Land: Preservation and History*. Jerusalem: The Hebrew University Magnes Press and Winona Lake, Indiana: Eisenbrauns, 2004.

The Epic of Gilgamesh. ca. 2100 BCE.

Erlander, Steven. "King David's Palace is Found, Archaeologist Says." *New York Times*, August 5, 2006. http://www.nytimes.com/2005/08/05/international/middleeast/05jerusalem.html?pagewanted=print

Fanon, Frantz. *Black Skin, White Masks: The Experiences of a Black Man in a White World* [1952]. Trans. from the French by Charles Lam Markmann. New York: Grove Press, 1967.

—— *The Wretched of the Earth* [1961]. Preface by Jean-Paul Sartre. Trans. from the French by Constance Farrington. Harmondsworth, England: Penguin, 1967.

Federici, Silvia, ed. *Enduring Western Civilization: The Construction of the Concept of Western Civilization and Its "Others."* Westport: Praeger, 1995.

Finkelstein, Israel. *Archaeological Discoveries and Biblical Research.* Seattle: University of Washington Press, 1990.

Finkelstein, Israel, and Neil Asher Silberman. *The Bible Unearthed: Archaeology's New Vision of Ancient Israel and the Origin of Its Sacred Texts.* New York: Free Press, 2001.

Finn, Elizabeth Anne. *Home in the Holy Land.* London: John Nisbet, 1877.

—— *Palestinian Peasantry: Notes on Their Clans, Warfare, Religion, and Laws.* London: Marshall, 1923.

Fischer, Steven Roger. *A History of Language.* London: Reaktion, 1999.

Foucault, Michel. *Language, Counter-Memory, Practice: Selected Essays and Interviews.* Oxford: Basil Blackwell, 1977.

Fowden, Elizabeth Key. "Sharing Holy Places." *Common Knowledge* 8.1 (2002): 124–46.

Freire, Paulo. *Pedagogy of the Oppressed* [1968]. Trans. from the Portuguese by Myra Bergman Ramos. New York: Herder and Herder, 1972.

Frye, Northrop. *The Great Code: The Bible and Literature.* New York: Harcourt Brace Jovanovich, 1982.

Fuller, Thomas. *A Pisgah-Sight of Palestine.* London: M. F. for John Williams at ye Crowne in St. Paules Churchyard, 1650.

Gabel, John B., Charles B. Wheeler, and Anthony D. York. *The Bible as Literature: An Introduction,* 5th ed. New York: Oxford University Press, 2006.

Gibson, J. C. L., ed. *Canaanite Myths and Legends,* 2nd ed. Edinburgh: T & T Clark, 1978.

Gitin, Seymour, Trude Dothan, and Joseph Naveh. "A Royal Dedicatory Inscription from Ekron." *Israel Exploration Fund Journal* 47 (1997): 1–15.

Golding, William. *Lord of the Flies.* 1954.

Gonen, Rivka. *Contested Holiness: Jewish, Muslim, and Christian Perspectives on the Temple Mount.* Jersey City, N. J.: KTAV Publishing House, 2003.

Graves, Kersey. *The World's Sixteen Crucified Christs: Christianity Before Christ* [1875]. New York: Cosimo, 2007.

Greenfield, Jonas C. "The Hebrew Bible and Canaanite Literature." Alter and Kermode, eds. *The Literary Guide to the Bible.* 545–60.

Guha, Ranajit. "Dominance without Hegemony and Its Historiography." *Subaltern Studies VI* (1989): 210–309. New Delhi: Oxford University Press India.

Gunn, Giles B. *The Interpretation of Otherness: Literature, Religion, and the American Imagination.* New York: Oxford University Press, 1979.

Hadley, Judith M. *The Cult of Asherah in Ancient Israel and Judah: Evidence for a Hebrew Goddess.* Cambridge: Cambridge University Press, 2000.

The HarperCollins Bible Commentary, rev. ed. San Francisco: HarperSanFrancisco, 2000.

Harpur, Tom. *The Pagan Christ: Recovering the Lost Light.* Toronto: Thomas Allen, 2004.

Hawthorne, Nathaniel. "The May-pole of Merry Mount" [1835]. *Twice-Told Tales.* n.p.: Ohio State University Press, 1974. Vol. 9 of *The Centenary Edition of the Works of Nathaniel Hawthorne.* 54–67.

Haynes, Jonathan. *The Humanist as Traveler: George Sandys's "Relation of a Journey Begun An. Dom. 1610."* Rutherford: Fairleigh Dickinson University Press, 1986.

Herbert, Sharon. "In Search of the 'Last' of the Phoenicians" (lecture). http://www. archaeological.org/webinfo.php?page=10224&lid=145

Herzog, Ze'ev. "The Bible: No Actual Findings." *Ha'aretz*, weekend magazine, October 29, 1999: 36–8.

Hirst, David. *The Gun and the Olive Branch: The Roots of Violence in the Middle East*, 3rd ed. London: Faber & Faber, 2003.

Hitchens, Christopher. *God Is Not Great: How Religion Poisons Everything*. Toronto: McClelland & Stewart, 2007.

Hitti, Philip K. *History of Syria, Including Lebanon and Palestine*. London: Macmillan, 1951.

The Holy Land: A Unique Perspective. Oxford: Lion, 1993.

Hornun, Erik. *Akhenaten and the Religion of Light* [1995]. Trans. from the German by David Lorton. Ithaca: Cornell University Press, 1999.

Hume, David. "Natural History of Religion," in *Four Dissertations* [1757]. Bristol: Thoemmes Press, 1995.

Hunt, E. D. *Holy Pilgrimage in the Late Roman Empire AD 312–460*. Oxford: Clarendon, 1982.

Huxley, Aldous. *Brave New World*. 1932.

Inventory of Cultural and Natural Heritage Sites of Potential Outstanding Universal Value in Palestine. Ramallah: Department of Antiquities and Cultural Heritage, Ministry of Tourism, Palestinian National Authority, 2005.

Kampftmeyer, Georg. "Alte Namen im Heutigen Palästina und Syrien." *Zeitschrift des Deutschen Palästina-Vereins* 15 (1892): 1–116; 16 (1893): 1–71.

Kanaana, Sharif. *Folk Heritage of Palestine*. Ramallah: Research Center for Arab Heritage, 1994.

Kaufman, Asher. *Reviving Phoenicia: The Search for Identity in Lebanon*. London: I. B. Tauris, 2004.

Kaye, Alan S. "Arabic." *The World's Major Languages*. New York: Oxford University Press, 1986. 664–85.

—— "Does Ugaritic Go with Arabic in Semitic Genealogical Sub-classification?" *Folia Orientalia* 28 (1991): 115–28.

Kennedy, X. J. and Dana Gioia. *An Introduction to Poetry*, 9th ed. New York: Longman, 1998.

el Khalidi, Leila. *The Art of Palestinian Embroidery*. London: Saqi, 1999.

Khalidi, Rashid. *Palestinian Identity: The Construction of Modern National Consciousness*. New York: Columbia University Press, 1997.

Khalidi, Walid. *All That Remains: The Palestinian Villages Occupied and Depopulated by Israel in 1948*. Washington, D. C.: Institute for Palestine Studies, 1992.

Kirsch, Jonathan. *God Against the Gods: The History of the War between Monotheism and Polytheism*. New York: Viking Compass, 2004.

Koestler, Arthur. *The Thirteenth Tribe*. New York: Random House, 1976.

Kokkinos, Nikos. *The Herodian Dynasty: Origins, Role in Society and Eclipse*. Sheffield: Sheffield Academic Press, 1998.

Krahmalkov, Charles R. *Phoenician-Punic Dictionary*. Leuven: Uitgeverij Peeters, 2000.

Kuklick, Bruce. *Puritans in Babylon: The Ancient Near East and American Intellectual Life, 1880–1930*. Princeton: Princeton University Press, 1996.

Lawrence, D. H. *Etruscan Places* [1932]. London: Folio Society, 1972.

Le Beau, Bryan F. and Menachem Mor, eds. *Pilgrims & Travelers to the Holy Land*. Omaha: Creighton University Press, 1996.

Leed, Eric J. *The Mind of the Traveler: From Gilgamesh to Global Tourism*. New York: Basic Books, 1991.

Leeming, David. *Jealous Gods, Chosen People: The Mythology of the Middle East*. Oxford: Oxford University Press, 2004.

Lehman-Wilzig, Tami, and Miriam Blum. *The Melting Pot: A Quick and Easy Blend of Israeli Cuisine*. Herzlia, Israel: Palphot, n.d.

Lemche, Niels Peter. *The Canaanites and Their Land*. Sheffield: Sheffield Academic Press, 1991.

—— "'House of David': The Tel Dan Inscription(s)." Thompson, ed. *Jerusalem in Ancient History and Tradition*. 46–67.

Levy, T. E., ed. *The Archaeology of Society in the Holy Land*. London: Leicester University Press, 1995.

Lipinski, Edward. *Semitic Languages: Outline of Comparative Grammar*. Leuven: Peeters, 1997.

Logan, Robert K. *The Fifth Language: Learning a Living in the Computer Age*. Toronto: Stoddard, 1995.

Long, Burke O. *Imagining the Holy Land: Maps, Models, and Fantasy Travels*. Bloomington: Indiana University Press, 2003.

Long, V. Philips, ed. *Israel's Past in Present Research: Essays on Ancient Israelite Historiography*. Winona Lake, Indiana: Eisenbrauns, 1999.

Lucas, D. V. *Canaan and Canada*. Toronto: William Briggs, 1904.

Lynch, W. F. *Narrative of the United States' Expedition to the River Jordan and the Dead Sea*. Philadelphia: Blanchard and Lea, 1852.

Maalouf, Amin. *On Identity* [1996]. Trans. from the French by Barbara Bray. London: Harvell Press, 2000.

McCurley, Foster R. *Ancient Myths and Biblical Faith: Scriptural Transformations*. Philadelphia: Fortress Press, 1983.

MacGregor, John. *The Rob Roy on the Jordan*. London: Murray, 1870.

MacLaurin, E. C. B. "A Comparison of Two Aspects of Ugaritic and Christian Theology." *Oriental Studies: Presented to Benedikt S. J. Isserlin*. Ed. R. Y. Ebied and M. J. L. Young. Leiden: E. J. Brill, 1980. 73–82.

McLuhan, Marshall. *Understanding Media: The Extensions of Man*. New York: McGraw-Hill, 1964.

el Mājidi, Khaza'al. *al āliha al kan'aniyya [Cana'anite Gods]*. Amman: Dar Azmina, 1999.

Makiya, Kanan. *The Rock: A Tale of Seventh-Century Jerusalem*. New York: Vintage, 2002.

Mandeville, John. *Travels of Sir John Mandeville* [1365]. Trans. with an introduction by C. W. R. D. Woseley. London: Penguin, 2005 [1983].

Margalit, Meir. *Discrimination in the Heart of the Holy City*. Jerusalem: International Peace and Cooperation Center, 2006.

Markoe, Glenn E. *Phoenicians*. Berkeley: University of California Press, 2000.

Martin, Ernest L. *The Temples That Jerusalem Forgot*. Portland: Associates for Scriptural Knowledge, 2000.

Masalha, Nur. *The Bible and Zionism*. London: Zed Books, 2007.

Maundrell, Henry. *A Journey from Aleppo to Jerusalem in 1697* [1703]. Beirut: Khayats, 1963.

Mazar, Amihai. *Archaeology of the Land of the Bible 10,000–586 B.C.E.* New York: Doubleday, 1990.

Melville, Herman. *Clarel: A Poem and Pilgrimage in the Holy Land* [1876]. New York: Hendricks, 1960.

—— *Journals* [1856–7]. Evanston and Chicago: Northwestern University Press and the Newberry Library, 1989.

—— *Moby-Dick; or, The Whale* [1851]. Evanston: Northwestern University Press and The Newberry Library, 1988.

—— *Typee* [1846]. Evanston: Northwestern University Press and The Newberry Library, 1968.

Meshel, Zeev. *Kuntilet 'Ajrud: A Religious Centre from the Time of the Judaean Monarchy on the Border of Sinai*. Jerusalem: The Israel Museum, 1978.

Metzger, Bruce M., and Michael D. Coogan, eds. *The Oxford Companion to the Bible*. New York: Oxford University Press, 1993.

Meyers, Eric M. "Israel and Its Neighbors Then and Now: Revisionist History and the Quest for History in the Middle East Today." http://www.bibleinterp.com/articles/emeyers.shtml

Millard, Alan Ralph. *Treasures from Bible Times*. Tring: Lion Hudson, 1985.

Miller, Perry. *Errand into the Wilderness*. Cambridge: Belknap, 1956.

Mitchell, T. C. *The Bible in the British Museum: Interpreting the Evidence*. London: British Museum, 1988.

Moran, William L. "The Hebrew Language in its Northwest Semitic Background." *The Bible and the Ancient Near East*. Ed. G. Ernest Wright. Garden City: Doubleday, 1961. 54–72.

Moscati, Sabatino, ed. *The Phoenicians*. New York: Rizzoli, 1999 [*iFenici*. Milan: Bompiani, 1988].

Mueller, Tom. "Herod," *National Geographic*, December 2008. http://ngm.nationalgeographic.com/2008/12/herod/mueller-text

Muhammad, Zakaria. *nakhlet et tay': kašf lughz el filasṭīniyyīn* [*Nakhlet Tay': Uncovering the Riddle of the Philistines*]. Ramallah: Dar esh Shurouq, 2005.

Murdock, D. M. (Acharya S). *Christ in Egypt: The Horus-Jesus Connection*. n.p.: Stellar House Publishing, 2009.

Nassar, Issam. *Photographing Jerusalem: The Image of the City in Nineteenth-Century Photography*. Boulder, Colorado: East European Monographs, 1997.

—— "Reflections on the Writing of the History of Palestinian Identity." *Palestine-Israel Journal* 8.4 9.1 (2002): 24–37.

Nebel, Almut, et al. "High-Resolution Y chromosome haplotypes of Israeli and Palestinian Arabs reveal geographic substructure and substantial overlap with haplotypes of Jews." *Human Genetics* 107 (2000): 630–41.

—— "The Y Chromosome Pool of Jews as Part of the Genetic Landscape of the Middle East." *American Journal of Human Genetics* 69 (2001): 1095–1112.

"Netanyahu to present Obama with Twain's Holy Land memoir." *Ha'aretz*, May 19, 2009. http://www.haaretz.com/hasen/spages/1086234.html

Nietzsche, Friedrich. *Beyond Good and Evil*. Chapter 3: The Religious Mood, Section 52. http://www.gutenberg.org/files/4363/4363-h/4363-h.htm#2HCH0003

Obenzinger, Hilton. *American Palestine: Melville, Twain, and the Holy Land Mania*. Princeton: Princeton University Press, 1999.

Onfray, Michel. *Atheist Manifesto: The Case Against Christianity, Judaism, and Islam*. 2005. Trans. from the French by Jeremy Leggatt. New York: Arcade Publishing, 2007.

Osband, Linda, comp. *Famous Travellers to the Holy Land*. London: Prion, 1989.

Owen, G. Frederick. *Abraham to Allenby*. Grand Rapids: Wm. B. Eerdmans, 1939.

Pagels, Elaine. *The Gnostic Gospels*. New York: Random House, 1979.

"Palestinian Costumes." http://en.wikipedia.org/wiki/Palestinian_costumes

Palmer, Edward Henry. *The Desert of the Exodus: Journeys on Foot in the Wilderness of the Forty Years Wandering*. Cambridge: Deighton, Bell, 1871.

Pappe, Ilan. *The Ethnic Cleansing of Palestine*. Oxford: Oneworld Publications, 2006.

Parker, Simon B., ed. *Ugaritic Narrative Poetry*. Atlanta: Scholars Press, 1997.

Peled, Yoav. "Inter-Jewish Challenges to Israeli Identity." *Palestine-Israel Journal* 8.4/ 9.1 (2002): 12–23.

Peleg, Yaron. *Orientalism and the Hebrew Imagination*. Ithaca: Cornell University Press, 2005.

Peters, Joan. *From Time Immemorial*. New York: Harper & Row, 1985.

Philip, Graham. Review of *Archaeology of Society in the Holy Land*. Ed. T. E. Levy *Palestine Exploration Quarterly* 130 (1998): 172–3.

Philo of Byblos: The Phoenician History. Washington, D.C.: Catholic Biblical Association of America, 1981.

Poe, Edgar Allan. "The Black Cat." 1843.

Prior, Michael. *The Bible and Colonialism: A Moral Critique*. Sheffield: Sheffield Academic Press, 1997.

Pritchard, James Bennett. *Ancient Near Eastern Texts Relating to the Old Testament*, 3rd ed. Princeton: Princeton University Press, 1969.

Qleibo, Ali. *Surviving the Wall: The Formation of Palestinian Cultural Identity from the Crimean War to the Wall*. Jerusalem: privately printed, 2009.

el Qumni, Sayyid Mahmūd. *an-nabi ibrahīm wa et tarīkh al majhūl* [*Prophet Abraham and the Unknown History*]. Cairo: Madbūli es Saghīr, 1996.

Ra'ad, Basem L. "Ancient Lands." *Companion to Herman Melville*. Ed. Wyn Kelley. London: Blackwell, 2006. 129–45.

—— "The Cana'anite Factor: (Un)Defining Religious Identities in Palestine and Israel." *Palestine-Israel Journal* 8.4/9.1 (2002): 108–20 [published in Hebrew in *Qeshet ha Hadasha* 4 (2003): 106–14].

—— "The Death Plot in Melville's *Clarel*." *ESQ* 27 (1981): 14–27.

—— "Editing in a Time of Dispossession." *Profession 2009* (Modern Language Association): 145–54.

—— "Primal Scenes of Globalization: Legacies of Canaan and Etruria." *PMLA* 116.1 (2001): 89–110.

—— "Subliminal Filmic Reflections of Ancient Eastern Mediterranean Civilizations." *Quarterly Review of Film and Video* 22.4 (2005): 371–7.

—— "Updike's New Versions of Myth in America." *Modern Fiction Studies* 37 (1991): 25–33.

Radhakrishnan, R. "Postcoloniality and the Boundaries of Identity." *Identities: Race, Class, Gender, and Nationality*. Ed. Linda Martin Alcoff and Eduardo Mendieta. Oxford: Blackwell, 2003. 312–29.

Raviv, Yael. "National Identity on a Plate." *Palestine-Israel Journal* 8.4/9.1 (2002): 164–72.

Redford, Donald B. *Egypt, Canaan, and Israel in Ancient Times*. Princeton: Princeton University Press, 1992.

Reinhart, Tanya. *Israel/Palestine: How To End the War of 1948*. 2nd ed. New York: Seven Stories Press, 2005.

Robertson, J. M. *Pagan Christs* [1903]. 2nd ed. London: Watts & Co., 1911.

Robinson, Edward. *Biblical Researches in Palestine, Mt. Sinai, and Arabia Petraea, a Journal of Travels in 1838, by E. Robinson and E. Smith, undertaken in Reference to Biblical Geography.* Boston: Crocker and Brewster; London: John Murray, 1841.

Rodriguez, Angel Manuel. "Ancient Near Eastern Parallels to the Bible and the Question of Revelation and Inspiration." *Journal of the Adventist Theological Society* 12 (2001): 43–64.

Rainey, Anson F., and R. Steven Notley. *The Sacred Bridge: Carta's Atlas of the Biblical World.* Jerusalem: Carta, 2006.

"Sacred Geography." *Quarterly Review* XLIV (March 1854): 353–84.

Saggs, H. W. F. *Civilization Before Greece and Rome.* New Haven: Yale University Press, 1989.

Said, Edward W. *Orientalism.* New York: Pantheon Books, 1978.

—— *The Question of Palestine* [1977]. New York: Random House, 1980.

Salibi, Kamal. *The Historicity of Biblical Israel: Studies in 1 & 2 Samuel.* London: NABU Publications, 1998.

Sand, Shlomo. *The Invention of the Jewish People.* Trans. from the Hebrew by Yael Lotan. London: Verso, 2009. First published as *matai ve'ekh humtza ha'am hayehudi?* [When and How Was the Jewish People Invented?]. Resling, 2008.

Sandys, George. *A Relation of a Journey Begun An Dom 1610, Containing a Description of the Turkish Empire, of Egypt, of the Holy Land.* London: W. Barrett, 1615.

Sarhan, Nimr. *al-mabāni el kan'ania fi filastīn* [Cana'anite Buildings in Palestine]. Amman: Dar el Karmel, 1989.

Schleifer, Yigal. "Where Judaism Began." *The Jerusalem Report,* June 16, 2003: 38–43.

Schlesinger, Arthur M., Jr. *The Disuniting of America.* New York: Norton, 1992.

Segev, Tom. *One Palestine Complete.* Trans. from the Hebrew by Haim Watzman. London: Little Brown, 2000.

Shaheen, Jack G. *Reel Bad Arabs: How Hollywood Vilifies a People.* New York: Olive Branch Press, 2001.

Sharon, Moshe, ed. *The Holy Land in History and Thought.* Leiden: E. J. Brill, 1988.

Shavit, Yaacov. *The New Hebrew Nation: A Study of Heresy and Fantasy.* London: Frank Cass, 1987.

Shehadeh, Raja. *Palestinian Walks: Forays into a Vanishing Landscape.* New York: Scribner, 2007.

Shlain, Leonard. *The Goddess Versus the Alphabet: The Conflict Between Word and Image.* New York: Viking, 1998.

Silberman, Neil Asher. "Power, Politics and the Past: The Social Construction of Antiquity in the Holy Land." Levy, ed. *The Archaeology of Society in the Holy Land.* 9–20.

Slyomovics, Susan. *The Object of Memory: Arab and Jew Narrate the Palestinian Village.* Philadelphia: University of Pennsylvania Press, 1998.

Smith, George. *The Chaldean Account of Genesis, Containing the Description of the Creation, the Fall of Man, the Deluge, the Tower of Babel, the Times of the Patriarchs, and Nimrod; Babylonian Fables, and Legends of the Gods; from the Cuneiform Inscriptions.* London: Sampson Low, Marston, Searle, and Rivington, 1876.

Smith, Mark S. *The Origins of Biblical Monotheism: Israel's Polytheistic Background and the Ugaritic Texts.* Oxford: Oxford University Press, 2001.

Sozomen (fifth century CE). *Historia Ecclesiastica*, Book II, Chapters 4–5. http://www.newadvent.org/fathers/26022.htm

Stanley, Arthur P. *Sinai and Palestine, in Connection with Their History*. London: Murray, 1856.

Stark, Freya. *The Journey's Echo: Selections from Freya Stark*. London: John Murray, 1963.

Stevens, Wallace. "A Mythology Reflects its Region." 1955.

Stowe, Harriet Beecher. *Uncle Tom's Cabin*. 1852.

Strange, John. "Herod and Jerusalem: The Hellenization of an Oriental City." Thompson, ed. *Jerusalem in Ancient History and Tradition*. 97–113.

Strauss, David Friedrich. *Das Leben Jesu* [1835]. *The Life of Jesus Critically Examined*. Trans. from the German by George Eliot. Reprint. Mifflinton, Penn.: Sigler Press, 1994.

Suolinna, Kirsti. "Hilma Granqvist: A Scholar of the Westermarck School in its Decline." *Acta Sociologica* 43 (2000): 317–23.

The Tanach. Stone Edition. New York: Mesorah Publications, 1996.

Thiong'o, Ngugi wa. *Decolonizing the Mind: The Politics of Language in African Literature*. Portsmouth: Heinemann Educational Books and London: James Curry, 1986.

Thompson, Thomas L. "Biblical Archaeology and the Politics of Nation Building." *Holy Land Studies* 8.2 (2009): 133–42.

—— *The Messiah Myth: The Near Eastern Roots of Jesus and David*. London: Jonathan Cape, 2006.

—— *The Mythic Past: Biblical Archaeology and the Myth of Israel*. New York: Basic Books, 1999. [*The Bible in History: How Writers Create a Past*. London: Jonathan Cape, 1999.]

Thompson, Thomas L., ed. *Jerusalem in Ancient History and Tradition*. London: T & T Clark, 2003.

Thompson, Thomas L., and F. C. Goncalvez. *Toponomie Palestinienne: Plaine de St Jean D'Acre et Corridor de Jerusalem*. Louvain La Neuve: Institut Orientaliste, Universite Catholique de Louvain, 1988.

Thomson, William M. *The Land and the Book*. London: Thomas Nelson, 1859.

Thomson, William. "Report of the Proceedings at a Public Meeting." June 22, 1865. London: Palestine Exploration Fund Archives (PEF/1865/2/8).

Thoreau, Henry David. "Resistance to Civil Government" ["Civil Disobedience"]. 1849.

Tracy, David. "Writing." *Critical Terms for Religious Studies*. Ed. Mark C. Taylor. Chicago: University of Chicago Press, 1998. 383–93.

Tubb, Jonathan N. *Bible Lands*. New York: Knopf, 1991.

—— *Canaanites*. London: British Museum, 1998.

Tuchman, Barbara. *Bible and Sword: England and Palestine from the Bronze Age to Balfour* [1956]. New York: Ballantine, 1984.

Turcan, Robert. *The Cults of the Roman Empire* [1992]. Trans. from the French by Antonia Nevill. Oxford: Blackwell, 1996.

Twain, Mark. *Innocents Abroad; or The New Pilgrim's Progress*. 1869.

Warburton, Eliott. *The Crescent and The Cross; or, Romance and Realities of Eastern Travel*, 2 vols. London: Henry Colborn, 1844.

Watson, Wilfred G. E., and Nicholas Wyatt, eds. *Handbook of Ugaritic Studies*. Leiden: Brill, 1999.

Watzman, Haim. "Archaeology vs. the Bible." *Chronicle of Higher Education*, January 21, 2000: A19–20.

Weir, Shelagh. *Palestinian Costume*. London: British Museum, 1989; Austin: University of Texas Press, 1989.

"Western Wall." *Encyclopaedia Judaica*, 1971 ed.

Wexler, Paul. *The Non-Jewish Origins of Sephardic Jews*. New York: SUNY, 1966.

Whitelam, Keith W. *The Invention of Ancient Israel: The Silencing of Palestinian History*. London and New York: Routledge, 1996.

Winthrop, John. "A Model of Christian Charity" [1630]. *The Norton Anthology of American Literature*, 6th ed. Vol. A. New York: Norton: 2003. 206–17.

Worth, Ronald H., Jr. *Bible Translations: A History Through Source Documents*. Jefferson, N.C.: McFarland, 1992.

Wyatt, N. *Religious Texts from Ugarit: The Words of Ilimilku and His Colleagues*. Sheffield: Sheffield Academic Press, 1998.

Young, Robert J. C. *White Mythologies: Writing History and the West*, 2nd ed. London: Routledge, 2004.

Index

Compiled by Nina Butska